More Advance Praise for *Just Call Me Mike*

"Mike Farrell proves that ferocious conviction is the organizing principle of an extraordinary life. In his memoir, *Just Call Me Mike*, he describes the fantastic, sometimes painful, and ultimately redeeming journey that his conscience has led him on. Like his life, the book dances seamlessly between his great passions—from fond memories on the M*A*S*H set, to nervous moments at military checkpoints on his way to help refugees in war-torn Central America, to scrubbing-in for real-life surgery on a prisoner of war in El Salvador. In a disarmingly honest and gentle voice, *Just Call Me Mike* collects an incredible diversity of experiences, so diverse that it's difficult to believe that one person could accomplish so much, in art and in service to others."
— Kamala D. Harris, District Attorney of San Francisco

"Each paragraph inspires . . . each page a sermon . . . the book, a history lesson not generally taught. Mike Farrell is both poet and fighter, his pen a sword that cuts through pretense and hypocrisy and enables each of us to be courageous in pursuit of justice. His greatest role is offstage acting on behalf of those who have been silenced . . . His book is a gift for all. I am proud to 'call him Mike'—friend to all."
— Rabbi Steven B. Jacobs, chair of the Progressive Faith Foundation

"Mike Farrell's passion for life and compassion for people are formidable. *Just Call Me Mike* is not merely an autobiography, but rather a road map and a book of directions for those desirous of affecting positive change. He makes believable the principle that one person CAN make a difference—we should all be that kind of citizen."
— Stanley K. Sheinbaum, economist

"Incapable of putting his conscience on hold, Mike Farrell beautifully articulates why he is a rebel without a pause."
— Larry Gelbart

"This book never, not for a page, emerges as self-congratulatory, and yet one cannot help but be overwhelmed by Mike Farrell's principles, his profound commitments, and his extraordinary courage. The account of his life experiences is so real, so moving, it went straight through my heart."
— Loretta Swit

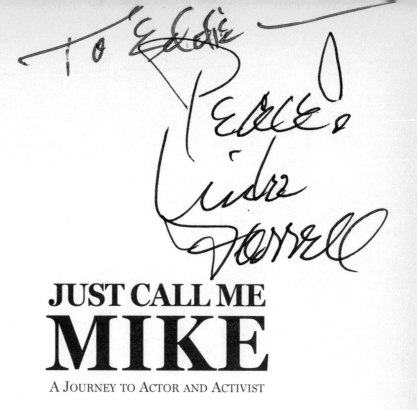

To Eddie
Peace!
Mike Farrell

JUST CALL ME
MIKE

A JOURNEY TO ACTOR AND ACTIVIST

BY MIKE FARRELL

RDV Books
New York

Published by Akashic Books/RDV Books
©2007 Mike Farrell

ISBN-13: 978-1-933354-08-8
ISBN-10: 1-933354-08-9
Library of Congress Control Number: 2006923113

First printing
Printed in Canada

Akashic Books/RDV Books
PO Box 1456
New York, NY 10009
info@akashicbooks.com
www.akashicbooks.com

To Shelley,
my hero

To Erin and Mike,
my inspiration

To Kathy, Jim and Karen,
semper fidelis

To Sal,
for the things I never said

For Agnes
&
For Joe

Acknowledgments

One doesn't, I have come to understand, write a book alone. In this case, there was quite a crowd around and it was wonderful to be able to visit with some of them again. Others, it was not so great. Ghosts, sylphs, spirits of the long and not-so-long dead rose to join me on this journey, and they swirl about me still. I welcome them all because, in some instances, there are debts owed, words that needed to be said, and this offered the chance. In other cases they remind me that, while this exercise has at least acknowledged their often bitter and painful existence, there is work to be done before they can rest. To them I offer my thanks and prayers, with full awareness of the debt I carry.

To all the friends who have accompanied me, sometimes guided me, through this complex process of living, I offer my thanks and my love.

To my family . . . I bow.

I had not intended to write a book. I was asked . . . no, nudged . . . no, hounded into doing it by Robert Greenwald, so if you don't like it, blame him. After seducing me into taking on this chore, this grueling experience that has turned out to be such a joy, Robert stepped back smiling and became a quiet but never-ending source of encouragement, support, and generosity. He and his RDV Books partner, Danny Goldberg, have simply never wavered in their determination to show me that, to them, this is an important and meaningful effort. I hope my appreciation comes through in these and the words on the pages that follow.

To David Shirley, the most gentle and painless editor conceivable, I doff my hat. His ability to strip away the chaff without drawing blood, coupled with his kindness in always buffering the deft surgical excisions with words of praise is an art in itself.

Johnny Temple of Akashic Books—whose ability to stay below the radar while seeing that everything comes out exactly as he wants it is unnerving—has been a gentle and appreciative midwife throughout this extraordinary gestation. And now he rises.

And to you, dear reader . . . if you've come this far, I bid you welcome. You, too, have my thanks.

TABLE OF CONTENTS

PREFACE

S o what do we call you, actor and activist?"

"Why don't you just call me Mike?"

It happens—usually when I'm about to be interviewed on television or radio—because these days the discussion may not be only about M*A*S*H, or *Providence*, or Hollywood. Since we're as likely to talk about war, or peace, or human rights, or maybe even how I could possibly object to executing some fang-toothed, slobbering monster, they want to fit me into a category.

But I don't want to be put into somebody's category. I'd rather just talk and let whoever's listening take it in, see if it fits and figure out how they feel about it—and maybe even why. Pigeonholing does the public's thinking for them, and kind of insults them in the process. I don't want to be part of that. Because it's been quite a trip, this journey of mine. So if someone wants to discuss—or debate—the issues, I'm happy to do that, but I'd rather not start off with a label that sets someone's teeth on edge.

Say I'm a "liberal" and some think they know my views on everything. They start dialing the phone or writing an angry letter without even knowing what I'll say. Or others think we agree, when we might not.

I've been around the block a few times now, and I think I've learned some things. A lot of these things have surprised me, and many have been painful, but mostly what I've learned is how lucky I am. This is some world we live in. I've been privileged to see a fair amount of it, and the more I experience, the more I realize the special place we inhabit in it.

Being an American, as I've discovered, is often a great privilege.

Being a privileged person in today's world—a world where much of what we take for granted here is unknown elsewhere—makes you think. It's made me think about the invisible people who live a quiet life of misery—and about those whose misery has made them unwilling to remain quiet.

Where do I fit in? becomes the question, and, *What is my responsibility here? What does it mean to be alive in the world today? What part do I play as an American?*

Like it or not, we Americans play a big part in the world, not all of it positive, as you'll note if—unlike our current president—you read the papers. So knowing who you are and what being a citizen of the United States means is important. I've certainly found it to be.

It's more than "Don't worry, be happy," or "Shop till you drop" and spend your way into debt. It's more than "Go for the gold" and drink hearty and cheer the team—singing the national anthem first, if you can remember the words.

It's much larger than that. It's what we aspire to and yearn for and what we owe to each other. It's about making the invisible visible, about salvaging those thought disposable, about recognizing and reassuring those who think they don't count, or perhaps fear they don't actually exist.

But there are some who don't really want us to know all this, or take it too seriously. These are the folks who want to make your decisions for you; who want to put you to sleep. Today it's friends of Karl Rove, tomorrow it will be someone else. They want power and money, and money and power, and they don't want—regardless of what they say—you to think too much. They want you out of the way, kicking back and relaxing, dreaming about winning the lottery.

They don't want you to think about life and love and responsibility: what I've come to think of as the spirit of America. They'd rather take charge, make the decisions and relieve you of all that. Because as the spirit of America awakens, as it struggles to find its way out from under the authoritarian cloud that's now attempting to smother it, as it reasserts itself as a beacon of hope for the world, we take back the power granted us so many years ago by those who invented the American dream. And those who would deny us that right have to go back into their caves.

That's what I've found in my journey toward becoming a citizen. I hope what follows will ring some bells for you.

Mike Farrell
Studio City, California
January 2007

Chapter 1
HOME

My growing up was done here in Southern California, in a small, unincorporated strip of Los Angeles County known as West Hollywood. That was before West Hollywood became a city of its own. There was no magic dividing line—at least none visible—but we were just across the tracks from Beverly Hills, where the houses were huge, the streets quiet, the cars new, and the police quick to check when anyone looked like he didn't belong. Everything was as it should be—complete with a veneer of entitlement.

West Hollywood included the famous Sunset Strip, though that was way above us, literally and figuratively, and the entire shootin' match was patrolled by L.A. County Sheriffs. They didn't bother us much, probably because they paid more attention to the small Mexican community living in an unpaved area of run-down pre-fabricated bungalows just south of Santa Monica Boulevard by the big barn where the streetcars slept. The streetcar tracks bisected West Hollywood and ran along Santa Monica all the way from the beach right through our section and on to downtown L.A., with a branch cutting up northeast at Fairfax through people's backyards and making a loop through Hollywood, down the storied boulevard, then connecting back to the downtown line. The streetcar was our link to the world.

We were a fairly typical working-class Irish Catholic family. My folks brought us—me, my younger brother and older sister—out from South St. Paul, Minnesota, when Jim was a baby, I was two, and Sally about seven, because Dad needed work, there was talk of war, and here, it was said, the streets were paved with gold.

Dad's younger brother Matt was already here. A dashing, handsome man, an ice skater with Sonja Henie's troupe, he had been an extra in movies and was now an even more arresting figure in the uniform of the Army Air Corps. He encouraged Dad to come west where jobs were plentiful and a hard-working man could do well.

Dad was a tough guy, the eldest of four kids brought up by a rigid, unpleasant mother and a father who, while a gregarious and popular fellow, traveled a lot, drank, gambled, and fought. He died in a fight, as the story goes, and Dad, still a young man, had to travel to the Dakotas or Montana or someplace to reclaim the body and bring it home. The oldest of three brothers and a sister, Dad's was a struggle against the forces that kept a workingman down. Sometime lumberjack, roustabout, deputy sheriff, and stockyard hand, he was a keenly intelligent man with little formal education who understood that work was the key to survival. Michael Joseph Farrell was my dad's name, same as mine. He went by Joe, while I've always been Mike.

Agnes Sarah Cosgrove Farrell, our mom, was one of ten kids. Raised in the Minnesota countryside in tough circumstances—read *poor*—that got tougher after her father was killed when she was still a child, Ag was a homemaker who never forgot that she came from a world where getting an apple in her stocking for Christmas was a thrill. Though her family was split up, first by World War I and then the Depression, the bonds never weakened. Eventually they all gathered in South St. Paul, where work was available in the stockyards, and they ended up living within blocks of one another, most for the rest of their lives. Agnes graduated high school, where she learned shorthand, and avoided the stockyards, for a while working as a clerk at the FBI office in St. Paul, something about which we teased her in later years. She said she had once seen John Dillinger—or was it Pretty Boy Floyd? Whichever, he was a handsome, dapper man who had the office in a flutter.

Agnes and Joe met at a dance, courted, married, and settled down. Work was not easy to come by as the war approached, so after struggling for a few years, Dad responded to the siren call of the West

Coast and packed up his family. Leaving her mother and siblings must have been terribly painful for Mom, who was notoriously easily moved to tears, but she was made of tough stuff and had a strong sense of loyalty. She stood by her man in the same way she stuck by her faith, with a deep and abiding commitment. If there were questions, none of us ever heard them. And once situated in California, she put all her energies into making a home. She cooked; she cleaned; she sewed; she bathed us and read to us and bandaged our wounds. She scrimped; she saved; she shopped; she cleaned; she cooked; she scrimped; she saved. She was always busy at something, and whatever she was doing, no matter how boring or tiring it might have been, she hummed as she did it.

She saved. I hated, hated, hated that she took us to the "Old Store," the Goodwill, to buy our clothes. This was long before used clothing was a fashion trend, and it stung mightily. The smell of that store, the idea of having to wear shoes, pants or a shirt that someone had cast off, the notion that the other kids we knew got to have their own brand-new clothes, all made me hot with shame. I dreaded the fact that someone might see us going in or out of the Old Store. It doesn't take a genius to understand why I now have more shoes than I can wear and a tough time throwing things away even when I no longer have any use for them.

We did live in a nice house in a nice neighborhood, money notwithstanding. Not ritzy, of course, this was the county strip. Mom cracked about the "lace-curtain Irish" and the "shanty Irish," and despite the work she did to keep the house and all of us clean, it was clear which ones we were. Dad had to borrow money for the down payment from his mother, whom we knew as "Gommie." In addition to having a room in our house that was off-limits to all of us whether she was there or not, Gommie also extracted a few pounds of flesh on an ongoing basis from both my parents for having made the house possible.

Gommie was a horror. Tough, mean, hard, bitter, bigoted, strict, doubtless miserably unhappy, she gave no quarter and, though none of us ever had the guts to check, probably asked none in return. She was a baby nurse—what we today call a live-in nanny—usually working for quite well-to-do families, sometimes for years. The thought horrifies me still. She was a neurosis-inducing machine if there ever was one, and I shudder to think of those poor kids today, trying to work things out on a psychiatrist's couch or in a bottle somewhere. On vacation or between jobs, Gommie came to live with us, periods in which the dread quotient at home rose perceptibly. She lived to quite an advanced age and softened considerably in the later years, poor dear, but by then the damage was done.

Grannie, Mom's mom, was Sarah "Sade" Cosgrove, who died not too long after we came to California. I remember a teary Mom getting on a train to go back for the funeral. She took Jim, who was too young to leave with us. I have few actual memories of Grannie, only that she was a sweet woman of considerable girth and an even bigger heart. Raising ten kids on her own was a monumental task in those days—in any days—and she succeeded to the degree that her memory is cherished and she was always spoken of with great affection. I'm told that when I was a tot in Minnesota, I was Grannie's "cookie boy."

We Farrell kids never knew either of our grandfathers, something that feels like more of a loss as I think of it today. As with Mom torn from her family and Dad thrust out on his own, we had to find our way without the guideposts some consider essential.

Sally was a very smart girl who suffered the particular difficulties associated with having been born blind in one eye, the blind one discolored. Our folks lacked the money to have the eye replaced with a false one that more nearly matched the good one, so she dealt daily with the humiliation of being "different" or, probably worse from her perspective, unattractive. Sally was an independent soul, doubtless toughened by experience. She was the only one of us who had the temerity to disobey orders from Dad, though even she would not do so openly.

Jim was cute, bright, cheerful, and enormously talented—good at everything, with an inner gyroscope that always had him landing on his feet. He was a charming kid who won friends easily and kept them. He suffered from being the little brother, of course, and I was so consumed by my need for attention and affection from Dad that I gave him short shrift, much to my later dismay. As a result, or perhaps simply because of his own adventurous spirit, he began early to blaze an independent trail.

In all, ours was what we thought of as a "happy" family. Except for the fear. Dad was a tough guy—he probably learned to fight from his father and to wield a wicked, sarcastic tongue from his mother. He was a big man, powerful and commanding, and like many men of his era, not given to tenderness or expressions of sentiment. He wasn't comfortable with emotion, his or other people's, and he protected himself well, clearly buying into the old cliché about the best defense. He wasn't physically brutal in the sense that we think of as child abuse today, but if any of us stepped out of line, one way or another, we quickly regretted it. Worse, we (or maybe I should speak only for myself) lived in terror of the devastation that would result if he were ever to truly unleash his arsenal.

Drinking wasn't just something that happened on special occasions in our house. It was pretty much a constant. Beer was the drug of choice; the hard stuff wasn't usually brought out unless friends or family were over. And when not at work, Dad (and sometimes Mom) could often be found at the local bar less than a block away.

A great deal was demanded of us kids, most of it stuff we had to intuit. Nobody talked about anything real, but it seemed we were expected to know everything. One learns in that situation to listen well, especially for the unspoken warnings. The antennae are always up. Certain things were understood, most of them negatives. You didn't cry. You didn't say certain words. You didn't do certain things. If you got into a fight, you were in trouble, but if you didn't win, it was worse. You learned by listening well, watching the signals, and being smart enough to stay ahead of the storm. Or you learned by doing it wrong and paying the price. To this day, whenever stepping into a room, I check things out carefully. I listen well and am good at watching for signals, sensing tension, picking up nuance. Survival instinct well learned.

Our deal was you went to church and to confession and to communion. You believed in the Virgin Birth and the Holy Trinity, and you got down on your knees and said your prayers morning and night. "Lord, I am not worthy . . ." was the mantra. You did those things because that was the way it was done. If you didn't, it was a sin, and you'd go to Hell. Since getting up and off to school on time was always a problem for me, I worked out what I thought was a pretty good compromise and tried saying my prayers twice at night to save time in the morning. Unsure if this was acceptable to God, I checked it through his emissary, the priest in the confessional. Not a chance, he said. So much for compromise; good intentions be damned.

It didn't matter that you didn't understand what was being said at Mass; you went anyway, and you knelt when they knelt and stood when they stood. And you struck your breast when the bells rang and made sure God knew you knew you weren't worthy. Sure it was a dead language, but there was a reason for doing it exactly that way. There must have been. To question meant Hell. It didn't matter, either, that you couldn't understand what Father O'Reilly said after Mass, though that was supposed to be English. He talked so fast with his brogue so thick that all I understood was that I was Michael the Archangel and a soldier of the Lord. I wasn't sure what a soldier of the Lord was supposed to do, but it became pretty clear what he wasn't supposed to do. The list of "don'ts" kept getting longer, the load heavier, but you couldn't ask why because that was one of the don'ts. What I "got" was that this was the way it had always been done and this was the way it was supposed to be done. There were a lot of mysteries, and there was a lot of fear: fear of God, fear of Dad, fear of pain, fear of failure, fear of not measuring up. It was hard to figure out exactly what we were supposed to measure up to, but it was probably hanging on the cross up there.

World War II was fought at home in a number of ways. Our door was always open to friends and family, some in uniform. Rose, one of Mom's sisters, came out and went to work at a war plant, a regular Rosie the Riveter. Mom shopped even more carefully, using scrip and little ration coins, and was excited when the chance came to buy meat. We had no bubble gum because, the story went, the Army needed rubber for tires for jeeps and trucks. My one clear memory is of pulling up in Dad's old Pontiac and getting out at the curb beside our house as the man on the radio announced, *"The war is over!"* That was good, I could tell.

Not too long thereafter, we got a call in the middle of the night—one of those you learn to dread. Uncle Matt, the dashing, handsome, uniformed hero, had been killed in an automobile accident. What followed was the first of what now seems a regular succession of Irish wakes at our house, with Matt's body there in our dining room in an open coffin, looking waxen and stiff, but sort of okay. There was a sickening smell of too many flowers; lots of adults shuffling around, lots of drinking, lots of murmured stories, and lots of tears, though mostly from the women. Of course nobody explained anything to the kids; we just got to watch and listen and try to figure it all out.

A couple of years later, when I was about seven or eight, Jim and I were taken out for a long ride by friends of the family. It was weird; we knew these people, but they didn't normally just take us for rides. I don't know where Sally was—and Mom was gone for some reason—but I knew this was a weird ride. Nobody told us where we were going, and, in fact, nobody seemed to have a very clear idea about that. There was a lot of chitchat, some coded words exchanged, and a lot of discomfort, all of which made me increasingly ill at ease and certain that there was something terribly wrong. But of course I couldn't say that. That's not what we did. Finally, after an hours-long, weird, boring, and unnervingly mysterious ride, it was apparently time for us to head back home. What a relief! And when we got there, Dad was bringing Mom home, and with them was a baby: our new little sister Kathy. That's how it works, we learned. People you don't know very well take you for a weird ride, and when you come home, you have a new baby sister.

Kathy was a cute kid and very smart. She was pretty and fun, and we were all family. Maybe she was all that was needed and everything would now become clear. But no; she added a few new notes, but it was the same tune. We watched over her and enjoyed her, always making sure she was okay. Kathy was, as she grew up a bit, the only one of us who had Dad's coloring. She had his dark hair and brown eyes, while Jim, Sally, and I all had blue eyes and light hair like Mom's side of the family. Maybe it was that, or maybe it was simply that she was his little girl, but Dad was always affectionate with Kathy, picking her up and hugging her when she came running as he got home from work. I envied her so much I ached.

I kept trying to win his approval. I was the nicest, the best little boy I knew how to be, smiling and hiding the fact that I hadn't yet figured it out. If being "good" would do it, I was going for the gold star. I'm sure I was a huge pain in the ass. I know I was a prig. But I so wanted him to let me know I was okay that everything else took a distant second. As I see it now, I was afraid that I didn't exist without his approval. He simply terrified me. I hated living in fear all the time, but the awareness that pain awaited any misstep—not necessarily physical pain, but certainly humiliation and rejection—hung like a shroud over everything, and it took years to recognize the rage it produced. It has much to do, I know, with the degree to which I simply cannot tolerate injustice.

I certainly never gave voice to it then; I never even recognized it. He was Dad, for Christ's sake, and I was just a kid. He was the biggest, toughest bastard on the block: great-looking, smart, charming. He was just a workingman, of course, but so popular and powerful that, to my mind, he was John Wayne–Plus. You crossed him, you were dead meat. I don't know how many times he came down the street from Bill Ruby's bar, the nearby saloon, burst through the front door and announced, "If the cops come, I'm not home," then headed for the bedroom, leaving us open-mouthed, full of questions we were unable to ask, deputized to cover for him. Mom dealt with it stoically. She dealt with everything stoically. Sometimes she was with him at

Ruby's or some other joint, sometimes not. When she was, another man paying her too much attention might end up flat on his back, initiating a quick departure and our deputization.

Don't get me wrong; it wasn't a constant brawl, nor was our home a place of horror. There were quiet times, good times. Dad coached our Cub Scout softball team, if rarely, and, when I took up the trumpet, used to have me play "Oh, My Papa" for friends after enough drinks were shared. There were certainly laughs; it's just that everything seemed overlain with a sense of potential explosion. Dad worked hard, worked constantly, it seemed. Mom too. And when Dad came home from work, we'd eat, he'd lie on the couch and fall asleep; and then, if we dared wake him because we couldn't hear the TV over his snoring, he'd get up and go to bed. I understand now that working himself sick to keep food on the table and a roof over our heads was his way of showing he loved us. The quick temper, the sarcasm, the fighting, while part of his personal legacy, were also signs of personal torment, probably frustration at not being able to do more for us. I get that now, after years of struggling and thinking and working and therapizing and fuming and weeping over it. *Now* doesn't help the terrified little kid I was then, except for the part of me that's still him. *Then* was when it would have really helped. He just never gave it words. Nor did he show it in a way I could understand. Mom was the same, I guess, though more gentle about it. She came from the same tradition and wasn't given to loving words or even loving pats. She showed up. But there were no hugs. We didn't touch. It's just the way they had learned it, I suppose. But God, it was lonely.

They arose before dawn. He ate; she heated water for him to pour into the radiator of his old car. Then he was off to work, and she got us up for school. She fed us, made our lunches, got us off, and then did her cleaning and shopping. During the war there was the rationing; after it there was still the rationing imposed by pocketbook, but she made do without complaint. From trailing along with her sometimes, we knew that she'd walk miles, from store to store, in order to save pennies on some needed item. She was a world-class shopper and a marathon walker. But she was always there when we got home from school, cleaning and cooking and humming. And dinner was on the table when Dad came home from work.

We grew up, and the dynamic didn't change much. We figured things out the best we could and caught hell when we got it wrong. When old enough, we got work, Sal being the first to have a real job. After high school, after she had saved enough money and, I assume, Mom and Dad helped out as best they could, Sal finally had the operation to remove her bad eye and put in a replacement that more resembled the good one. It still wasn't the same, didn't move correctly with the other one, but it was closer.

After mowing lawns or doing odd jobs enough to save for a used bike, I got a paper route. Jim went with me until he was old enough to have his own. Mom would often help us fold the papers before we took off to deliver. The headlines were about war in Korea and the Commies here at home, but none of it had much impact on our lives from what I could see, except to begin my fascination with the Marines as the embodiment of everything manly and tough. I still wanted Dad's approval and recognition, though try as I might, the most I could get from him was the occasional acknowledgment, more often ridicule or a cutting, embarrassing remark, too often in front of friends. Nurturing was not in the vocabulary back then.

Left alone, for the most part, to find our way in the world, we looked outside for our lessons, hoping for counsel and support, each bearing in our own way the cross of unmet hopes and dreams. For me it was the aching need for acceptance and appreciation, for love—if not from my dad from someone somewhere, but really from my dad— that would validate my existence, help me understand this life I feared and was sure I was getting wrong. And somewhere in my subconscious, I held onto the sound of my mother humming.

That's hardly an exhaustive description of home and family, of course. It's only a cursory glance at the early days, but it's in these days that images, ideals, and concepts are formed, character begins to be defined, and one's sense of life's purpose takes shape. For me it was a daunting world in which disaster lurked. Things were not at all clear. What I knew without question was that those with power were often cruel to those without. I hated that more than anything but had no idea what I could do about it except learn to smile ingratiatingly, dance when necessary, and duck. I played by the rules as best I could make them out and tried not to be extinguished by the interplay of powerful forces around me.

Our core group of friends from school and the neighborhood was largely from the same social and economic class and was basically comprised of good kids. Jim and I got particularly lucky when a coach at West Hollywood Park where we hung out saw a group of us running around unsupervised and organized us into a club. Marvin Bass was his name, and it should be inscribed in the pantheon of heroes. Marv got the club, which we named the "Banshees," into a "Y" league to give focus to our physical energies, but he aimed higher than that. His genius was in organization and direction. Our club had meetings, dues, and rules to follow; we elected officers and learned a form of discipline enforced by swats—not, in that sense, unlike home, though different in that the rules were clear. Most importantly, Marv introduced us to "the chair," a process that cracked open doors of thought and communication largely unknown to us at the time.

Once a month our regular weekly club meeting was devoted to "the chair." Each member would take his turn in a chair in the middle of the room while the rest of us, one at a time, would offer some kind of "constructive criticism." No one was allowed to pass; everyone had to offer some thought, however mild. Marv made clear that this was an important part of friendship and that we had to be careful to be both honest and fair. This was not the time to take a cheap shot or vent a petty grievance; it was an opportunity to help each other grow. It would be good, he counseled, not only for the one in the chair, but also for each of those participating. And it was. It was very hard at first, because most of us had never learned to deal honestly with one another in this way, but with Marv's careful guidance, we were introduced to the value of candor, of caring, and the true nature of friendship.

At home the status was quo. Hormones began to rage, tormenting me with all the pressures and desires that my religion said assured damnation. Sneaking peeks at Sally's movie magazines in hopes of seeing an ad for bras or girdles exposed me, pun intended, to another fantasy world. People, I learned, became famous for being actors, some of them young people. And with fame, it was clear from those slick pages, came attention—lots of it—and what must certainly be love.

Well, hell, went my secret thoughts, *I can probably do that.* Had I the insight at the time, I'd have realized it was what I'd been doing all along: acting like I wasn't terrified. And here we were, living in the middle of the world of movies and stardom and fame. Dad was becoming more regularly employed as a carpenter in the studios. When we went to Carl's Market up on Doheny, didn't we sometimes see movie people from Beverly Hills shopping there? And when I was in Mrs. Loops's second grade class at West Hollywood Grammar School, didn't I have a big crush on Natasha Gurdin, better known as Natalie Wood? How could I ever forget that once, when we were in line, she a few people ahead of me, someone told her that I *liked* her. She turned, beautiful even then and incredibly self-possessed, and smiled, saying, "Why, Mike, why didn't you tell me?" I, of course, immediately beet-red and utterly tongue-tied, was unable, to my everlasting regret, to say a word in response.

Thus was born the secret dream of being an actor; a dream, however, that had to be kept secret because I was painfully shy, terribly fearful of being exposed and ridiculed. To give voice to such a fantasy was to ensure humiliation from Dad and risk it from others. "Shy," in fact, hardly describes it. It was grotesquely painful. Every new experience threatened disaster. In what was probably my first date, I somehow asked young Jackie Skeba, a girl we knew from the park, to go to the movies. On the appointed day, I headed to her house, and we walked together to the streetcar. I paid our fares as we got on, but when we went to sit down, I couldn't muster the courage to sit beside her, so sat instead in the row behind. She tried to talk me into coming to sit beside her, but I, poor fainthearted dunce, simply couldn't. I have no memory of the rest of the date and can only assume I was able to go into the theater with her, but where I sat has receded into the mists of memory.

Throughout junior high school, I did my best to obey the rules and hoped I was doing things right. I was, for the most part, a "good boy," pathetically so, in retrospect. Not that I should have been bad, but pathetic in that the good was only a product of fear. I figured that if I was good enough, sooner or later somebody would let me in on the secret. I didn't understand it in exactly those terms at the time; all I knew was that there was something I was supposed to know and that so far I hadn't gotten it. I was a good, fairly bright if unimaginative student and in social situations increasingly something of a leader, though always dreadfully aware of the fact that I was only one step ahead of disaster. At any moment I might be unmasked. I didn't know the secret. Every class I went into, every new situation was the same. Everyone there was comfortable. Everyone there seemed to know what needed to be done, when it had to be done, and how to do it. Everyone knew but me. Seeking affirmation, I ran for and was elected Student Body President at Bancroft Junior High School. True to form, once elected I had not a clue as to what one did in that role. But I was nice.

As I grew older and got into more involved social situations, I simply became better able to fake it. I still didn't have a clue. I dated and was terrified. At Hollywood High, the "Banshees" became the "Saracens," and our group, though larger, still provided the safety zone inside which we could operate with a reasonable understanding of our own rules. We weren't the tough guys, nor were we the star athletes or the lovers, and I know that some regarded us as squares and goons. But it was a cocoon that protected us and allowed us to operate in an increasingly complicated world, and I was grateful for it then—as I am now.*

The mother of Blair White, one of the guys, was a psychiatrist, and she organized those of us who were interested into a weekly teen group session that opened my eyes just a bit to what psychotherapy might have to offer. But I wasn't willing to expose my fears in front of my friends. What I had besides the guys was God, or at least what I had been taught to believe about God. And I clung to that tenaciously, sometimes ferociously. I read the Bible and theologians like Hans Küng and tried to figure out where a miserable sinner like me could hang his hat, could hope to be able to keep hoping. If I truly didn't matter, perhaps didn't even actually exist—a possibility I feared—I simply had to have something to believe in, for God's sake.

After high school we established a tradition, again at Marv's suggestion, of meeting for dinner once a year. For fifty years now, as many as can make it gather every spring and touch base. And we still do a form of "the chair"—though without the critique— where each member brings the rest up to date on his life, loves, family, successes, trials and tribulations.

Chapter 2
LESSONS

I still had to work after school. I had graduated from the paper route to selling papers on a corner—and was terribly embarrassed by this when a high-school classmate once drove by with her parents. After a temporary move to soda jerk, I finally got a "real" job driving a delivery truck for Sales Fulton Market, a Beverly Hills grocer whose clientele included some big show-business names. Taking groceries in through the delivery entrances of the homes of Groucho Marx, Jack Benny, Lucille Ball and Desi Arnaz, Rosemary Clooney and José Ferrer, Jimmy Stewart, Jane Russell, Jimmy Durante, and many others was heady stuff. I'd fantasize about being "discovered" as just the young potential star someone was looking for. During one of my deliveries, the beautiful Dorothy Malone came into the kitchen and was kind, made small talk, and asked me what I eventually wanted to do. To my confession that I wanted to be an actor, her sweet response was, "Oh, yes, you should." I was a goner.

But back in real life, it went unstated. In the evenings and on weekends, the guys and I cruised and roughhoused, expanding our horizons a little at a time. But even within the safety of the club there was this sense of inadequacy, this lack of completeness dogging me. I had my little secret, and I still didn't know the big one.

It was soon to become crushingly clear that I might never be able to learn it. When I was seventeen—a senior at Hollywood High, a virginal yet throbbing sexual time bomb sure to soon explode, a devout Catholic terrified of eons in Purgatory, a fairly popular guy with a still-secret desire to become an actor yet too shy to stand and address his public speaking class, and a boy on the cusp of manhood who hadn't yet developed the courage to ask a probing question of his father, let alone confront him—my dad died. Died as in dead. Died as in subject rather than host of an open-coffin Irish wake at our house with requisite flowers, drinkers, mourners, friends, stories and tears, if mostly from the women. Dead, waxy, and slightly off-looking as he lay in his coffin at fifty years of age. My dad, the biggest, toughest, smartest, strongest bastard on the block—gone from a heart attack. John Wayne–get-outta-the-way Dad, dead. And to top it off, as the eldest son I was now, they told me, the man of the house. Take his place. Right.

He had not been well, but none of us thought it was serious. How could it be? He was Dad. He'd had stomach problems for years. He would suddenly pull the car over, get out and cross behind it to puke. But in another moment, he'd throw the car door open to threaten some "horse's ass" who had cut us off or honked impatiently or followed too closely. He was Dad. He'd had surgery a couple of years earlier to remove an ulcer, and he drank some pretty awful-smelling crap to deal with it, but he was Dad, this monolith, this overwhelming, imposing, threatening, all-powerful, surely eternal force.

And now he was gone.

Somehow the world seemed to go on. Mom, as always, was stoic. We all sucked it in and made it clear she'd be okay. I graduated from high school and went to work, knowing that my eighteenth birthday would soon mean a draft notice. College was not on our family's agenda, never had been. Given the odds, I took a deep breath, followed the fantasy fed by watching John Wayne in *The Sands of Iwo Jima*, and with my buddy Pat Merrifield, joined the Marines. Being a Marine meant you were tough, capable, and a man. After all, "the Marine Corps builds men," and if I could do it, that proved something, right? Pat and I had read *Guadalcanal Diary* and seen *Battle Cry*, and had hyped each other on the lore of the Corps for years. Joining the Marines was part of this dream that we had built up for ourselves. Being in the Marines was a different thing entirely.

* * *

Boot camp at MCRD, the Marine Corps Recruit Depot in San Diego, was, as advertised, brutal. I had graduated in January and Pat not until June, and I waited so we could go in together. This, cleverly, had us starting boot camp in July, the hottest, most miserable time of the year in San Diego—only to be followed, as it happens, by August and September, which are worse.

The process of making men, as defined by the Marine Corps in the late 1950s, was to grind you down physically, humiliate and degrade you emotionally, abuse you psychologically, and destroy you spiritually. Then they could build you back up into their ideal: a lean, mean fighting machine that would attack and destroy the enemy on command, with no questions asked, no matter how suicidal the mission. They didn't want smart-asses who thought for themselves and who might, when ordered to charge the hill or destroy the machine-gun nest, say, "Uh, sarge, that doesn't sound like such a good idea to me. A guy could get hurt doing that." They started grinding us down from the day we came through the gate and never let up.

Pat and I were separated immediately, which was not part of our plan. He was put into Platoon 373 and I into 374. Unlike our fantasy, we saw little of each other for the duration; bucking each other up was limited to the occasional quick sighting. The guys in my platoon were all young and the usual mix of fat and thin, tough and not so, big and little, somewhat smart and not very. Our head Drill Instructor (DI) was Sergeant Kelly, a big, mean, hard-assed Irishman very much like my dad, who made no secret of his contempt for us and for our chances to become real Marines. Number two was Sergeant Reyes, also hard-assed and mean, a Mexican-American. By way of introduction, Reyes announced that he'd kick the shit out of all of us until we failed and went crying home to Mommy. He promised that at some point during boot camp every one of us would want to kill him. I thought he was being dramatic. Number three was Corporal Stark, a Southerner who was nearer our age and clearly determined to demonstrate the difference between us puny-ass, chickenshit recruits and real Marines like himself. Not the brightest bulb in the chandelier, Stark had a lot to live up to in his two superiors, and we were the vehicles by which he could show his stuff.

Life, as expected, was tough. More than tough, it was miserable. By any reasonable standard, it was fucking awful. We were scalped, shot full of vaccines, screamed at, laughed at, poked, prodded, jeered, stripped, clothed, humiliated, made to run and run and run, then stand at attention in the blistering heat until some passed out, then run some more—and that was the first day or so. Because I was one of the taller recruits, I was made a Squad Leader, thus given responsibility for those in my command. If they screwed up, I ate it. In the ensuing weeks, we learned the history of the Corps, ran the obstacle course, took tests, ran the "grinder" (the half-mile-long by quarter-mile-wide asphalt parade ground that made men weep), hit the sack exhausted at taps and arose exhausted at reveille, tried to stay awake as we learned military protocol, learned close-order drill, learned to carry, sleep with, field-strip, clean and fire weapons, and throw hand-grenades. The occasional breather was always marked by the command, "The smoking lamp is lit," making smoking the only "luxury" afforded us amidst the assault. This encouraged many who had never smoked to start and made the term "breather" rather ironic. My dad having been a heavy smoker—Camels—I wasn't tempted. We marched, ran, beat each other with pugil sticks (simulated bayonet/rifle butt combat), completed the obstacle course in ever-better time while carrying any shitbirds who slowed us down, learned hand-to-hand combat, learned to care for equipment and uniforms, took a required swimming test, stood inspections, withstood humiliation, abuse, the occasional beating, and generally struggled to survive. Some failed. Some went "over the hill," a few cracked up, one decided I was the enemy and threatened to kill me. No one in our hut took the threat too seriously until Sergeant Reyes discovered in a surprise inspection that the guy had squirreled away live ammunition. The poor bastard was taken away under guard and we never saw him again.

We lived in Quonset huts, corrugated tin, half-round structures that look like someone sliced an oil can in half, top to bottom, and laid it on the open side. Everything inside and out had to be spit-shined and polished, the racks (bunks) tightly made, footlockers perfectly arranged. A door at each end of the hut opened onto a concrete step to the asphalt walkway, a few huts down from which was the head (latrine/toilet). On each side of the concrete step was a patch of "grass," per the DIs, the only ones with the right to step on it. For one of us to do so was an invitation to disaster. This strip of "grass" was actually sand, probably four feet wide by eight feet long, and part of our duty was to maintain it by raking it into perfect, symmetrical, undisturbed rows. A DI would, of course, walk right across it coming into or going out of the hut for a snap inspection or some other harassment, and if one of us failed to immediately spot and repair the damage by raking over the footprints and restoring the perfect furrows, there was hell to pay.

Because boot camp was on a set schedule of weeks, new companies of recruits arrived regularly and provided a basis for comparison. On the grinder or on the obstacle course, progress became easier to measure as we noted the sloppiness of the others in close-order drill, the number of those who fell out, collapsing in sobbing or unconscious heaps as we double-timed past them looking sharper and feeling more fit by the day. On one occasion, the hierarchy of priorities came clear as we marched smartly in close-order drill on the grinder near a new platoon undergoing inspection by their DI, who was savagely berating a recruit at the top of his lungs: "You are a filthy-assed pissant excuse for a Marine, private! You are a disgusting, chickenshit insult to this platoon, boy! You know what this is in your ear, boy? This is dirt, boy! Dirt! Do you hear me, cockroach? Dirt! D-E-R-T, dirt!"

One of the few moments of real, if hidden, delight came when we realized we could outrun Stark. On the grinder, when he got tired and would stand in one place and run us in circles around him, he could gloat, but when we got to Camp Matthews for rifle range training and had the long, cross-country runs, we realized we had him. He had the authority, of course, and could call a break when he needed it, so there was no way we could take advantage or make an issue of it. But there came a time when we had him and he knew it. Small victory, much needed. Kelly, on the other hand, was a rock. Reyes ran us in some circles as well, but Kelly matched us step for step.

Eventually, I was promoted from Squad Leader to Left Guard. A big recruit named Moreno had been named Right Guard, and I was now his counterpart. Left and Right Guards are the two most senior positions in the platoon of recruits. Right Guard marches at the head of the platoon, carrying the Guide-On (flag). Left Guard brings up the rear, keeping things tight and ensuring there are no stragglers.

Breaking down, going crazy, or going over the hill weren't in the cards for most of us, though I suspect everyone gave each some thought. After Sergeant Reyes clobbered me with the butt of a rifle, I swore to myself, *I'm going to kill that son of a bitch*, making clear his first-day promise wasn't simple theatrics. But what was a real possibility at all times, and probably the thing we most feared, was being "set back." If you got sick or were injured and had to go to "sick bay," got put in the brig, or maybe just weren't cutting it and fell into disfavor with the DIs, you were reassigned, once out or recovered, to another company of recruits who had started later than we had. Being thus set back in the schedule meant, aside from losing the minimal comfort of being with the guys you'd gotten to know and having some understanding of the idiosyncrasies of the DIs who'd been your torturers up to now, being sentenced to a longer term in boot camp. The idea was almost unimaginably awful, yet the prospect loomed large for all of us.

And one day it happened to me. Summoned to the DIs' hut with Moreno and the Squad Leaders, I stood rigidly at attention with the others as we listened to our orders. As the room got lighter around me and began to rotate, I started to lose my balance. Feeling myself start to go, I put out a hand, hoping to steady myself on Sergeant Kelly's oil stove, a breach punishable by death when standing at attention.

Instead of screaming or going for my throat, Kelly barked, "Farrell, you okay?"

"Sir, yes, sir!" I responded, loudly, as was the routine. Then I fell over.

Sick Bay was just another Quonset hut like the one we'd been living in for weeks. Guys were there with bandages, casts on arms and legs, and a few, like me, with what was apparently some kind of flu. *Shit, shit, shit!* I thought through the haze of fever and fugue. I didn't want to be there. Couldn't I just go back to 374 and gut it out? Anything but being set back. I'd rather die. After a couple of days with the only word from a Navy Corpsman who took temperatures and dispensed medicine, I figured it was all over. Then a miracle happened. Someone from the platoon came in to check on me. It was probably Stark. I know it wasn't Kelly, and it wouldn't have been Reyes. Whoever, he wanted to know how I was doing and if I thought I could get back on duty soon.

"Yes, sir," I muttered, hope stirring faintly.

"Kelly wants you back," he said. Or at least I think he said that, if it wasn't all a dream.

However it happened, whatever was said, the next day I was back in hell. But it was 374, the hell I knew, and I was, go figure, grateful. The routine was just as awful, but I was quickly back in shape and able to keep up. We were getting to be "short-timers" at this point with only a few weeks to go before graduation, and there was a general heightening of tension along with a quickening of the pace of training and testing. Something that we knew would come before graduation was an inspection by the Commanding Officer of the base, a big deal. One of the tests we took, while not an IQ test, gave a result that in some manner was supposed to conform to an intelligence rating. When we got our scores, Sergeant Reyes came up and asked what mine was. After I told him, he did a take and said, "What?" I told him again, and he nodded, made a face, and walked away. I didn't know what to make of that, but one didn't question a DI.

Later I saw Pat for a minute. He said the CO inspection would be, in part, a test of the company's DIs and that a recruit from one platoon would be selected as "honor man," presented with a set of dress blues (the formal Marine Corps uniform), and promoted to Private First Class. Word had it, he said, that 374 was favored, with Sergeant Reyes pushing Moreno and Kelly promoting me.

Scuttlebutt is hard to comprehend. I'll never understand where Merrifield got his information, but our inspection went well and I was able to handle the CO's questions. Then, about a week before we were to graduate, Sergeant Kelly called me into his hut and said, "Farrell, you got the blues," and nodded, his face immobile as ever, not so much as a hint that he gave a shit.

I said, "Sir, yes, sir. Thank you, sir," did an about face, and stepped smartly out. And on graduation day, when our company marched onto the parade ground before officers and family members there for the big event, the Left Guard of Platoon 374 was wearing the U.S. Marine Corps' Dress Blue uniform with a single stripe on the sleeve. Honor man without a clue.

It was odd, I have to say. I was now officially a man, so certified by no less than the United States Marines, but all I could figure was that I had once again somehow managed to skate by. I remember thinking, as some of us talked later about where we'd be stationed afterward, that after three months of misery and pain I'd rather stay here at MCRD and go through boot camp again than head on to someplace where I didn't know the rules. Better the devil you know.

Going home on the first liberty allowed me to step out a bit and show off the uniform (not the Blues, which were saved for formal or special occasions—and remain in my closet today), yet back in the real world nothing seemed changed. I now knew how to kill with my bare hands, but when I went to see some friends from school, in particular a couple of the girls from my class, I was still the jerk who didn't know the secret.

Advanced Infantry Training (ITR) at Camp Pendleton was similar to boot camp in that they ran us and marched us all the hell over the place. Here, though, other than when we were on bivouac in the field or had guard duty, we had nights and weekends off. And if we thought our DIs could run, these guys were mountain goats. Up, down, no matter the incline, they were tireless and didn't mind showing us how much tougher we had to get before being Marines in their eyes. But the thing that sticks with me from that time is the shipping out of a Bogart. There were two of them and they were brothers. They may have been fraternal twins; one was a big, well-built, good-looking kid, the other shorter, smaller, scrawny by comparison, with glasses. They had joined together, gone through boot together, and been promised that they'd stay together throughout their time in. One day, however, orders came down for the little one, who was told to collect his gear and get in the back of a waiting truck to be taken to his new station. They were both stunned, couldn't believe it, but the bigger one clearly felt responsible and tried to argue. He said he was sure there'd been a mistake—the recruiting sergeant had promised they'd stay together, it was written into their enlistment papers. *Tough shit, Marine; they lied to you, man.*

I hated it. No honor in the Big Green Machine. Say anything to get 'em in, and if they've got a bitch, tell 'em to write their Congressman. I can still see the big guy's face, trying to hide the tears as his brother rolled away in the back of that truck.

My orders were not good news either, as it happened. Every Marine is basically a rifleman, as we were constantly reminded, but the Corps has to meet its own needs so there are other jobs that have to be filled in addition. You're assigned an MOS (military occupation specialty) based on some unknown criteria, and can request certain areas or jobs based on interest or talent. I had no particular interest in specializing. I simply asked to be a basic rifleman, assuming I'd be assigned to the First Marine Division at Camp Pendleton and be able to play war during the week and go home most weekends, unless my country needed me to go fight Commies somewhere. Never assume. My orders were to the Third Marine Division in Okinawa, news that I took very hard. Fact was, it scared the shit out of me, but no matter what clever idea I came up with, I was as helpless as Bogart. And once

ITR was over, I was transferred to a staging area at Pendleton and then put on the U.S.S. Gaffney and shipped overseas.

Being seasick on a troop ship is not a pleasant experience. But then, a troop ship is not a pleasant experience no matter how you feel. I was lost and lonely and scared, but once the seasickness subsided, the trip at least became more bearable. I was still trying to be a good Catholic and went to Mass regularly aboard ship, busily imploring God for just a tiny little heavenly intercession that would magically whisk me back home. But I guess the line was busy. There were, though, a couple of sunsets, when the sea was calm and there was a moment to be alone and quiet on deck and simply take it all in, that were profoundly moving. An overriding sense of peace was possible in spite of everything, I found.

Other than those few moments and the puking and the praying, the trip was noteworthy only because we were informed at one point that we had been put on alert, ordered to circle awaiting a possible change of destination. We might, we learned, be off-loaded in a place known then as French Indo-China to assist a friendly government against an insurgency. Happily, further word shortly came that sent us on to our original destination: Naha, Okinawa.

Okinawa figures large in Marine Corps history. Occupied by the Japanese for many years, it was considered the stepping-stone to an invasion of Japan by both sides in World War II, and the battle to secure it was ferocious and costly. There was still, we were told, festering resentment on the part of many, and certain parts of the island were off-limits. I'll assume, with the benefit of hindsight, that at least part of that resentment arose from a wish for independence, national integrity, and an end to what was seen as an occupation by American forces.

My first assignment was to a typing school in Koza. I was eventually to be the clerk in some company, but first I had to be a typist. Sweet duty, at least for a while. We lived in typical barracks, had an easy schedule, and spent our liberty time in what was known as Koza's

"BC" (business center), a strip of bars, restaurants, clubs, souvenir shops, and whorehouses. I was still incredibly naïve, a virgin, didn't drink or smoke, and was trying hard to be a good Catholic lad; the temptations of BC were more a source of discomfort than excitement. I was certainly aware of attractive women, but mostly embarrassed by the fact that any attention from me was seen as solicitation. I was "one of the guys," certainly, but made uneasy by the behavior and some of the things said by young studs away from home for the first time with money in their pockets and too much to drink. Interestingly, rather than busting my chops about being a "straight arrow," some of the guys, between bouts of giving me shit, toasted and saluted me, accepting my choices as my own and not a condemnation of theirs. Others, perhaps a bit relieved, chose to stick with me. I was so busy trying to find my own way that I didn't spend a lot of time analyzing theirs, but was glad to be accepted as I was.

Typing school finished, I was assigned to Charlie Company in an ONTOS battalion up north at Camp Hansen. ONTOS was a motorized anti-tank vehicle, sort of a combination half-track and recoilless rifle that seemed to break down more than it ran, but if the enemy was going to come at us with tanks, it was thought to be an important part of the defense. Hansen was a tent camp, and the conditions were pretty basic. Without knowing it, I was living a precursor to the life I'd later portray on M*A*S*H, if without the still and most of the laughs. There was a village nearby, but it was off-limits, said to be controlled by Communists and unfriendly. On weekends when we had time to go on liberty, the favored place was Kadena, the U.S. Air Force base near Naha, the capital. It was a schlep, but living in a tent and slopping through mud on a regular basis made the air base at Naha seem a bit like heaven. They had a movie theater, a soda fountain, a PX (post exchange) where we could buy things to send home, and virtually all the comforts of a modern stateside facility. The only thing wrong with it, besides the fact that it was in Okinawa, was that we had to leave and go back to Camp Hansen.

After a few months, I was sent to the hospital at the Navy base in

Yokosuka, Japan, for a problem with my foot. Japan was exotic and interesting, much more modern than Okinawa, certainly, and duty at the hospital was cushy. The cherry blossom trees in bloom are extraordinary, and liberty allowed treks through Yokosuka, a visit to Tokyo, and a ride on the bullet train to see a bit of the country. While there I got to know a Marine named Tyus who was from Ohio. He was a good guy, and we spent some time together at meals, went into town, and had some laughs. Oddly, I noticed some discomfort among the troops around us on the base and finally realized that it was because Tyus was black (or, given that it was the late 1950s, because he was a "Negro"). Nothing was overt, because the services had been integrated for a few years, but our friendship clearly crossed a line.

All of this seems odd now. West Hollywood had not been an "integrated" community in the ideal sense. Though David Espinosa, Tony "Chuy" Estrada, Gloria Rojos, and other Mexican-Americans had been classmates and friends in grammar school and beyond, they pretty much lived separate lives, many of them in the barrio down by the car barns. While our group, the Banshees, was a "club," theirs, the Black Stars, was a "gang." Yet in spite of the differences, we were friends. My dad talked casually about "niggers" and "Heebs" and "shines" and "kikes." But our next-door neighbors, the Rosses, were Jewish and our friends, and we were in and out of each others' homes all the time. Clearly there was a gap between social attitudes and behavior. There were black kids and Latinos at Bancroft Junior High and Hollywood High, though not in great numbers, and while the social separation was indisputable, there was no animosity that I was aware of. Maybe it was naiveté on my part. Certainly it was ignorance as I look back on it now, but racial tensions were not part of my understanding. Palling around with Tyus came naturally and easily because he was a nice guy. And he seemed to feel the same way about me. Go figure.

After a while, as happens in the service, Tyus shipped out. Later I got to know another Marine in Yokosuka, a fellow by the name of

Morgan, and he also became a friend. Sort of the other side of the coin, though I didn't understand that until later—Morgan was white and from New Orleans, Louisiana.

From Yokosuka I was sent back to San Diego, first to Balboa Naval Hospital, where I did guard duty. Morgan arrived there later, and he and another Marine named Mahler came home with me on liberty, stayed with my family, got to know my pals, and became life-long friends.

Coming full circle, after a few months at Balboa I was transferred back to MCRD where I could see recruits going through their ordeal, and then received my discharge.

Chapter 3
BEGINNINGS

Home after the service, things were in many ways the same. Sally was married and out of the house; Jim and Kathy were at home with Mom; Kathy still in school. Mom was working part time for a local realtor, and between her earnings, Dad's Social Security, and what Jim and I contributed—as well, I'm sure, as periodic help from Sal—she was secure and the house was safe. She was still able to make the five-mile walk once a month to make the mortgage payment if one of us couldn't do it for her.

It was an odd time. Many of my friends were off at college, in relationships, a couple actually married. The service was behind me and real life was staring me in the face. College wasn't an option, so I got odd jobs and kind of marked time for a while, trying to figure it out. I eventually got a good job doing what I had done while in high school, delivering groceries. This time it was for Hazan's, a bigger company with a fleet of trucks that brought me again through the back doors of some of the stars' homes I'd delivered to before, plus those of Anthony Quinn, Jerry Lewis, David Janssen, Broderick Crawford, and lots of others. I was helping out quite a bit at home while privately nursing my secret dream of being discovered, and trying to see what life held. At Hazan's, the guy who oversaw everything, routed our deliveries, and generally ran the place was an openly gay man named Bud. He was very smart, quite together, and not in the least shy or apologetic about who he was. Knowing Bud made me begin to take another look at some things.

This being Hollywood, homosexuality was part of the scene. Gays, or "queers," as we knew them, were everywhere, sometimes flamboyantly so, sometimes more or less covert. Often, I came to realize, they were invisible and simply a productive and dignified part of the community. Two men, whom Mom simply referred to as "the boys," bought the house across the street from ours and were thoughtful, polite, perfectly respectable neighbors for years. Her quick acknowledgment and acceptance of them and their lifestyle, like her acceptance of many of the changes she faced in an increasingly complex world, was a testament to her character. My friends and I were often less accepting, particularly when we were younger. Subject to all the fears and fancies of young males, we often behaved hatefully, if truly not intending any harm. Walking home from grammar school, I remember with embarrassment, it was considered an act of daring when passing the Chinese hand laundry just off Santa Monica Boulevard to shout "Ching-chong Chinaman" into the door and run like hell as the proprietor dashed after us screaming epithets of his own. I'm also sure we made life uncomfortable, if not miserable, for a very effeminate kid named George who lived down the block. While we certainly never hurt him physically, we teased him without any real appreciation of the pain we were inflicting.

During junior and senior high school years, hitchhiking was the transportation of choice, and in my case the odds were high that the ride I'd be offered would be from a gay man who, somewhere before dropping me off, would either openly ask if I was interested in having sex or make a sly allusion that would open the door to same. It happened so often that it got to be a standing joke that I was "queer-bait," but all I knew was that it was an easy, convenient, and free way to get a ride. Whenever and however the proposition came, all I had to do was say, "No, thanks," and the subject was closed. In retrospect, however, unlike the situations with the Chinese laundryman and George, where I had been a rude and offensive perpetrator, here I was, if passively taking advantage, simply ignorant of the loneliness, longing, and desperation that propelled these overtures.

All of that was still marinating when I walked toward the bus stop, heading home from work at Hazan's, and a man stopped his

Cadillac on the corner, got out, made some lame excuse, and offered me a ride. Now an ex-Marine with nothing to fear, I said sure. As we headed west on Santa Monica Boulevard, he made conversation and then asked me what I wanted to do besides drive a truck. When I ventured that I wanted to be an actor, he produced his business card, and introduced himself as Henry Willson, an agent. He said he thought I had potential and would like to talk further.

No pass. Not yet, anyway. I thought this was interesting and actually kind of exciting, so I reported it to the family when I got home. Sally, who was there at the time, warned me off, saying this was the way he snared young men. I knew that, of course, but said I could take care of myself. I figured I'd call him and see what happened. Henry Willson, I soon learned, was well known and quite successful in the business, famous for discovering and establishing stars like Troy Donahue, Tab Hunter, and Rock Hudson. His trademark was renaming his actors, dubbing them with cute and hopefully catchy first names. So when my friends got wind of what was happening, I was showered with clever possibilities for new names, most of them unprintable.

For the next few weeks, Henry and I did a kind of minuet. I continued to work, and life went on. But now there was this flirtation with Hollywood and, in my wildest, most secret dreams, stardom. I was invited to Henry's office, plied with gossip, taken to lunch, and eventually invited to his home. He was respectful, full of Hollywood stories, and never insinuated anything other than a professional relationship. I'm embarrassed now that I was willing to go along for a while in the hope that maybe this was somehow legit, that there really was a shortcut to having a successful career as an actor that didn't involve compromising myself. After some time and much discussion of the way in which stars are made (pun perhaps intended), Henry actually set up an interview with a producer for a role in an upcoming war picture.

The producer, who may have been Hal Wallis, was kind. He asked a few questions about my nonexistent acting background. Then he asked about my relationship with Henry, which, I made clear, was strictly business. Skeptical, he asked if I expected it to remain so. I insisted it would. He then explained, very generously as I think about it now, that even if the situation was as I had described it, everyone I met in the business would assume otherwise. Was I ready to live with that? Was I, indeed? I thanked him and left. In retrospect, I don't believe I thanked him enough. I'm not sure it would have been possible to do so.

Later, I told Henry what the producer had said and asked if there was, in fact, an unspoken quid pro quo here. Of course there was, he said. He would fully expect me to show my appreciation for whatever he was able to do for me. This was the way things worked in Hollywood, he explained, and I should wise up. I'd never get anywhere in this business without "cooperating" with him or people like him. I said, "Thanks, but no thanks," and left.

Suddenly I was back at square one, if a bit wiser for the experience. I continued to work and hang out with pals, but my secret was out. Everyone now knew I had the dream of becoming an actor. My buddy Pat, also back from the Marines, was working nights at a gas station on the Sunset Strip, and I often stopped in to see him and shoot the bull about life and the world. Bud Boyle, a Canadian who worked the late shift with Pat, had come to Hollywood, like so many, with the dream of a career in show business. More honest about his ambition than I, Bud had signed up at an actor's workshop. In one of our late-night lament sessions, he said, "You know, Mike, if you're really serious about being an actor, maybe you ought to do something about it." Though the idea of performing in front of people still terrified me, I accepted his challenge and agreed to see for myself what the workshop was about.

Jeff Corey, a well-known and respected character actor, held a highly regarded series of classes at his workshop. Jeff's place was the base for a number of actors, dreamers, and hopefuls, some of whom had great potential, while others had little or none. Some were incredibly beautiful, some "interesting," some ordinary. Some were simply hucksters and hangers-on; too many thought fame was the magical solution to their unresolved personal problems. As I sat in the back of Bud's class silently watching, I didn't yet know which category I fit into. But watching soon became participating, as my shyness was gradually overcome by the lure of the work. Little by little I began to feel that this was actually something I could do—and that I enjoyed doing. This led to other classes, workshops, schools, relationships, connections, and, eventually, a part in a play. The play was Somerset Maugham's *Rain*, and I was cast, ironically, as U.S. Marine Sergeant O'Hara. I was terrible—not because I didn't know how to be a Marine but because I didn't yet know enough about being an actor. Terrible or not, an agent saw the play, felt I had potential, and sent me out on a few interviews. This offered the exciting possibility of actually working as an actor. It also meant I had to be available for more interviews and even work, in the event I got a part. That was the end of punching a clock and the beginning of my new role as "unemployed actor." There were lots of us around. Scratch any soda-jerk, pizza cook, waiter, doorman, bouncer, car-repossesser, or process-server in L.A., and you'll probably find an aspiring actor just beneath the surface. I did all of that to keep money coming in during the long gaps between interviews and the occasional one-line role on a TV show or in a movie.

Still trying to be a good Catholic, I was fascinated by the attention being paid an Irish Catholic politician named John F. Kennedy. Politics and the world situation had meant little to me up to that time. The drumbeat about "Commies" had been pounded into us in the Marines, but politics meant boring old white guys talking about things I didn't understand. I did "like Ike" in junior high school, probably because it rhymed with Mike, but Mom said not to let Dad hear that. Dad was a union man and a Democrat who said Republicans were for big business and Democrats for the worker, and I guessed that's what I was too. Kennedy, however, was something new: smart, young, good-looking, Catholic, and Irish, though of the "lace curtain" variety. He was a war hero, the perfect image of a dutiful, God-fearing public servant dedicated to family and country. And a Democrat to boot! The derision he dealt with only raised him in my eyes. Questioning whether a Catholic should be elected President was simple bigotry—insulting and infuriating. I watched Kennedy's progress, was delighted at his nomination and excited that he was the first presidential candidate I'd be old enough to vote for.

Around this time, I took what turned out to be a meaningful road trip. Ron Allcott, one of the guys from the Banshees/Saracens, was in the Army at Fort Bragg, North Carolina, and needed his car. His parents offered to pay me to drive it there. It was winter, which made this a challenge, and Morgan, my old Marine buddy, was now home in New Orleans, so if I timed it right, I could see Mardi Gras, too.

The drive was an experience in itself. Piloting Ron's Ford through a huge storm in Oklahoma meant learning to maneuver over icy roads as cars and trucks slid off the highway before me. That was a dicey time, but heading down through Arkansas and into Mississippi, Alabama, Georgia, and the Carolinas was even more unsettling. For the first time, I witnessed the overt manifestations of segregation in my country. *White only* restrooms and drinking fountains were not, as I had mistakenly assumed, things of the past. Though insulated by a nice car, I was mortified by the preponderance of blacks living in poverty. Insulated by white skin, I was ashamed that what was readily available to me would not have been to my friend Tyus, had he been there with me. I drove through beautiful country lanes and city streets that seemed, to all outward appearances, to be the America I knew, yet a monster hid just beneath the surface. I sensed that I would never see things quite the same way again.

Turning over the car to Ron, I was happy to discover that Rick Williams, another of our childhood chums, had stopped to see him, too. A West Point grad and now an Army officer, Rick was driving back to the West Coast; he dropped me in northern Louisiana, and I hitched south from there.

The visit with Morgan was a mixture of fun and confusion. As he had been welcomed into my home in Los Angeles, his doors were opened to me in Metairie, a New Orleans suburb. His folks were gracious examples of Southern hospitality, but I couldn't escape the sense that his mother felt my presence an intrusion. New Orleans was beautiful and exotic, and, though I still didn't drink, Mardi Gras was a crazy, dazzling, extraordinary spectacle. Morg was a good guy, but our views of the racial situation were very different. As a non-Southerner, I "didn't understand," he insisted, the reality of living there. And, in fairness, that was true. I didn't understand how otherwise reasonable, intelligent people could justify or tolerate, much less condone, the bigotry and abuse that seemed to be the order of the day in the South.

During Mardi Gras, parades and balls were everywhere. One of the local customs involved throwing toys and trinkets from the floats to excited crowds of onlookers. Morg told me that as a prank, young white men would sometimes wrap up bricks to look like presents and throw them out at the crowds in the black communities. I found it shocking, incomprehensible, that such a thing could be laughed off. Yet Morg was my friend. While I hated what he was saying, I understood on some level that, just as I was a product of my experience, he felt forced to defend the culture in which he was raised. I was sickened, but I lacked the ability, and frankly the courage, to fully express my feelings, raw and confused as they were. My dad, after all, had used ugly words to describe black people, who weren't seen in large numbers in our community. Was this simply a more blatant version of what we lived at home, or was it something more serious and ingrained? All of this was aggravated by the fact that these were the days when people rarely discussed religion or politics in polite company.

Thankfully, our friendship survived. Morg came back west with me and spent years there before returning home. Today, his views have moderated, along with those of many in the South, and he now runs an interracial sports camp for children.

* * *

At this point, the presidential race was in full swing. JFK even came to L.A. He attended Mass at the Church of the Good Shepherd in Beverly Hills, where our family went when we wanted to dress up, pretend we belonged, and share prayers with the swells. It was so crowded that day that Kennedy was hustled out the side door before Mass ended. I didn't get a chance to see him, but I could still say I was there. When he was elected, with a little help from my vote, it was a great day for the Irish. The bigots had been beaten back and Americans were inspired by the hope JFK represented.

On the career front, I continued with classes, found parts in plays, and did what I could to become a working actor. I was prodded, I think, not only by my own needs but also by the desire to prove Henry Willson wrong. In order to make a living, I still needed outside income, so I did more work for Ron Allen, a private investigator who kept me busy as a process-server. Ron was a big guy, about my height of 6'3", but he had me by thirty or forty pounds, tipping the scale at around 230. We got along well. I think he liked me in part because I was an ex-Marine and had picked up some martial arts experience. Ron provided full service for the attorneys who were his clients: filing papers in court; seeing that summonses and subpoenas were served properly; locating people who had skipped out on bills, trials, or sometimes spouses; repossessing cars and other goods; following errant husbands and wives; protecting clients against those they feared meant them harm; and routinely dealing with the seamier side of life. Helping Ron brought in money, but I often felt lousy about having to serve notice that someone's marriage was over or his car or furniture was being taken away for non-payment. And being the proverbial "messenger," I was cursed, threatened, chased down the street by one very angry man with a very large knife, held at gunpoint by another until the cops—thankfully—came, and, on one memorable evening, shot at by a true lunatic. Not a fun time.

One day, Ron smiled and said he had "just the thing" for me. An attorney handling a divorce said his client feared her soon-to-be-ex-husband might become violent. She wanted a bodyguard until things were settled. The husband was, Ron said, a well-known actor with a reputation for being a tough guy. Did I want the job? "Who's the guy?" I asked. He gave me the name. "No thanks," I said.

Meanwhile, I was meeting, studying, and in some cases working with beautiful and charming women, and I was quick to develop huge crushes on more than one of them. At the suggestion of a friend, I audited a course on musical comedy at UCLA, taught by John Ingle, the renowned drama teacher from Hollywood High whose class I had always been too afraid to take. John chose me to partner for a scene with a very attractive blonde I'd been watching with great interest. Though I was lousy in the scene (singing scared me silly), the rehearsals resulted in a serious romance.

Judy Hayden, a great-looking, very talented graduate of Oklahoma State University, had come west to get her master's degree in theater before applying to teach high school. She had been part of a popular singing trio in school, but wasn't sure about pursuing a career in the business and thought teaching would be both smarter and more secure. Our romance quickly had me doing loops, but because Judy had been raised in a strict Baptist home, we butted heads over religion. As we grew more serious, it became a painful dilemma: two young people more and more sure they were in love, yet held apart by belief systems that were at war. We both believed "in God, the Father Almighty, Creator of heaven and earth," as the Apostle's Creed had it. So why couldn't she just accept that Jesus had established the one true faith with the first Pope in Rome? Seemed clear to me. Hadn't Father O'Reilly and later Father O'Callaghan said so, for Christ's sake?

The religious obstacle course was a tough one, but we tried our best to run it. Judy had met my family many times, so I accompanied her back to Edmond, a suburb of Oklahoma City, to meet hers. Floyd and Eleanor, her parents, were good people, warm and hospitable, and made me feel at home. Her sister Marge and brother Jack came to say hello as well. David, a younger brother, was still living at home.

All were, as I understood it, "Bible-believing Christians" who took the Good Book as the literal word of God. Its proscriptions and admonitions had to be believed and obeyed literally and were not subject to interpretation. That was pretty tough from my point of view. I certainly considered myself a Christian and had read the Bible. But I thought that evolution, if a "theory," was a pretty well-established one, while the Bible, a pretty fair guide for one's life, laid down some confusing and outdated rules, laws, and ideas that could well use a bit of thoughtful interpretation.

Fortunately, we didn't spend our time discussing the Bible, but instead just got to know each other. Floyd was a good man, quiet and conservative, with a wry sense of humor. Eleanor was quite something. Well educated and open to new ideas, she had studied child development to teach special education. Her quick mind and joyful outlook were a delightful surprise. Her ability to marry a modern, sophisticated, and humane perspective with fundamentalist religious views was, if confusing, nonetheless impressive. Jack, a former jock, was now in business. He was friendly, with a ready smile and a joke always on his lips. Marge was bright, wry, with a devilish wit. She struck me as the one most willing to question dogma of any stripe. David was a child of television who would repeat commercials and do impressions. Their social group was a kind of closed circle comprised of school and church. Jack was married to a very pretty woman named Marie, a schoolmate, who seemed suspicious of me. But in all, the meeting was a success. They realized I wasn't a Papist Dog conniving to drag Judy from their Way into my One True Church, and I saw that they weren't ignorant hicks from the sticks. In fact, we liked each other. Floyd's concern turned out to be the most prophetic. In his experience, he said, people of different religions who can't come to agreement on one or the other usually ended up with none.

Back in L.A., life continued. I was getting older and perhaps a bit wiser, but was still pretty much without a guidebook. There was religion, of course, but it seemed more and more to create, rather than solve, problems. There were my friends, more of whom were marrying or at least pairing off, leaving less and less room for the old relationships. There was home and family, which seemed okay as long as no one was sick or in trouble. But the emotional support I longed for still had to be assumed; it was neither spoken nor demonstrated. Home, so the story went, was the pad from which my life was to be launched; the rest was up to me. Still awash in confusion and indecision, I tried my best to follow the rules as I understood them.

On top of all of this, there was the increasingly volatile, bigger world of which I was only dimly aware. Kennedy had assumed the presidency and walked right into the Bay of Pigs fiasco. From what I could tell, he behaved honorably by assuming responsibility and taking the heat. With Ed Berghino, another Banshee/Saracen pal who had joined the Marines, Pat and I mused over the Communist threat posed by Castro and whether going back into uniform might be necessary. Judy graduated and got a job teaching English and drama at Laguna Beach High, in a beautiful coastal city sixty miles south of L.A. in Orange County. Seeing her now required a long schlep and time away from home, work, and whatever was happening with my career. But Ron Allen's business was expanding to Orange County, which meant I could earn some money while spending time with Judy. Soon I was there more than in L.A.—putting a serious strain on what was at best the sputtering beginning of an acting career.

Judy rented a house with another new teacher, a cute blonde named Gaye Thorpe. A couple of lookers, they were quickly pulled into the social world of Laguna High's faculty, and I had to protect my interests. Already sure I was dumber than the next guy, my lack of a college education was an added embarrassment as I found myself fighting to stay afloat in the intellectual combat of faculty society. Between dinners, parties, and events at school and working for Ron Allen's company, the time for making the rounds in Hollywood became increasingly scarce. Gaye was generous and understanding of our relationship, so I soon found myself doing what the Church called "living in sin."

Laguna was a pretty progressive community. At a local NAACP meeting, I met Dennis Madison, who managed Orange County for Ron Allen. A committed liberal, Dennis was recruiting people to go down South to take part in the Freedom Rides. Recalling the *White only* signs and the gift-wrapped bricks, I thought about going. But it was a scary proposition, and I let my immediate needs override my conscience.

Acting jobs were hard to come by in L.A. When I was lucky enough to get one, there often wasn't a lot of acting involved. As one of a group of soldiers in the hospital in *Captain Newman, M.D.*, I earned a day's pay for jumping up and down and screaming like a sex-crazed fool when the beautiful Angie Dickinson came into the ward—not all that hard to do. A day's pay then for this proud member of the Screen Actors Guild was a little over a hundred bucks. That was a lot of money at the time, but if one was only able to work one day every month or two, it sure wasn't enough to live on. Working for Ron and doing other odd jobs was a necessity.

I was thrilled around this time to get a one-line role in *The Americanization of Emily*, starring James Garner, Julie Andrews, and James Coburn. I had a chance to say hello to Coburn on the set and was knocked out when he was pleasant enough to return the greeting and ask how I was doing. I played a reporter at a press conference. A scandal had erupted around the identity of the first American soldier killed at the D-Day invasion, and my character asked the key question: "You mean the first dead man is alive?" When the picture came out, I excitedly took a group of friends to the Warners Theater in Beverly Hills to see my motion picture debut. As the scene came and went with no sign of me, I discovered the pain of being "left on the cutting-room floor."

With my career showing little promise and Judy living in Laguna, I was open to Dennis's suggestion that we partner in a new firm, Madison and Farrell. We bought out Ron's interest in Orange County and set up our own attorney service, figuring we could expand the client base in what was clearly a thriving area. We arranged with Ron to work under his license when doing anything of an investigative nature, thus offering our clients a full-service company. With this as a potential financial base and our relationship coming to the "do-or-don't" stage, Judy and I decided to get married. The need to get on with our lives, the social pressure to commit and make something of ourselves, and the press of time (though neither of us was yet twenty-five) brought Floyd's concern to reality. In August of 1963, the Baptist and the Catholic said their vows in a Presbyterian Church.

Three months later I was struck dumb by the news that President Kennedy had been killed. Horrified, shocked, disbelieving, I wept along with most of America, unable to tear my eyes from the pictures pouring into our living room. This heroic figure, this leader who gave us hope, this man I so admired and with whom I identified on so many very personal levels, had been ripped away. Newscasters told us that Lee Harvey Oswald, a twenty-four-year-old ex-Marine, may have been the lunatic responsible. This single fact touched me deeply, as I was also a twenty-four-year-old ex-Marine. Two days later I watched bleary-eyed as Oswald was himself murdered before my eyes on live TV. But something seemed wrong, terribly wrong. This was simply bad theater. Were we to believe, as they were saying, that there was no connection between Jack Ruby and Lee Oswald? Did no one see anything peculiar about this chain of events? The whole thing stank to high heaven, wasn't that obvious? Was I nuts? Could it simply be tragic coincidence and ineptitude that an emotionally overwrought Ruby somehow managed to slip through dozens of well-armed police to eliminate Oswald? Come on! I sat there and stared, aghast, waiting for someone to stop this nonsense and tell us what was really happening.

In the days following, the news media—the same news media that had for the past three years painted Vice President Lyndon Johnson as an uncouth, embarrassing, jug-eared hick—now began to recast him as precisely the hero the nation needed. LBJ was all at once the stalwart, his history the Great American Story. He was the loyal, seasoned, fully capable Leader-in-Waiting that we were lucky to have. What a country!

What a country, indeed! *What is this?* I wondered. Is it the media's job to pat us on the head and lull us to sleep with tidings of good will and assurances that all will be well? I thought their job was to tell the truth. I thought they were there to sift through the facts, to ask the tough questions, and, if not to determine the truth, at least to present what they knew and let us come to our own conclusions. But this was neither. *What's going on here?* I asked myself. *Who's making these decisions? And why?*

Disturbed and unable to just let it go, I began to listen, to read, to ask questions, to try and separate the loony from the legitimate. Painful as it was to adjust to this new reality, I had to also live my life. As with my dad's death, I had the vague feeling that somehow what had happened was unfair, that I was being robbed of something important, that there was a lesson I hadn't been given sufficient time to learn. This wasn't the way it was supposed to work. Yet I had little choice but to go on and do the best I could.

Madison and Farrell grew steadily and I was eventually able to offer my brother the chance to come work with us. As with everything, Jim excelled at the work. He was popular with our clients and quickly became an indispensable asset to the company. Judy and I made an effort on the religious front, trying different churches and services for a while, but I began to feel that what I had been taught about Jesus didn't square with these rigid choices, these absolutes that faced us. If Jesus had been who they said he was, wouldn't he just love the little kid who wanted to do the right thing so much that he said his prayers twice at night in case there wasn't enough time in the morning? Wouldn't he appreciate two young people who were struggling to find a compromise that would allow them to work out their lives together without being condemned to hell for breaking rules that had been imposed on them in his name? Eventually Judy and I came to feel that our relationship with God, evolving as it was as a result of this examination, didn't seem to fit into the available superstructures. Attendance at church on Sunday became less meaningful to us than how we lived our lives.

Judy had quickly become the toast of Laguna High, with her school plays winning plaudits and awards, and I was handling a growing business. I became interested in natural food and the effect of diet on one's health, probably in subconscious reaction to what had happened to my dad. Judy and I began performing at the storied Laguna Playhouse, a local theater with a long history and a big reputation. The Playhouse was run by an extremely talented young actor/director named Douglas Rowe, who became one of our closest friends. Over the next couple of years we did a number of shows there, became deeply involved with the theater community, and gradually emerged, if on a local level, as a celebrated couple. Though I now took a drink once in a while, I was still a square to some of the theater crowd—and a bit of a scold because I not only didn't smoke "grass" or do other drugs but actively disapproved of both. Graduating from a health-food dabbler into a serious vegetarian, I was trying to maintain a clean lifestyle, and dope didn't square with it. Still, Judy and I enjoyed the plays, the endless rounds of parties, and the time spent with the theater's troupe of actors, which briefly included a young Harrison Ford.

Within a couple of years it became clear that this life, as successful as it seemed, was not everything I wanted. That other possibility was still pulling me. After talking it over with Judy, who was thrilled with things as they were but understood that I needed to scratch this itch, I called a family friend, Jack Albertson, the venerable character actor who later became an award-winning Broadway, motion picture, and television star. Jack understood completely. "If you don't give it a try, you'll never know," he observed, and offered to arrange a meeting with his agent, Jack Weiner. The agent agreed to set up some interviews, if possible, so I sold Dennis my part of the business and began to make the rounds in Hollywood again.

As I strained to find out if I really could make a living in the business, the country was going through its own struggle. The moral authority of the civil rights movement was undeniable no matter how

Bull Connor, Lester Maddox, and the White Citizens Councils tried to resist it. Long-held resentment and frustration burst into flames in many cities across the nation. In South Central Los Angeles, Watts erupted, destroying property, inflaming fears, and dismantling the myth that racism was limited to the South.

Jack Albertson and his wife Wallace, who lived across the street from my mom in West Hollywood, had long been active politically. As Jack tried to help me develop a career, he and Wally offered political insight as well. With the embers still glowing in Watts, they held a series of interracial dialogues in their home, inviting friends from South Central to meet people from the West Side.

At one of their meetings, I met a man who ran "Operation Bootstrap" in Watts, providing learning opportunities for anyone interested. He invited me down, thinking I had something to offer people trying to find a life beyond the dead-end streets. I met with some community activists and other folks just looking for a straw to cling to, but with neither the organizing skills nor the experience to run a program myself, I wasn't sure I could help. "Anybody who cares can help," they said. The experienced leaders had other priorities though, and we set up an actor's workshop with me as the sole teacher, barely a step or two ahead of any smart or talented person who showed up. After a while the project felt a bit silly in the face of the serious problems people were dealing with, and our little studio died on the vine. I never forgot the experience, however, or a lesson I learned in a sensitivity training session I took part in at Bootstrap. Amid the fear and pain, men and women of varying ages, colors, life experience, social position, and education sat together trying to figure out a way to bridge the gap that separated us. While acknowledging our differences, the group leader focused on the common motivation shared by people trying to make a difference in the world. Love was ultimately what service was about, he explained, and "loving implies taking a risk." In order to love someone you have to be willing to run the risk of rejection, of being hurt, of having your heart broken, or, in some instances, having your face pushed in. It was a hard thing to hear at that time, and I wasn't sure I understood it. But it stayed with me.

During this period things improved a bit professionally, and I began to feel that maybe a career was out there somewhere. A couple of commercials paid well. A few acting jobs didn't, but they helped build a résumé and keep the flame alive. One of those early jobs stays with me today. I was hired to do a bit part in *The Graduate*, the film in which Dustin Hoffman burst onto the scene. Spending the day watching Mike Nichols direct was exciting. Seeing Hoffman sitting on the floor talking with the actors and extras like a regular guy was inspiring. In my scene (I still think of it as "my scene"), Hoffman's character had been using an alias while having an affair with Anne Bancroft at a hotel at the same time as he was trying to wangle a date with her daughter, played by Katharine Ross. Finally agreeing to the date, Ross informed him she wanted to go to dinner at that very hotel, which he claimed never to have visited. As the couple entered the lobby, I was the first of a number of bellhops who greeted him, saying, "Hi, Mr. Gladstone; nice to see you." It was great fun, if unremarkable, but when building a résumé, you include everything. Years later, a reporter said he remembered my performance. Sure he was blowing smoke, I asked, "Oh really? What did I do?" He stuttered, blushed, and finally guessed, wrongly, that I was in the frat house scene with Richard Dreyfuss. The credit remained in my résumé.

Chapter 4
THE HOUSE

Being in the grind took time and attention away from other aspects of life. With Judy continuing to fly high in Laguna, my commitment to scraping by in Hollywood took its inevitable toll, and our marriage collapsed.

It was as though the bottom had dropped out. I was devastated. Suddenly I was floundering, questioning everything, and nothing made sense. We had gone in separate directions in our lives, and I was as much to blame as she was, but I was nonetheless furious and inconsolable. I wanted to strike out, to blame somebody—anybody. My marriage wasn't supposed to fail. I was living by the rules as I understood them. I had tried to be honest and honorable, served my country, and worked hard. But instead of a thriving, happy, fulfilled, successful person, I was suddenly a failure, a miserable, confused, deeply troubled wreck. It had to be fixed. But how? If the marriage was broken, perhaps I could just put it back together. But Judy, though also sad and confused, was satisfied with where she was. Should I drop everything and forget my dreams? Or was I supposed to be a "man" and drag her away with me? I went in circles. What could I do to get my life back on track?

Seeing my pain, my friend George Russell suggested The House. I'd known George slightly in school, but we had become close after the service. He and his girlfriend Jessie Rex were part of a program called The House, and they felt it might help me. Jessie was a very bright and self-assured woman whom I was at once drawn to and somewhat afraid of because of her candor. George and Jessie had already told me a bit about The House because of what it had come to mean to them, but it hadn't been of particular interest to me at the time. Seeing the state I was in, George pressed the issue, insisting there was no danger in giving it a try. What did I have to lose?

Technically known as The Manhattan Project, The House was a therapy-oriented self-help program funded by the Salvation Army. It had begun as a drug-rehabilitation program and was run primarily by graduates, people who had come there out of need and found both purpose and hope. Though drug addiction remained a core concern, the program quickly expanded its vision, recognizing that addiction was only one of many choices people made to dull the pain of loneliness, misery, doubt, and self-hatred. A psychologist and a psychological social worker were the managers of the program, but The House was really a self-directed community to which people in trouble came for help.

At that point I knew none of this but was open to anything that might help. George and Jessie's recommendation was encouragement enough. George told me who to call and left the rest up to me. He said there would be an initial interview and that I'd be expected to "stand up and make a commitment" if I decided to give it a try.

I didn't understand much of what he said, but I was desperate. I called and made an appointment. The next day I went to an office in Norwalk adjacent to the state mental hospital, where I met with Ed Boyle and Ernie Saenz. Ed was the social worker, a good-looking, silver--haired Irishman who projected an air of privilege. Ernie was the program manager, a Latino with Mexican or Indian blood, or both, a former drug addict with a pockmarked face and fierce dark eyes. The office was bare, institutional, with a desk and a couple of chairs. They asked how they could help. I didn't know. I told them that my marriage had fallen apart and that my world seemed to have gone with it, that I was angry and confused and didn't know what to do. They responded by telling me a little about the program and the kinds of people who came through it. Some were from mental institutions, some from jail, some from the streets, and some, like me, from "straight society."

"What we've found," Ed explained, "is that regardless of their experience, no matter what the problem is that sends them to us, everyone wants the same thing. Everyone wants to be loved, to be respected, and to have attention paid. What do you want?" I said I wanted to get my wife back and get my life in order, but I wasn't sure how to do that. Ernie replied that their experience with people from all kinds of circumstances with all kinds of problems broke down to the same basic thing: "Everybody wants love, attention, and respect. What do you want?" Weren't they listening? I said that I needed to figure out how to get my wife back and put things back together so that I could breathe again and get my life on track. They both looked at me intently, smiling slightly. Ed said that people often look for what they think will stop their pain immediately, but it always goes deeper than that. "People all want the same thing. They want love, respect, and attention. What do you want?"

After another false start or two, I finally got the message. I took a deep breath and said, "I want to be loved and respected, and I want to have attention paid."

The two looked at me, and I heard one of them say, "I can't hear you." So I said it again. Then Ed shook his head, saying, "I can't hear you."

I thought of George's comment about standing up and making a commitment. They wanted to know I meant it. So I stood up and began to shout, "I want people to love me and respect me . . ." Suddenly I was sobbing out the words as if a dam had burst. Tears were running down my face as I sputtered out ". . . and pay attention to me." Before I realized what was happening, both men had their arms around me and were holding me tightly as I wept.

I don't remember ever having been held by a man before that, let alone two men. Yet there was nothing uncomfortable about it. I was sobbing out my misery, and these two men I didn't know were holding me as if it was the most natural thing in the world. Whatever it was I needed to do to get through this miserable, painful time, I knew that these men would help me.

After a few moments, the wracking sobs eased, Ed and Ernie backed off, and I sat down. As I pulled myself together, we talked a bit more about how people got to The House and what happened there. Many people—especially those who came out of prison or other institutions or off the streets—lived in. As a non-resident member, I could go there anytime to meet people or help out and otherwise learn the ropes. But Tuesday and Thursday nights were the group sessions where the work was done. I said I'd be there Tuesday.

And I was. The House was an old three-story Tudor-style structure between 6th and Wilshire on Manhattan Place in Los Angeles, just a block off Western Avenue. The neighborhood was run down but not awful, and the house was the same. My first meeting was scary, but I was there early, unusual for me. One is not late to meetings at The House, I was told. A commitment is a commitment.

Up a half-dozen steps was a wide porch. The front door opened into a good-sized living room with a fireplace on the left wall. Through folding doors to the right was a dining room, with a pantry and kitchen toward the rear of the building. Directly behind the living room were an office and a common room. A flight of stairs led up to the second floor where the residents lived, one wing for the men, the other for women. Above that were a couple of small rooms used for additional group sessions when needed. There was a kind of antic energy here, but also warmth and a sense of musty restlessness.

People were already there; others followed me in. They were men and women of assorted ages and colors, some of whom introduced themselves and welcomed me. Some of the welcomes were stiff and rather formal, and I later realized that certain people had been given the task of learning to be polite. George and Jessie were there, thank God, and were relaxed and comfortable, which made it a bit easier for me. I saw Ed and Ernie as well. Ed welcomed me, and Ernie said hello, his smile contradicted by hard eyes that, I was to find, missed very little. More than anyone, Ernie seemed taut with the knowledge that one small slip for many of these people meant death. Jessie introduced me to Bill Cozens, the psychologist. A big, sweet bear of a man, he had a ready smile and eyes that mixed knowledge with sorrow and empathy. Bill exuded the sense that he knew who he was, that he was okay with the world, and that, painful as it could be at times, he was ready to accept what came because there must be some purpose to it all. It felt good to be near him.

Everyone settled down as Ernie stepped up in front of the fireplace. He asked one of the newer members to read "The Purpose," the mission statement of the project. It was a declaration of personal responsibility, stating that each of us was committed to becoming a responsible and productive citizen, that the process required not only living up to our own commitment but being aware of the needs of those around us as well. One of the fundamental premises of The House was that we were all our brothers' keepers, responsible not only for our own well-being but also that of others.

I was introduced, and it was explained that I had made a commitment to Ed and Ernie. Everyone applauded. New members who had not yet made a commitment did so at these meetings, which can be pretty tough. After seeing people go through it a number of times it became clear that "I can't hear you" meant that the person making the commitment hadn't truly communicated a sincere desire. When someone did succeed in making an acceptable commitment, everyone applauded and the new member was received with hugs. Because I had made mine with Ed and Ernie in that office, I was accepted by the applause. The hugs would wait until they "got" me.

The House had its own hierarchy and language, some of which I learned quickly and the rest over time. Because the people here had never received the love, attention, and respect they needed, most had learned to "game" for them—cheating and lying and contorting themselves into unmanageable emotional and physical wrecks in order to get some twisted version of what they longed for. Lacking these essential ingredients of life, they sold themselves—sometimes literally—for whatever seemed to fill the void. They'd lied, cheated, stolen. They'd shot themselves full of dope or pumped themselves with alcohol to deaden the pain. They'd twisted themselves into unrecognizable human shapes, accepting abuse, degradation, torture, perversion, or virtually anything that promised to stop the pain of loneliness and the misery of self-hatred born of believing oneself unlovable.

But I learned this over time. At first, all I knew was that this was a world very different from the one in which I had lived. Here were whores and thieves, junkies and gang members, loud, angry men and women just out of prison. There were weird, shy types stepping tentatively out of mental institutions, drunks, kids here as a condition of parole, and confused "straight" types, like me. Some were lost and trying to find solid ground again; some angry and bitter at a failed relationship, a cheating spouse, an unfair lot in life. Here, if the term could ever apply, was a collection of social detritus. To the world I had known, certainly to my dad, these were bums, throwaways, misfits, crooks, perverts, and nuts. And we were here to help ourselves by helping one another.

Keeping busy was the rule. Work, stay active, do the program, keep focused. "Indulging" was not allowed. Playing head games about "the old days" and "the old ways" was a step backward. We were to "pull up" anyone who was indulging. To let somebody get away with hiding, cheating, lying, indulging, was to give her a "pass," and that was a cop-out, allowing her to slip back into self-defeating behavior. And for many, slipping back meant death. Giving a pass meant you didn't give a shit if he or she died. And even if you truly didn't give a shit, the program taught you to "act as if" you did. "As iffing"—doing it until you felt it—was the way you learned.

The big lesson was to take responsibility for who you were and what you wanted. If you want something in life, ask for it. Don't cheat, don't steal, don't con and game; don't be a chickenshit. Ask for what you want. If you have the courage to ask for it, you might just get it. Most people don't have the guts until they learn to try. If the answer is no, you have to be strong enough to take it, to learn to deal with that rejection and move on. The goal is to get yourself to a place in life, with real, responsible people with whom you can have an honest relationship, asking for and getting what you need. Like many, these people came from situations where nothing was given—or even made available—to them. "Don't give me that 'rehabilitation' shit," Ernie once said, "these people have never been habilitated in the first place."

People who don't know enough to ask for what they want are "stupid." Those who do are "responsible." Too stupid to know how to ask for what we wanted, those new to The House were in the "Stupid Group." When we had been there long enough to learn how to know what we wanted and have the courage to ask for it, we'd graduate to the "Responsible Group." It was all very confusing and very scary. But something about it made me want to come back, to find out what they could teach me.

Every Tuesday and Thursday night, I attended Group, the therapy sessions where we checked each other out and worked each other over. This was not "the chair" that Marv had introduced our club to when I was a kid. Nor was it Andy White's mother's teen group or sessions with a psychologist to help work out some issues. This was life-or-death stuff, and it was very tough. Sometimes I'd come during the day or on weekends to help with an outing or an event, or just to be at a meal or a birthday party. Other times I'd be there for a crisis, when someone freaked out or a new member came in loaded and had to "kick"—go through the sick, heavy-flu-like process of getting off heroin or some other drug. But it was in Group where the hard work was done.

At first I tried to just listen and watch, but the others would bust me for hiding. As a straight member, with a life outside and privileges most of the residents didn't have, I learned there were things I knew how to do that could be helpful to others. In the Stupid Group, we'd go around the room and deal with whatever was happening for each one at that moment. Sometimes we'd take up an issue that had been brought to the group leader's attention by Ernie, Ed, or Bill, if they weren't leading the group themselves.

As scary and painful as it was, I began to learn, little by little, to trust, to understand the value of opening up and letting deep, dark secrets out into the light. Some of the members had done group therapy in prison or at the hospital, so they knew all the games. But The House was different: It was the end of the road. Most people were here because they had tried everything else. Failing here meant going back—and probably death in a gutter somewhere. So they were tough on themselves and tough on each other. And they were tough on me.

"Why you here, man?" *My wife and I split up.* "So what?" *So I want to get her back and get my life together.* "So do it." *Well, she's not sure she wants to.* "Why not?" *Well, she's . . .* "She bullshit! What about you?" *Well, she . . .* "She bullshit! What about you? If she's so fucked up, why'd you pick a lemon?" *What do you mean?* "I mean, who the hell are you, man? Don't give me this bullshit about your wife being the problem. If she's the fucking problem, why'd you pick her? What the fuck's the matter with you? You don't come here to tell us to fix your fucking marriage for you. Fix yourself, asshole; then take care of your own problems. What kind of an asshole picks a woman who messes him over? Who the hell are you?" *I'm Mike.* "What?" *I'm Mike.* "What the fuck is a Mike?"

Good question, as I came to understand. They didn't want names and didn't play games. They wanted your guts, your fears, your secret self. Sometimes after a long struggle, when you exposed the pain, the fear, the self-loathing, that thing you knew in your heart of hearts made you completely unacceptable and irredeemable, they'd reach out, letting you know your secret was no worse than anyone else's, that there was "nothing new under the sun." They'd give you the gift of their embrace. And then, having acknowledged that place where your secret hell hides, you would realize they wanted not to punish you for it but to teach you that getting down to the root and exposing yourself is an act of courage. They led you to realize that to own the puny, sniveling, misshapen miserable cur behind the masks is to acknowledge the real human being inside you. Your job was first to own that being, then to present him to another and ask that he be accepted. That was the authentic way to gain the love, respect, and attention you long for.

Stripping away the masks and owning the hidden fear, rage, and pain that have trapped you is a birthing process. In any such process, there is pain and loss that seems insurmountable before there are explosions of insight, of soul-deep joyful discovery. I experienced it all because whores and junkies and drunks and bums and queers and crooks cared enough to demand it of me. They accepted me for the terrified, unloved kid I finally revealed myself to be. They helped me see that I was creating my own misery by wallowing there, unwilling to accept the part of me that I always feared my dad would disown. They helped me see that I truly did exist, if in a form I detested, and that owning that frightened, miserable wretch—acknowledging his existence—would free him to grow into the man I wanted to be. They opened themselves up to me in turn—in priceless moments of exquisite human contact that will never leave me—and love was born.

Always there were hugs. Men embraced men, women embraced women, men and women embraced each other and wept. More simple, honest, and immediate expressions of pure, unadulterated human love passed between people under that roof than I ever knew existed.

After I'd been there for a few months, Ernie made a judgment about a member and came down on him hard, as only Ernie could do. He was ferocious and everyone stepped lightly around him. Ernie had been a down-and-out junkie for many years and this place had saved his life. His was often the final word. In this instance, however, Ernie was wrong. I saw it, took a deep breath, and stood up to him. I was terrified, but I called him on it. And I was made "responsible."

Being a responsible member carried with it—surprise—responsibilities. Before too many months passed I was leading groups, helping people strip away the masks they thought were keeping them alive. One night, we were working with a newer member who had come from prison but had made little progress. He was a repeat offender and another fall meant life imprisonment, so he made a commitment to the program and insisted he wanted to change. He was a quiet, homely man with a slightly misshapen face and buckteeth, a loner who didn't mix in easily and wasn't at all forthcoming. He was tough and resistant, and we couldn't get beneath the surface. We'd noted his discomfort with the opposite sex, so after many hours and many sessions, one of the women in the group began probing. He clearly had trouble connecting with her and couldn't meet her eyes. After a long effort, she demanded that he look at her. When he finally did, she simply asked what was wrong. His eyes appeared to moisten; he tore them away, shaking his head, and looked at the floor. But she kept after him and, little by little, got him to open up a bit. He told us about his work, but little about his life and less about what was going on inside. The woman shifted gears. She observed that the straight work he'd done so far hadn't been satisfying because he kept slipping back onto the wrong side of the law. So what, deep in his heart, would he really like to do with his life? He was quiet for a long moment and seemed to go somewhere while thinking about her question. Then in a small voice, this homely man began to explain that what he'd really like to do, what he had long dreamed of doing, was to find a way to work with the blind. And as he said it, he began to weep, as did many of us. Life's mysteries can be so simple at times.

Being responsible meant being part of delegations to prisons to introduce inmates to the program, letting them know there was an alternative to going back to the old neighborhood, the old life. Prisons are cold, rigid, dispiriting. Few I've visited—in those days or since—offer hope. Deadness and hopelessness color the walls. From behind the bars a palpable sense of twisted, constrained, muted but powerful, angry passion reaches out in waves laced with fear and cunning. Souls are crushed in these places, yet in spite of everything some survive. Hardened cons lied through their teeth about wanting to come out to the program. They wanted out and would promise anything to gain access, but then, it was clear, they'd do the same numbers and scams they'd been doing all their lives. Because "you can't con a con," we had members with us who knew these games and called them on their stuff immediately. On my first trip, Ernie warned me to not let anyone intimidate me. He said they'd try.

Sitting with a group of inmates that night, I was engaged by one who was intent on challenging the straight guy. He lashed out with tough-guy con jive, but I'd heard enough from people at The House by that time to be able to answer him directly, giving as good as I got. The contest got hotter. Apparently frustrated at being unable to cow me verbally, he suddenly leaped up and charged. It all happened so fast that no one had a chance to do anything. Remembering Ernie's words, I sat where I was and stared him in the eyes instead of reacting in fear or jumping up to confront him. Fortunately, he stopped just as he got to me and stood there, shaking with anger (or fear). I remember noting that his false upper dentures had come loose as he charged. Suddenly he seemed pathetic and vulnerable rather than threatening. Motionless, we locked eyes for a few moments; then he huffed a couple of angry words that seemed addressed more to himself than to me. As it became clear he wasn't going to do anything, I told him to go back and sit down. Amazingly, he did. Later, when I had gotten over my own shakes, some of the group told me I had handled it well. When I said I had damn near peed my pants, they laughed and assured me no one could tell.

During these months at The House, my life outside continued. I was still trying to build a career as an actor and was, by that time, sharing a rented house in Burbank with my friend Doug Rowe, who had taken time away from his job as director of the Laguna Playhouse to breathe life into his own acting career. I discovered that my experience at The House was having an interesting impact on my life in general. Bill Cozens had once said that, though this was not the reason to be there, the work I was doing at The House would make me a better actor. He was right. In fact, I was finding that acting itself became not only easier but, in an odd way, less meaningful. It wasn't that I didn't care about having a career, or that I no longer enjoyed acting. It was just that I could now enjoy doing it without feeling that the success it could bring was necessary to give my life meaning. I wouldn't find the love I had so wanted by having my picture in movie magazines or from the approval of an audience. None of that was real. The love I wanted was out there in the world, available to me just because I was who I was.

Judy and I decided to try to work it out again. She soon left Laguna, and for a while she and Doug and I shared the house in Burbank.

My family had been pulled into the orbit of The House as well. My mother and my sister Kathy came to some of the holiday and birthday parties we had there. Kathy says I introduced hugging into our family as a result of what I learned.

During this period, Kathy became involved with one of my friends. Bob Lucas was a bright, good, strong young man who had been a heroin addict and thief for years. He worked hard in Group to make sense out of his life, which, up to the time he came to The House, had been a picture of failure. Repeatedly hooked, he stole from his family and everyone else to buy the drugs he needed to dull the pain of his own worthlessness. He eventually ended up in jail. Once out, he returned to that life and, again hooked, was quickly back behind bars. Finally, disgusted with himself and vowing to straighten out, he came to us, worked the program, and soon became one of our favorites. He also became my friend. After some time he met my family, and shortly thereafter, Bob and Kathy began to date, eventually fell in love, and decided to marry.

I was thrilled. I adored my sister and loved Bob, and seeing them so happy together was wonderful. It was an exciting thing for The House, too, a true success. As the two settled down to establish a life, we were all full of hope. But after some time, the stresses of maintaining a straight life, a relationship and a job began to show. On parole, Bob had to take a regular oral dose of methadone, a control drug intended to ward off the craving that heroin addicts experience. He also had to submit to regular urine tests to show that he was staying clean. Bob hated having to take the methadone, claiming it was keeping him in the world of drugs. Whether it was the resentment or doubt or some character flaw that triggered it, Bob slipped back into "chipping" with heroin, ran afoul of the tests, and went back to jail.

It was a blow to all of us, but for Kathy it was devastating. I'm sure she feared that she had somehow failed him, though that was certainly not the case. We visited Bob, listened to his apologies, and held out hope that once free he'd find his way back to a productive life. Sad to say, he didn't. Kathy tried hard to work it out, but somehow it was all too much for him and they split. Late one night she got a call from the police. Bob had been found in his car, dead of a heroin overdose.

I've always had a negative reaction to casual drug use, but it was probably because "nice boys" didn't do them. Now, having seen up close the tear-stained horror of lives ruined, I simply hate them.

The successes were sweet at The House, but the failures hurt like hell. Bill once explained that out of every ten lost, maimed, angry people in need to whom we extended ourselves, four would respond and be significantly helped. The temptation, then, was to be more selective in choosing those to whom we extended ourselves. The problem, Bill noted wryly, was that out of the ten more carefully selected people, four would respond and be significantly helped. The job of anyone in the helping professions, he said, is not to select the most likely successes but to reach out to an ever-wider universe of people in need and do what we could to improve those numbers. Quite a man, Bill Cozens. He continued to love all within reach and to encourage growth and the development of a hopeful and productive life for everyone.

Things were moving for me after more than a year of work at The House. During a period in which they were making changes in the program, I took my leave. I stayed in touch for a while, but I've always felt that in a sense I took it with me out into the world. I think that was the intention: You don't really leave The House; you take it with you as you go. So I went. But I'll never forget the debt I owe to Bill, Ed, and Ernie. And to Ellen, Rick, Suzy, Jeannie, Irma, Ken, Peggy, Mary, Sarah, Ray, Gordon, Robert, Mario, Roger, Jim, Gary, Bob, and so many more. And especially to George and Jessie. I'm trying to repay it the way they would want me to.

Chapter 5
BIRTH

I began to enjoy a fair amount of success in finding work, much of it in television commercials and in slightly larger parts on TV shows. I was also having some luck with good roles on stage. In those days, working on stage was a way to get casting directors and agents to come see that you could actually act. I got a break when a young agent who had seen me in a play at the Glendale Center Theater wanted to represent me. His name was Phil Arcara, and he was with the Hiller Agency, a small but highly respected office in town. Phil was smart, energetic and dedicated, and he seemed enthusiastic about helping to build my career.

For the first time, I was earning enough money as an actor to support myself without another job on the side. Judy and I were patching up our relationship, and our friend Doug had caught fire in the commercial world and moved back to New York. The lessons from The House had opened up a vision of the world that sensitized me even more to the injustice and dishonesty I had instinctively reacted to earlier. Rather than passively accepting it, I now felt an obligation to those who had helped me—to apply what I had learned from them on a larger scale. Just as stripping away the masks of deceit in group sessions could free the human trapped inside, it seemed logical that insisting that we practice what we preach in society—fairness, honesty, decency and justice—could have the same result on a larger scale.

This being the 1960s, there was no shortage of opportunities to get involved. Responding to an ad in the *L.A. Free Press*, I went to a gathering of people interested in promoting a full, public investigation of the assassination of JFK. Thus began the Kennedy Assassination

Truth Committee, a clumsily named but dedicated group of which I was elected co-chair. The committee obtained a copy of the Warren Commission's twenty-six volumes of evidence, met and shared information, heard theories from some who had written books on the subject, conducted events questioning the Warren Report (which, White House tapes have revealed, even Richard Nixon once called "the greatest hoax that has ever been perpetrated"), worked to promote public interest, and provided speakers to groups small and large. We obtained one of the first copies of the Zapruder film and used it to show the shocking act that robbed us of the last national leader to truly inspire Americans.

The Vietnam War was raging and I wrote letters, marched in demonstrations, and argued the case for withdrawal. I read *The Autobiography of Malcolm X*, among other works, and tried to develop a better understanding of the huge social stresses that had been made manifest in my life by my father's use of racist terms, my fellow Marines' discomfort at my friendship with Tyus, and the loathsome reality of segregation both in the South and here in Los Angeles. I felt an increasing sense of fury at the casual indifference to racism, injustice, and insensitivity demonstrated by elected and appointed leadership, increasingly referred to as "the power structure." When the Black Panthers were under siege in Los Angeles, I rented a truck, filled it with food, and delivered it to a home in South Central L.A. where they were holed up, expecting an attack by the police (which later occurred). I supported César Chávez and the United Farm Workers' lettuce and grape boycotts, believing that those who worked in slavelike conditions to pick the food for our tables deserved the right to organize for better wages and working conditions. With friends, I organized a public showing of the documentary film *A Time for Burning* to help generate discussion of the white opposition to integration that suffused the nation and would only be overcome by recognizing and confronting our most fundamental fears. I supported Eugene McCarthy for president and was confused and frustrated by Bobby Kennedy's late entry into the race. At a rally for Bobby's candidacy, a black man I had met earlier told me of an interracial gathering in South Central. I attended the meeting with a group of interested friends, only to be confronted by the other side of racism in the form of taunting, insulting and threatening behavior by the very man who had invited us.

It was a time of learning, and everything I learned underscored the importance of the values taught at The House. Everyone does want love, respect, and attention, but the damage done to those who have been deprived of them isn't easily remedied. It takes hard work and dedication to bind the wounds of the abused, the neglected, the misshapen, the dysfunctional. It takes love. And the scars are sometimes so deep even that doesn't succeed. When it does, though, you know the risks were worth taking.

This was definitely a time for taking risks. Pressure for civil rights continued against stiff opposition. JFK's killing didn't slow the movement, but as it grew the opposition became ever more fanatical. It was a bloody time. James Chaney, Andrew Goodman, and Michael Schwerner died trying to make America live up to its promise. Malcolm X was murdered; Muhammad Ali unleashed a torrent of outrage by refusing induction into the Army on the basis of his religious beliefs. Pressed to explain, he spoke directly to the point: "No Viet Cong ever called me nigger." Martin Luther King was murdered in Memphis, shaking the foundations of society. Months later a momentarily triumphant Bobby Kennedy was gunned down, and despair threatened to trump hope. But when Tommie Smith and John Carlos stood on the winners' platform at the Mexico City Olympics, shoeless, heads bowed, and fists raised during the playing of the National Anthem, the message was clear: We are here, we will not go away, we will not submit.

For some, the brutality at the Democratic Convention in Chicago meant the end of everything. For others it was the beginning. Did Mayor Daley and the Chicago police represent our country? If Senator Abe Ribicoff could condemn the "Gestapo tactics in the streets of Chicago," surely others could express their fury at this outrage and declare that neither the Vietnam War nor the Chicago police represented the true America. But it was hard to know the right thing to do. Hubert Humphrey was unwilling to stand up to Lyndon Johnson on the war, so Richard Nixon was elected president by claiming to have "a secret plan" to end it. Disgusted with the process, I helped elect Nixon by casting a protest vote for the Black Panther Eldridge Cleaver. Clearly, I was making mistakes as I worked my way through this turbulent time, but I was learning in the process.

I was also building a career. Phil was moving things along, getting me interviews and sometimes offers to do more meaningful parts. These more significant roles were important, exciting steps. But having moved beyond the stage of two- or three-line roles in television shows, I was frustrated to get a call from him one day with an offer for a quite small role on an episode of a popular series. Irritated at what seemed a step in the wrong direction, I got up a head of steam and told him I thought the offer was an insult.

I'll never forget his reaction: "Don't ever let me hear you say that again. There are a lot of actors in this town who are not working and would be thrilled to get this offer. The casting director had the chance to offer this job to a lot of people, and out of all of them, he chose you. It is never an insult to be offered a job; I don't care how damned small the part is. If you don't want to do it, that's fine. That's your choice, and you have every right to make it. But you are not ever being insulted when someone offers you a job. Any job. It is a compliment, and you need to understand that and respond appropriately."

I absorbed it all, took a deep breath, and replied, "You're right, I apologize. Please tell him that I very much appreciate the fact that he thought of me, but I think I'll wait and hope that something better will come along."

"Good," Phil responded. "You've made the right choice. I'll call him right back."

He was a hell of an agent. We were together until he left the business.

One day, Phil called with an offer for me to read for a part on

Days of Our Lives, a daytime soap opera on NBC. I interviewed, read, and was offered the part of Scott Banning, an architect involved in a typical soap-opera situation. Because the producers weren't sure how the story line would play out, they didn't offer a contract, explaining that the role guaranteed at least a couple of appearances a week for the next few weeks. After that, they'd know more. If I took it, I'd be working as a "day-player," earning AFTRA (American Federation of Television and Radio Artists) minimum wage for each day worked. That was fine with me.

It was my first regular job, and I was thrilled. I'd be playing a recurring character for at least a little while. As it turned out, the story line caught on, and I was on *Days* for almost two years. By the time they got around to offering more money and a guaranteed term of employment, Phil thought I was better off as a day-player, thus free to leave if something better came along.

MacDonald Carey and Frances Reid, two veteran actors, played the heads of the Horton family, around whom the program revolved. My story line was emotionally complex, as soaps tend to be, with my wife (played by Joyce Easton) dying of a brain tumor and the care of our adopted baby (Chad Barstad) left to our neighbor Susan (Denise Alexander), who was secretly in love with me. The adopted son, of course, was actually the illegitimate child of Julie Horton (Susan Seaforth), granddaughter of the Hortons, with whom I was, after the death of my wife, to be lured into a marriage of convenience for the sake of the baby. Got it?

Soaps have become an industry in and of themselves. While still a springboard for some careers and a pasture for others, they're now a separate world, with magazines, awards shows, and huge and loyal followings. In the late '60s, however, they were still primarily half-hour shows thought of, at least on the West Coast, as the industry's stepchildren. Be that as it may, I was happy to have the role. The atmosphere on the set was utterly professional, the job demanding, and the company hard-working, pleasant, and fun. The actors were gifted and dedicated to their craft, but I was in particular awe of Mac

Carey and Frannie Reid, both of whom received me with grace and were wonderfully supportive throughout my time on the show.

After two years of suffering, weeping, worrying, fighting off lustful advances, and conniving to save my child, I was offered a chance to leave the soap for a role in *The Interns*, a pilot for a prime-time series on CBS. Luckily for me, the job of finding an actor for this particular role went to the same casting director who had put me in *Days of Our Lives*. The show's creator, Bill Blinn, knew my work from a Hollywood showcase and had actually written the part of a married young physician, slightly more settled than the other young docs in the ensemble, with me in mind. As he was casting it, however, Bill thought I was under contract to the soap and not available. The casting director, aware that I had no contract and might be interested, called Phil, and it was goodbye Scott Banning, hello Dr. Sam Marsh.

In the tradition of life imitating art, as the transition from *Days of Our Lives* to *The Interns* was taking place, Judy and I became determined to make it work. We bought a house in Sherman Oaks, and she was soon pregnant. I was ecstatic.

Yet nothing's as easy as it looks in this business, and an important lesson was in store on the way to becoming an "intern." The network offered us a "test deal." This involved going in to shoot some scenes from the show and then waiting while the show's producers and the studio and network executives pondered over their creation, our future, and whether the two were connected. Because I hadn't known what to expect, I was excited to discover two things. One was that the series had already been ordered; we wouldn't have to go through the torture of doing a pilot episode and then sweating about whether or not it would make the schedule. The second was that while the first day of shooting was a "test," they were only testing one actor for each part. This suggested that we were the producers' choices and, if things went as intended, I was going to be Dr. Sam. That was the good part. We five would be the interns, and the young actress playing my wife would be a regular in the series as well. She was, as I discovered that day, not only very attractive but also quite smart and exceptionally talented. So when I reported to work a couple of days later, I was shocked to learn that they had decided to replace her with another actress. Dumbfounded because I thought she was so good, I asked the producer what had happened, and he said they (it's always the faceless "they" who make these decisions) had decided she was "too sexy." God. How quickly and easily parts—and sometimes careers—slip away as a result of some fool's whim.

Being one of the leads on a prime-time network television series is a heady experience. The quick shift from unemployed actor hustling to get work to "star," however overused the term, can put one off stride. Both the network and the studio (Screen Gems in this case) have publicity departments to crank out stories about how wonderful you are, where you've been, and where you're going. And if you're not interesting enough, they'll make it up. Studio executives who wouldn't have given you the time of day yesterday come around to glad-hand and say hello; photographers record your every move on the set, and if the machine has created enough of a buzz, the paparazzi do the same outside. You're making more money than you've ever made; reporters call; people want to take you to lunch. It can be very seductive. The big danger is falling into the trap of believing your own publicity and getting the idea that you're more than just another widget being processed through the system this season.

The head of the cast was Broderick Crawford, an Academy Award–winner probably best known for the long-running TV series *Highway Patrol*. Brod played Dr. Peter Gold, a crusty, tough-talking, no-nonsense surgeon with a harsh manner and a good heart who pummeled his neophyte medicos into crackerjack doctors. In reality, Brod was a crusty, tough-talking, no-nonsense drunk with a harsh manner and a good heart who, if his work wasn't completed before noon, would as likely as not become incomprehensible on the set. I think no one was greatly surprised by Brod's behavior, as his reputation preceded him. I was least of all. A few years earlier, I had delivered groceries to his house and had seen him come into the store where I worked so drunk he was barely able to stand. He was a crotchety but warm guy with a serious problem. The producers had been promised that he was off the sauce and on good behavior. When that proved as true as such assurances often do in the business, they began shooting his stuff early in the day and tiptoeing around him.

Not content to ignore the elephant in the room, I attempted the impossible. Taking Brod aside on more than one occasion, I said he owed it to himself and the company to see that we got the work done. Once past his first blustery denials, he actually began to open up a bit and gradually expressed a gruff affection for me. Though his drinking continued, I was touched by the appreciation he showed. Long after the show was cancelled, Brod would call periodically to make sure I was doing okay. Never failing to thank me for my concern on the set, his calls continued for years after the show ended, right up to the time of his death.

The young actors playing the interns were, despite considerable talent and experience, primarily "unknowns." We were a diverse group, chosen with an eye to wide appeal. Hal Frederick, a great-looking black man, played Dr. Cal Barrin. Hal had been working in TV for a while, but this was his first series. Sandra Smith was a smart redhead with a sexy New York savvy. It was her first series as well. Christopher Stone was a shaggy-haired, blond he-man with great teenybopper appeal. Stephen Brooks was a bright and handsome man and, in my estimation, the best actor in the group. If memory serves, he was the only one who had done a series before. I believe that Elaine Giftos, who came in to play my wife Bobbe, had been a dancer. If not, she certainly had the legs. While shooting an early episode, she asked if I knew why the first Bobbe was dropped. Without thinking, I repeated what I had been told: "They said she was too sexy." Elaine looked at me for a moment, blinked, and said, "Thanks a lot."

It was a good bunch, congenial and hard-working. There were no memorable displays of the Hollywood "temperament." We younger cast members were so glad to be working in a series that we never even thought about causing trouble. Even Brod's problems didn't result in the kind of craziness the tabloids feast on today. I was glad to be in a good show and hoped it would catch on and stick around for a while.

It was a good year, and I learned a lot. Brod taught me a particular lesson about what it means to be a professional. When working in film, each scene usually requires a master shot and "coverage," which is breaking down the scene and doing close-ups and other shots of the people involved. Then the editor cuts them together to emphasize whatever points the director or writer wants made. When shooting coverage, the actors spend a lot of time waiting while the lights are adjusted and the set is prepared. This can be tricky—in the case of someone like Brod, it meant he could go back to his dressing room and have a snort. When shooting a close-up of one actor, the others in the scene perform their roles off-camera.

This is where you find out who the pros are. Some actors give less of a performance when off-camera, which can create real problems for the actor being filmed. Some simply lose focus, but a few are either disinterested or so self-obsessed that nothing matters but their own on-camera time. Some so-called stars, particularly when it's an inconsequential scene with an "unimportant" character, don't show up at all, leaving it up to the script supervisor to read their off-camera lines. Brod, however, always made it a point to be there for his off-camera work. He may have been somewhat slurry with the words at times, but he always showed up and gave it what he had to give, no matter how small the scene. It's a lesson that has always stayed with me.

During the first few episodes, as we were getting to know each other and trying to define our characters, the head of publicity came to talk to me. With the war in Vietnam raging and the antiwar movement growing, I had been wearing a peace symbol for some time. The stunning slaughter of peacefully protesting students at Kent State by National Guard troops convinced me that Dr. Sam Marsh should wear it as well. Mr. Publicity, however, disagreed, saying he thought it inappropriate.

"How so?" I wondered aloud.

"Blah-de-blah-de-blah," he offered.

"Really?" I countered. "It seems to me to be perfectly logical for a young man in Sam's profession to be openly expressing his views at a time like this."

"Well, perhaps," he said, "but blah-de-blah-de-blah."

"Sure," I agreed. "People do have different points of view. This is Sam's."

"Yes, but blah-de-blah-de-blah."

"Oh, I certainly understand that we want to reach a wide audience," I agreed, "and I suppose it's possible that someone out there might be unhappy about Dr. Sam's peace symbol. That same person might not like the length of Chris's hair, too. You gonna ask him to cut it?"

"Well, blah-de-blah-de-blah."

"Right, part of his character. Same with the peace symbol."

"But the network blah-de-blah-de-blah."

"Equal-time provision? Does that go for every character in every show, or is it ultimately a matter of balance?"

"Well, blah-de-blah."

"Uh-huh. Then what do you suggest? You think maybe in every other episode I should wear a bomb?"

He went away shaking his head, but I heard no more about the peace symbol. I suppose that's the way stories about temperamental actors are born. I remember with pride, though, when Lew Ayres played a guest role on one of our episodes. A major star from the early years of films, he had been seriously impacted by working on the film *All Quiet on the Western Front*. Declaring as a conscientious objector at the outset of World War II, Lew served as a medic under fire in the Pacific. Despite his heroism, public outrage at his unwillingness to fight hurt his career deeply. He was a true gentleman. It was an honor to work with him and a thrill when he told me he liked the peace symbol.

In November of 1970, when we were about halfway through the season, my son was born. My golden boy, we named him Michael Joshua Farrell and called him Josh. (That only lasted until he was old enough to decide he didn't want to be Josh. He went through various incarnations over time, from Josh to Michael Josh to MJ to Michael, where it stayed.)

It was pouring rain the day he was born. I've always loved rain, so it seemed right. Judy and I had done the Lamaze training, which was relatively new at the time, so I stayed with her throughout the labor, providing ice chips and keeping her on track with the breathing. I was in the delivery room when he was born, something that's not unusual today, but was very much so then. Judy was extremely brave. It was an incredibly tough, wonderful, beautiful experience, and I made a vow that this sweet, squalling, helpless little guy would never, if I could prevent it, lack for love and touching and hugging and attention. And respect.

I was a whacked-out father, madly in love with this little guy, happily babbling and showing pictures of him all over the set. I'm sure I bored people to distraction. One of the many guest stars that came in to do an episode shortly after he was born—thus getting the full lecture and slide show—was a lovely young actress named Shelley Fabares. I remember being struck by her beauty, which is not an unusual commodity in Hollywood, but also by how sweet, quiet, and unassuming she was, which is.

Production ended in the spring of 1971, and we all said our most optimistic "see you laters," hoping that our reasonably good ratings meant we'd be back to intern for yet another season. But it wasn't to be. Judy, Josh, and I were motoring across the desert in our VW van on the way to see her folks when I got word to call the studio and was told the show was over. It wasn't good news, of course. I was an unemployed actor again. But somehow it wasn't devastating. Things had been moving along nicely, career-wise, and there seemed to be no reason to think they wouldn't continue this way. And besides, if it didn't work out I could always make a living doing something else. I'd done it before.

It's odd now to look back on that optimistic moment and wonder where it came from. I had certainly seen by that point that this was a *business* I was involved in—a cruel and heartless one at that. So many of the talented young people I had studied with, worked with, and in some cases admired, were still struggling mightily to eke out a living, while I had been lucky enough to keep a roof over our heads for a few years. But here I was: unemployed, with a new baby, and the show in which I had been a "star" cancelled. Yet somehow I felt okay—even protected. I think the sense of calm came from what I learned at The House: Success in this business wasn't necessary to provide the things that had been missing in my life. In fact, it *couldn't* provide them. That was my job. And I was up to it. A wonderful feeling of liberation came with that knowledge.

Not long after returning from Oklahoma, Phil called to say that some people at Universal Studio were interested in talking to me about another series—*The Man and the City*—starring Anthony Quinn, the motion picture star. Quinn would play the mayor of a small Southwestern city, and I was being considered for the part of his aide. If interested, I'd have to take a screen test, which seemed a bit silly since I had just done a series. And the deal would include a seven-year contract with the studio. It all required some thought. If the series failed, I'd then be obligated to stay at Universal and, in theory at least, do what they wanted me to do.

After thinking it over, though, I decided to go ahead. The chance to work with Tony Quinn, one of the giants of the business, was simply too good to pass up. I really couldn't imagine him staying tethered to a television series for long, so I didn't have high hopes for an extended run. And once we were cancelled, they probably wouldn't want to keep paying me and would agree to drop the contract. At least that's what I told myself.

But first things first. The "screen test" was essentially a personality test. There were no lines to learn; I wasn't asked to play a scene with another actor. I simply sat on a stool on a stage in front of a camera while some people behind the lights asked me questions. I answered them in a straightforward manner, tried to be charming, and hoped I wasn't coming across as terminally goofy. Then I left.

And waited. Waiting is the worst. You think about all the things you said and wish you'd said. You feel sure you've blown it and the response will be bad. It's like waiting for the doctor to call after you've had a test for something awful. And it usually happens on a Friday. It's completely out of your hands; there's absolutely nothing you can do but wait. Finally, Phil called. Goodbye Sam Marsh, hello Andy Hayes.

There's a reason Tony Quinn was a giant in the industry. Getting to know him was an experience. There was an animal energy around him that was palpable. His focus was intense, his presence undeniable. When we did interviews together, it was as though he sucked all the air out of the room. He was like a hungry force that devoured every person and every idea within reach. Once I got past being intimidated by him, it became fun to watch people—particularly women—be pulled into him. He was like a giant sexual magnet. I remember, during one episode, the incredibly attractive and wonderfully sexy Angie Dickinson was playing a guest star role. I left the stage during a break to go to my dressing room and found Tony and Angie walking just ahead of me. He had his arm around her as they headed for his trailer. I had no idea what, if anything, was going to happen in there, but I remember thinking, enviously, *My God, this guy is amazing.* At that moment, Tony looked back over his shoulder at me, smiled, and said, "Give it time, kid; your turn will come." He laughed that big, raspy laugh and headed off with Angie.

On the set, Tony was a wonder. He was always finding the guts of a scene, sniffing out the germ of an idea. He knew how to play the scenes and how to transform the often trite and wooden dialogue that results from the time pressure on the writers in television into genuine human conversation. In one episode his character was confronted with racism. During the scene the mayor asked Andy, "Do you think of me as a Mexican?" We talked about the scene and about the thrust of the show as we went over the dialogue. Tony was quiet for a few moments. Finally, he looked at me and asked, "Do you think of me as a Mexican?" For a moment I was paralyzed. His question was so simple, so pure, and so real that I suddenly didn't know if Tony was asking Mike if I thought of him as a Mexican or if the mayor was asking Andy. It was one of those rare, pure moments of utter honesty that creates magic in theater. He was brilliant.

During another episode, Tony and I were left standing together at the end of a scene in which the mayor was hurting over a difficult experience. There was a silent beat before the director called, "Cut," and I was moved to put my arm around him. We had to do the scene again, and just before we began, he turned to me and said, "You know that moment when you put your arm around me? Next time, want to, but don't." He was right, of course. The scene played beautifully. The audience was left wanting that contact to happen rather than having me solve the problem for them. He was truly a master.

And he was a complex character. He told stories all the time, many of which were utter bullshit. He kept felt-tipped pens of different colors nearby and would dash off wonderful pieces of abstract art between scenes. Later he developed a reputation as an admired artist, making me wish I had kept a few of the sketches. He had an assistant who ran errands for him and always carried a chessboard so they could play whenever Tony felt so inclined. After watching their games for a while, I noted that Tony would cheat rather than lose. There was nothing the assistant could do. He was the Washington Generals to Tony's Harlem Globetrotters: paid to lose. Full of stories, full of bravado, full of life, full of bullshit, Tony was something! When I brought Josh on the set, Tony became as soft and gentle as he was loud and powerful at other times. He held my boy and became a big, blubbering grandpa, whirling with him and dancing. I could see the tears in his eyes.

During a break one day, I was reading a script and Tony asked about it. I told him I'd been offered a part, so I was looking it over, hoping it was good.

"Want my opinion?" he asked.

I said, "Sure," and handed it to him.

He leafed quickly through the pages, clearly not reading any of it.

"Know what I'm doing?" he asked.

"No," I answered, puzzled, "what?"

"Looking for long speeches. If it's got long speeches, fuck it."

One day we had to reshoot a scene because of a sound problem. Tony took the opportunity to ham it up a bit, demanding to know how we could have sound problems with all this wonderful equipment and this huge soundstage with its padded walls. He had once done "a little film" by the seashore, he declared, and that soundman had only a simple recording device that he strapped over his shoulder. That's all he had, Tony insisted, and "we never had to loop a line." (Looping is a process in which actors can rerecord dialogue after the filming is over. It can be tricky matching the lip movements, but it's sometimes necessary to take out extraneous noises or to repair a goof.)

"What little film was that, Tony?" I asked, playing along.

"Oh, a little film called *Zorba the Greek*," he replied, breaking into Zorba's wonderful dance.

During the season with Tony, I was asked to take part in an event to raise funds for the defense of Daniel Ellsberg and Tony Russo. Ellsberg was the former Rand Corporation analyst who had, aided by Russo, copied and leaked the Pentagon Papers to the *New York Times*. Their hugely courageous act, while traitorous in the eyes of some, ripped the mask of legitimacy off the Vietnam War. Though Ellsberg bore the brunt of the scrutiny, both men were pilloried and lionized, depending upon one's point of view, and were savagely attacked by the Nixon Administration. It was later discovered that the campaign against them included a super-secret team called "The Plumbers," who broke into Ellsberg's psychiatrist's office searching for information that would discredit him. Once completely exposed, the Watergate scandal destroyed Nixon's presidency and later revealed his arrogance, prejudice, and utter lawlessness.

The invitation was exciting and a little scary. Up to that point, my political activities had been below the radar for the most part, limited largely to personal decisions like the peace symbol, participating in demonstrations, and statements in support of a candidate or against the war. There was a lot of pressure on people in the business to lay low. Even a small gesture like adding the word *Peace!* when signing an autograph raised eyebrows. Signing autographs had always struck me as odd anyway and a little embarrassing. But I figured if that's the way the game is played, I could at least attempt to communicate something meaningful.

The Ellsberg event was to be a huge, well-publicized gathering at the Los Angeles Sports Arena. It was organized by a group of dedicated civil libertarians and war protesters led by Stanley K. Sheinbaum, an economist and publisher who had become a leading figure in the movement to end the war. Taking part in the program, onstage with a small group of actors reading pertinent political and historic statements, meant being very public about a decidedly controversial issue. The event was to feature heavyweights from business, politics, and entertainment, including Jane Fonda, Donald Sutherland, Sally Kellerman, and Burt Lancaster. It was exciting as hell to be asked; apparently someone had noticed that I gave a damn about what was happening and wanted to see if I was willing to risk being public about it. Either that or they were really hard up for actors. Whatever their reasons, the invitation was thrilling.

When I agreed to take part, they asked me if Tony would consider coming as well. Aha! Now I understood their real reason for contacting me. But that was okay. I was certainly realistic enough to know that I wasn't going to bring a lot of juice to the effort on my own. If I could bring Tony, I was still doing a service. But unfortunately, he wasn't available. When I called to say Tony wasn't going to come, I was pleasantly surprised to learn that they still wanted me.

I arrived early enough to rehearse our presentation and then sat backstage to watch the place fill up. It was a great event, with a huge and highly charged crowd anxious to express its indignation at the lies and insulting, brutal, and high-handed behavior of Nixon and his henchmen. I was thrilled to be there. There was a lot of press, which, aside from the fundraising, was the point of the exercise: to let Nixon and the world know that the people here saw what was going on and were willing to stand up and condemn it. It was fun, if a bit intimidating, to hang around backstage before the small troupe of which I was part went out front. Fiery speeches provoked roars of approval from the crowd and wonderful cracks allowed us to laugh at the cruel absurdity of the clowns in Washington. And I had a ringside seat. Finally, my troupe was tapped to go on, and four or five of us read words chosen to underscore the importance of the mission we were embarking on that evening. I remember Bob DoQui, a black actor I knew, reading a powerful statement from Frederick Douglass, the emancipated slave whose searing indictments of American hypocrisy scorch the soul as they lay bare the gaping chasm between the easy rhetoric of patriotism and the bitter reality of life in America for so many. I have no idea what I read, but apparently I got through it.

It was exciting, heady, and deeply inspiring, and then it was over. Ellsberg and Russo graciously thanked us for being part of the evening; I was touched by their simplicity and dazzled by everything. To be in the company of these courageous men who had put their careers, their freedom, and possibly their lives at risk in order to do what they believed necessary for the safety of their country was intoxicating. To be in the company of stars who risked public censure by standing up for what they believed in was stirring. I felt a combination of embarrassment that I had done so little while they risked so much and a sense of hope at seeing the difference that one who has access to the public forum can make.

Back at work, Tony asked who was at the event and how it had gone. I was surprised when he expressed regret at missing it and admitted that his excuse had been a cop-out. He ruminated about the terrible days of the House Un-American Activities Committee hearings and the Hollywood Ten, implying that his experience of those times was the reason he hadn't taken part. He didn't exactly apologize for not going, but he came close. While I've never seen any evidence of his being singled out during the Red Scare, I'm sure the fear permeating the industry in those days impacted everyone in some way. In any event, his admission was touching; more so was his expression of admiration for my having been there.

The Man and the City ended more with a whimper than a bang. Tony was in discussions with the studio as we wound down the season. Our ratings had not been as high as had been hoped, and it was clear we were on the ropes. I wasn't surprised, frankly; the limitations of the show were too constraining for an actor of his power. But I could see that the idea of failing troubled him. As the show developed, David Victor, the Executive Producer, tried to fashion Tony into another version of Marcus Welby, the lead character in a very successful show he was producing at the time. But that approach was exactly wrong for Tony. In abandoning its focus on real political issues, the show became meaningless, and no one was happy. I wasn't privy to the high-level conversations, but it was clear that Tony was losing patience with the studio's inability to find a direction for the show. He took me aside one day and explained, apologetically, that he wasn't interested in making the changes suggested by the studio. Their latest brainstorm had been to junk the format entirely and have us become some sort of cop or detective team.

"I know what they want," he confided. "They want me to be the tough guy, knocking the bad guys around the way we used to do it at MGM. But that's bullshit; I'm not gonna do that anymore."

Keenly aware of how lucky I was to be working with this man, I wasn't anxious to lose the job, but it was clear that Tony was right. They were trying to fit a giant into a little box. The more the "geniuses" tried to twist and squeeze him into a shape that made sense to them, the more likely he was to explode. So we simply said goodbye. What a force he was. What a joy to know him. And how proud it made me, years later, to have him express approval of my efforts on behalf of social justice.

Chapter 6
QUEST

With the show over, I awaited word that my contract with the studio was terminated, as I had expected—and hoped—would be the case. But, "Not so fast, Johnson!" The old joke from Marine Corps days came back to haunt me: The parents of a guy in boot camp are killed in an automobile accident. The DI has to tell him. Not the most sensitive of souls, the DI ponders his options and orders the platoon to fall in. With them all at attention before him, he commands, "Everybody whose parents are alive take two steps forward! . . . Not so fast, Johnson!"

And so it was. The executives in the Black Tower, the infamous office building dominating the Universal lot, decided that my contract was a good investment if they could find something else for me to do. For me, it was a kind of good-news/bad-news call. Much of what the studio was doing didn't interest me, and staying under contract meant I wouldn't have the option of saying no. On the other hand, they were paying me every week.

Phil, ever the pragmatist, said, "Look, they can't force you to act. If you say no, they put you on suspension, you sit home for a while, it goes away, and they find something else."

"Does the time I'm on suspension count against the contract?"

"Nope. It gets tacked onto the end."

"Shit, I could be here forever!"

But there was home and family to consider. I had signed the contract. And there were a lot of actors in town who would have been happy to trade places.

As it turned out, the seven-year contract, now reduced to six, only lasted three more. And they weren't bad years. I was being paid, after all, except when I was on suspension. During those times I found other things to do, like standing on a busy corner, a human billboard supporting the lettuce and grape boycotts of César Chávez and the UFW. When working, things could have been a lot worse. I did a few episodes of Universal's TV shows. I had my own dressing room where I set up a chessboard in case I could find someone to play. One morning I came in to find that someone, most likely one of the night cleaning crew, had made an opening move. I countered it. The next day another move had been made. Great fun! The game went on for some time before it suddenly stopped, and I never did find out who the phantom player was. I guess she or he was transferred or something. It's weird to lose a friend you've never met.

George McGovern ran against Nixon that year, and I worked on the campaign. Though I didn't actually meet Senator McGovern until it was over, I was attracted to it by his straightforward, heartland civility. He was a truth-teller, a war hero, and a fundamentally decent human being who, had he been elected, could have moved us back toward being the hopeful nation John Kennedy inspired. Having now known Senator McGovern for years, I feel a deep sense of loss whenever I think of the extraordinary opportunity America missed by not putting him in the White House. Instead, the Vietnam slaughter continued, though even Nixon had secretly begun to look for a way out. Documents now disclose that he and Henry Kissinger actually discussed the impending loss of the war early on, but felt it might jeopardize their election prospects to pull out too soon. How many thousands died because of their chicanery?

I was asked to do some speaking for the McGovern campaign, helping to explain what was right with his approach and wrong with the war. It was a new experience, so I was careful to stay within the parameters of the campaign's message. It was heady stuff. More than once I found myself out of my depth when asked to explain complex economic issues and had to beg the questioner's indulgence and call for help. I was much more comfortable, though still in new and exciting territory, introducing proxies for the candidate, like economist and former ambassador John Kenneth Galbraith. Then I could just do my job, shut up, listen, and learn. I wish more had paid attention.

At work I alternated between being "Peck's bad boy" and working on projects I found interesting. After yet another suspension for turning down yet another silly script, Phil and I were summoned to the Black Tower by one of the executives. His mission was to make clear that I didn't have script approval in my contract.

"Well, you send him the scripts, don't you?" Phil asked.

"Yes," he admitted, "we do."

"So Mike reads them and decides if he wants to do it or not and lets you know."

"Yes, exactly," the exec agreed, talking to Phil as if I wasn't there, "but that's not the way it's supposed to work. We're just sending him the script to let him know what he's going to be doing."

"Right," Phil said, "and if he doesn't want to do it, he tells you."

"But he can't do that."

"Sure he can. He just did."

"But then we have to put him on suspension."

"Right. You just did."

"Yeah, but we don't want to do that."

"So don't."

"But . . ."

"It's up to you. Anything else we can do for you?"

Meetings with executives can be so interesting if you have a good agent.

In one of the jobs I did agree to do, I played John Denver's brother. John loved chess and hated that he couldn't beat me. We laughed and became friends as he kept saying, "That's not how this is supposed to go!" A lovely man and an inspiring performer, I was thrilled to call him friend.

Universal finally found a pilot to stick me in, yet another version of *Marcus Welby, M.D.* I was to play the Jim Brolin role, the younger sidekick of the lead doctor. Such an obvious rip-off had little shot at succeeding, but it gave me the chance to play opposite the Oscar-winning actress Jane Wyman, who was simply great. Warm, open, friendly, and utterly professional, Jane gave no hint that television was beneath her or the working hours too demanding. She set a tone on the set that was pleasant and comfortable, respectful of the crew, the material, and the opportunity the show presented. For me, it was another in a string of chances to watch and learn from talented, highly regarded veteran actors who had taken on iconic status. Unfortunately, my relationship with Jane was short-lived because my guess was right. The show wasn't picked up.

The next summer another miracle entered my life in the form of Erin Elizabeth Farrell. Judy and I were already notorious as overly attentive and nauseatingly doting parents. "Judy and Mike aren't fun anymore" was the refrain. But we were in synch, and I don't regret a minute of it. That the kids are now wonderful, bright, healthy, well-adjusted, successful young adults makes it all worthwhile. It's the greatest achievement I can ever hope to enjoy. Just as with her brother, we talked and sang to Erin before she was born, did the Lamaze training, and were primed to go the night she arrived. We thought we had it so under control, though, that we nearly cut things too close. Judy was well into labor as I screeched into the hospital lot, so I rushed her into the hands of the staff and ran to park the car. When I came racing back, she was already in the delivery room, hollering, "Get my husband in here!"

Back at work I got a great break, playing opposite a terrific actor named Robert Foxworth in a movie for television, a Gene Roddenberry project called *The Questor Tapes*. Roddenberry, riding high as a result of the phenomenal success of *Star Trek*, saw this show as a way to deal with some of the world's problems in a contemporary setting. Foxworth played Questor, an android designed by an extra-terrestrial intelligence to help the human race toward its rightful destiny. I was Jerry Robinson, one of the scientists working on the super-secret project that created Questor. With the deft Roddenberry touch, this unlikely science-fiction scenario created a kind of buddy movie, with Foxworth and I dashing around the world to stave off disaster and promote peace, while avoiding the bad guys who were trying to shanghai the android and use his powers for nefarious ends.

Typical of Roddenberry's genius, the show gave us the chance to deal with very political issues in a format that, as *Star Trek* demonstrated, engaged people's imagination while asking them to reflect on important issues they might have resisted reading about in the newspaper. Bob and I had great fun doing the picture. He was aware of the impact of words, which I appreciated. One exchange he had with the director, Richard Colla, said a lot. Bob had a line describing Questor's vision, what his work could mean to the world. As written, it said something like, "This will be very important to the future of man." Bob wanted to use the word "humankind," or at a minimum, "mankind," instead of "man." Dick, trying to protect the writer, said they all meant the same thing. If that was so, Bob wondered, why not use one of the others?

"What's wrong with 'man'?" Dick asked.

"We're not only talking about men," Bob explained.

While this might seem a small point, I was extremely impressed with Foxworth's sensitivity. Here was an actor who thought deeply about the impact of the words we use in a medium with such extraordinary power.

Gene Roddenberry was very happy with the finished picture, as were the studio and the network. The audience liked Questor as well, and it was ordered as a series. This was exciting. I liked Bob, I liked our characters, and I liked the relationship between them. I certainly liked the idea of being one of the leads in a good series, and I was looking forward to having a lot of fun doing a show that might actually have something to say. Things were moving swimmingly. The wardrobe person took me out and we bought thousands of dollars worth of clothes. I talked to the producers about concepts, stories, and shooting in distant locations.

Then one day I called the producer, as I had done dozens of times, and was told he was busy but would get right back to me. He didn't. I called back a little later to be told the same thing. He still didn't. It was a Friday, as I recall. These things always happen on Fridays in Hollywood, and I began to experience that gnawing insecurity that is always right at the edge of the actor's consciousness. I called yet again. Now it seemed the producer had gone home. Beginning to sweat, I contacted Phil, who knew of no problem. Eventually I called everyone I could think of, except my congressman, and would have called him if I'd known his number. Everyone was either not home or not available. Over the weekend, I finally reached Gene Roddenberry; all he knew was that there were "discussions" going on. This is nightmare time for an actor. Every insecure bone in your body goes into overdrive, and even the secure ones aren't so sure anymore. After a couple of very sleepless nights, Phil called to say that we had been asked to come to another meeting in the dreaded Black Tower.

By this time the writing was on the wall. In blood. Mine. It didn't take a genius to know that this would not be a good-news meeting. And there were no surprises. As the executive explained, the premise of the movie was that Questor, being an android, had all the intelligence that science could instill in him, but had no feelings. Jerry, then, was the heart in the equation. But I knew that; I'd seen the movie. However, for the purposes of the television series, the studio felt that Questor would be in more jeopardy while on the run from the bad guys if Jerry wasn't there to help him out. Aha. So, the series would be going forward, but instead of Bob and Mike being Questor and Jerry, there would only be Bob being Questor. Questing.

You know that feeling in the pit of your stomach when the worst thing you can think of actually happens? Not fun. Later, when nursing my wounds and reflecting on why I felt so completely crappy, I realized that all of my "buddies" in this new adventure, who treated me like I was the greatest guy in the world, had to have known at some point that this was being considered. But not one of them—not one—had the decency to warn me.

The fact is, this business is full of that kind of artificiality. Fred

Allen once said, "You can take all the sincerity in Hollywood and put it into a flea's navel and still have room left over for three caraway seeds and an agent's heart." I've been lucky in the agent department, dealing with honest, caring people who've worked hard on my behalf, so I don't buy into all the bitching about bloodsucking agents. Some may be, but agents too often become the vessel for all the anger, disappointment, frustration, and envy that this business generates. It's fear again, the old enemy. Everyone is worried that his job will disappear, that it will be discovered that he really doesn't have any talent, or she's too old or too young or slept her way to the top. People fear they'll be pushed aside by the next one to come up with a bright idea—or a dumb one that someone will buy. It's at base a business and, despite the glossy coating of song and celebration, a heartless one at that. And I was sad. Disappointed. Depressed.

But I still had my home and family. I had a contract and a regular paycheck. It wasn't like I was broke, hopeless, and on the street. I just needed to lick my wounds and find the bright side again. And speaking of bright sides, it gave me more time to play with my kids. When all is said and done, that's a lot more important than whatever comes in second. And I knew that pretty soon the studio would have another stupid part for me to turn down and the status would once again be quo.

Chapter 7
M*A*S*H

A couple of interesting things did actually happen in the following months. First, a producer sent me a pilot script for a half hour situation comedy called *Jerry*, and asked if I'd be interested in playing the lead. That was very flattering, but the script really didn't ring my bell. I told him thanks, but no thanks. He was surprised and asked why. It was a joke show, a comedy that relied on gags, silly situations, and odd characters to carry the audience along. I was hoping for something with substance, something that had a base of reality out of which comedy or drama would grow naturally, rather than being imposed. But rather than go into all that I said, "Well, it's not M*A*S*H."

I had loved the Robert Altman movie M*A*S*H, a hard-hitting, topical indictment of the insanity of war that came out at the height of the collision of Vietnam and the American antiwar movement. I hadn't expected the TV series to live up to its promise, but I'd been surprised and very impressed with what I'd seen. Not only did a terrific company of actors play very human people trying to survive under harrowing conditions, but the writing and production values were first rate. I remember catching part of the show one night, and the young man playing Radar carried a scene with such honesty, innocence, and integrity that I was both moved as an audience member and thrilled as an actor. M*A*S*H demonstrated that you could work within the sitcom framework and still be about something—in this case, something wonderful and real, human and touching—rather than superimposing a false reality on a fake premise. *Jerry*, on the other hand, was just about jokes.

Ironically, Phil called not long after this with an interesting query. At the end of the second season of M*A*S*H, some problems had arisen in the renegotiation of Wayne Rogers's contract. Phil had been asked, unofficially, whether I'd be interested in taking his place if things weren't soon resolved. I was interested, of course, but had learned by now not to put a lot of stock in "possibilities." I simply logged it and moved on. The contract difficulties, whatever they were, apparently got resolved, as I heard no more about it in the ensuing months.

What I did hear about was the ongoing Watergate scandal in Washington. While I felt a bit cheated that the entire sordid tale wasn't played out for the lesson it could provide America, I breathed a big sigh of relief when Richard Nixon resigned on August 9, 1974. Sadly, it was too late to elevate George McGovern to the presidency, but it vindicated the values articulated by the McGovern campaign and allowed us to hope, if only temporarily, that the days of corruption and venality in government were over.

I also learned that the *Questor* series had been pulled from the schedule. Though I tried not to gloat, I later enjoyed a great story about it. After many false starts, Merv Gerard, an experienced writer, was called in to figure out how to make the show work. As he later related it to me, Merv got all the concepts, information, and input from the executives, then sat down to watch the original movie. After doing so, he confronted Frank Price, then head of television, with the question, "Who's the idiot that dropped Mike Farrell from the series?" After a pause, Price responded, "You're talking to him." Something about "laughing last" came to mind at hearing this, because I recalled a point during all of it when someone came to me and asked if I would consider coming back to the show. Never one to hold a grudge, I said, "Not on your life."

Another season passed and nothing came along that knocked me out. One morning, I read in the paper that Wayne Rogers was again talking about leaving M*A*S*H. Hmmm, I thought. *I wonder if that's true. And if it is, I wonder if we'll get another call.* Once again, I logged the information and let it go. But then Phil called to say that the folks at Twentieth were worried about Wayne's possible departure and would like to meet with me. Was I interested? Was I! But could I? I had a contract. "One thing at a time," Phil counseled. "We don't need to worry about that until we need to worry about it." Made sense to me.

I'd been on the Fox lot before, had actually worked there a couple of times. By now I'd done two years on a soap, guest-starred in a number of TV episodes, starred in two prime-time television series and a successful movie. Then why was I so nervous? I felt like a kid on my first date. I assume I checked in and waited, sweating profusely, but I remember nothing. Suddenly there was Burt Metcalfe, a casting director I'd known at Universal. Burt introduced me to Gene Reynolds and Larry Gelbart, the show's Executive Producers. Gelbart was also the show's primary writer. All three were warm and friendly and I was a zombie! I finally confessed that I was nervous as hell, but I was sure glad to be there and I liked their show a lot. They laughed and thought that was great, which helped me calm down— a little.

As I tried to breathe, they explained their situation. Negotiations with Wayne Rogers were not going well, and they had to prepare for the possibility that he would not be back. In that event, they'd need someone to fill his shoes as Hawkeye's buddy. It was clear that they hoped Wayne would come back. That only made sense. Why mess with a winning combination if you didn't have to? I said I understood, and in the event they did have to make a change, I'd be thrilled to be considered. I added, though, that I would not be interested in replacing Wayne in the role of Trapper John. That, I thought, would be a big mistake. They quickly agreed; that was not their intention at all. What they had in mind was to replace Trapper with a guy who was newly married, probably had a child, and fully intended to remain faithful to his wife—someone different from the womanizing Hawkeye and Trapper. "Does that sound interesting?" they asked. Did that sound interesting?! It sounded too good to be true. I summoned all my *savoir-faire* and tried not to slobber while stuttering through the rest of the conversation or step on my feet as I made my way to the door.

A few very long days later, Phil called to say they wanted me to do a test. There would be at least two other actors testing for the part, he said. Again, the test wasn't about acting ability, it meant doing a test scene with Alan Alda to see what kind of chemistry, if any, happened in the pairing.

"Oh my God. Can I do it?"

"You can," he responded. "If it works, Universal says they'll let you out of the contract for however long you're there, with the understanding that you'll come back to them once it's over."

"But . . ."

"Don't worry about it. Worry about that later. Worry about this now."

When the day came for the test, I reported to the set at Fox and suited up. I had spent so much time thinking about the scenes between B.J. and Hawkeye that I now had absolutely no idea how to do them. After being made up and donning a set of Army fatigues, I tried to remain cool, calm, and totally under control. Just before I panicked completely and ran screaming from the soundstage, Alan Alda came over and introduced himself. He talked; I mumbled. He talked a bit more. I grunted, my stomach growled, sweat seeped through my shirt. Finally, they were ready for us. Gene Reynolds talked us through the scene. I remember virtually none of what he said or what happened. I do seem to recall that a basketball was involved, though I have no idea why. The camera rolled; we got through it; then we tried it again. At least I think we did. At some point, it was finally over and people were saying goodbye to me in those distant voices you hear when you're coming back to consciousness. I probably said thanks. I'm sure I left.

In the car on the way home, I couldn't stop talking to myself, asking question after question: "Why did you do that?" "Why didn't you think of . . .?" "What in God's name is wrong with you, you half-wit?"

"It's a comedy, for God's sake! Don't you think it would have been a good idea to be funny?"

A day or so later—it felt more like a year—the call finally came. I was at my mom's house in West Hollywood when Phil delivered the news: "You got it."

I was very cool, saying simply, "That's great. Thanks." Then I hung up the phone, gave my mom a kiss, ran out to my car, raced up to Phil's office on Sunset, ran screaming into his room, and grabbed him in a bear hug. Phil was thrilled; I was thrilled; Wally was thrilled; people in the next building were thrilled. Everybody was thrilled. Everything was great! And it just kept getting greater.

That same afternoon I got a call from Alan Alda, asking if I could meet him for dinner that night to give us a chance to get to know each other and talk about the show, the characters, and the future. We ate at a Chinese restaurant in Hollywood, and I pretended I wasn't nervous as we talked and laughed and ate until well into the night. And at some point I stopped being nervous. *This is a nice man*, I kept thinking. *He didn't have to do this.* Of course, it could just be good business to warm me up this way, but it was soon clear that this wasn't about business. The guy really cared about the show and the characters. He wanted the relationships to mean something, and he wanted the show to succeed. And not just with good ratings and awards, though there's nothing wrong with that; he wanted the show to succeed by honestly and honorably exploring the lives and relationships of the real people who had been in this terrible situation, while at the same time entertaining the audience.

The following Monday morning, I reported to work on Stage 9 at Twentieth Century Fox. In spite of Alan's generous welcoming dinner, I was still nervous. After all, I was replacing a guy who had been part of this company for three years and had certainly developed strong relationships with everyone. I was worried that I might, on some level, be resented. I'd also been around long enough to know that television series, even successful ones, can fail at any time for any number of reasons. I was haunted by the recurring thought that if

M*A*S*H were to fail in its fourth year, I'd be wearing its failure around my neck for the rest of my life.

Other than that, it was a walk in the park.

The first person I saw on the set was Gary Burghoff, who played Radar with such sweetness and charm. He stuck out his hand and greeted me warmly. Next Loretta Swit walked over and introduced herself; then came Larry Linville, Jamie Farr, and Bill Christopher. After Burt introduced me to the other members of the company, Gene Reynolds, who was directing *Welcome to Korea*, the hour-long special episode that introduced B.J. Hunnicutt, called us all to the table for the reading of the script. Reading through a script with the rest of the company is a great thing for everyone involved. It gives the writers, producers, and director a chance to see what works and what doesn't. It gives the script supervisor the chance for a first real timing. And for me on this particular occasion, it was a wonderful icebreaker.

After we'd completed the reading, Gene announced, "Okay, page one." Seeing my quizzical look, he explained: "After the first read-through, we go back over it page by page to see if anyone has any questions, problems, or suggestions." I could hardly believe my ears. These people actually wanted to hear what the actors thought? Though I'd been very lucky in my working experience, it was generally felt that producers, directors, and writers regarded actors as over-paid, self-important narcissists, often as dumb as posts, who should hit their marks, say their words as written, and otherwise shut up and stay out of the way. Sadly, there are far too many actors whose selfish and unprofessional behavior encourages this view. My experience, however, was that for every actor who behaves like a jerk, there are twenty other smart, creative, talented, decent players whose generosity and experience can be an asset to any production. Unfortunately, those who don't call attention to themselves often go unnoticed and remain unheralded. The willingness of Gene and the M*A*S*H producers to hear what the actors had to say, even to the point of encouraging their input, was so extraordinary that I kept thinking it couldn't be real. But it was.

It stayed that way for the next eight years. I came to regard M*A*S*H as a creative community, where the quality of the work was primary and the contributions of all were encouraged and appreciated. While Alan's Hawkeye was clearly the lead, it quickly became evident that in everyone's mind the star of M*A*S*H was M*A*S*H.

Alan's intelligence and generosity stand out in my mind. He's as bright as anyone I've ever known, wonderfully analytical, gifted with a great sense of irony and brilliant comic timing. His generosity was evident in the way he shared the spotlight. We all knew that he was the star, the drawing card, the big *macher*. He could have had anything he wanted, including his face in every scene and himself as the fulcrum of every story. In the show's later years, Alan's agents are said to have asked him and his wife Arlene, "What'll we ask for this year?" to which Arlene is said to have responded, "How about Tennessee?" While probably apocryphal, the story gives a sense of how highly he was prized by the network and how much power accrues to one in that position. He knew, though, that the spirit of the show would be better served if each of the characters was fully dimensional, and he saw to it that everyone was served in that way.

Gene, Larry, and Burt, with the able assistance of Alan, were the creative trio (plus one) that kept the show on course. Gene, a former child actor, has a keen mind and a great eye, and was a real force behind maintaining the show's integrity. He directed many of the episodes and had an unerring sense of truth. Larry is rightly credited as the comic genius responsible for the high quality of writing for which the show is known. Unusual for one so incisive, antic, and spontaneously hilarious, Larry is generally soft-spoken, thoughtful, and quite sensitive in person. Burt, a Canadian-born former actor, had made his mark as a casting director and continued to find smart, talented, interesting actors throughout all the years of the show. He quickly moved up in the M*A*S*H hierarchy—directing, overseeing the writing, seamlessly assuming the role of Executive Producer after

Larry's and then Gene's departures—and flawlessly maintained the show's quality during its last few seasons.

The cast, as I regarded them then and think of them now, was perfect. Loretta Swit came out of the theater and, for the most part, returned to it after the show closed. Her power as an actress combined with her personal growth over the years to create the evolution of her character from the rank-obsessed, snarky, sexpot "Hot Lips" into the tough, dedicated, yet lovely nurse-of-men's-dreams, Margaret Houlihan. Watching Loretta on the set, shifting effortlessly from sitting demurely in her chair needlepointing to taking a good Irish swing at Hawkeye in response to the director's call, was a lesson.

In real life, Larry Linville was as personally intense as Frank Burns. Fortunately, Larry's intensity was focused on living and acting rather than conniving and playing Frank's power games. Larry found a way to humanize a thankless character, but it was not an easy task. Frank was a great comic foil for us, but over time it became harder and harder for Larry to play and for us to make fun of a character whose bizarre behavior devolved from neurotic to what teetered on the brink of psychotic.

Gary Burghoff's Radar O'Reilly never failed to touch me. From the first time I saw the program to the episode in which Radar finally said goodbye and shipped out, Gary's ability to convey truth, simplicity, innocence, and a continuing astonishment at the audacity of war moved me endlessly.

Jamie Farr's gifts made a one-joke character into a revolutionary, turning Corporal Max Klinger into a beloved example of man's unwillingness to knuckle under to rules, regulations, and regimentation. Jamie's personal energy was palpable; his enthusiasm brought a smile to everyone's face the moment he walked on the set. His love of the lore of show business made him our personal ambassador of goodwill.

Both William Christopher and his character Father Mulcahy were personal favorites of mine. Bill's very droll sense of humor and Mulcahy's good-hearted vagueness always tickled me silly. The image of Bill sitting on the set totally caught up in reading *The Iliad* in the original, ancient Greek and pausing to laugh in delight at some impossibly obscure Homerian joke never fails to bring a smile. The dedication that he and his wife Barbara brought to the challenge of raising an autistic child cemented my love for both of them.

Two regular cast members came to the show after I arrived, one only a week or two later. Harry Morgan's Colonel Sherman Potter, reporting in as the unit's commanding officer after the departure of the much-loved MacLean Stevenson (Colonel Henry Blake) had big boots to fill. And fill them he did. Harry's career apparently included a role in every classic American picture ever made and more television series than you can count. He walked in and sat down on the first day, took everyone's hearts, put them in his pocket and never gave 'em back. Given his wealth of experience working with every major star in the business, we expected him to be a treasure trove of stories, but this elfin creature with the foghorn voice also had an impish sense of humor, a wry wit, and timing you could set your clock by. As Alan put it so perfectly, there simply is "not an unadorable bone in the man's body."

A few years later, when Larry Linville decided to hang up Frank Burns's jersey, Burt was faced with the challenge of finding someone capable of taking on Hawkeye and B.J. He found his man in Major Charles Emerson Winchester, III, a cutter with class, played to the stuffiest of nines by the wonderful David Ogden Stiers. Stiers, who arguably had more classical theater training than the rest of the cast combined, had a rapier wit, a ferocious power of concentration, and the ability to break up other actors. David got every member of the cast at one time or another, while none of us could break him with a hammer—except for Harry. Harry would clench his jaw, flare those nostrils, and pin Stiers with a look that would reduce the man to a helpless, semi-hysterical puddle of jelly, unable to say or do anything for minutes. It was a wonderful thing to watch, revenge by proxy for the rest of us.

Add occasional guest performances by Allan Arbus as Captain

Sidney Freedman, the shrink everyone wishes they had; Ed Winter, the slyly dense intelligence officer; and the adorably corrupt and decrepit Sergeant Rizzo, played by G.W. Bailey. We also enjoyed the dedicated support of Nurse Kellye Nakahara, Roy Goldman, Jeff Maxwell's Igor, Bob Hill, Jennifer, Shari, Dennis, and the rest of the Mini-M*A*S*H. It was a company of which I was proud—and incredibly lucky—to be a part.

Once accepted as a member of the company, the next hurdle was the audience. Would they buy the new guy? My fears increased as we neared the broadcast of my first season, but fortunately we were working so hard that I didn't have time to obsess about the potential for failure until it was too late to worry. Before I knew it, the season was upon us, the ratings were excellent, and we were off to the races. Aside from being thrilled to be working in a group of happy, talented and dedicated professionals, I was giddy at being able to say the lines that were written for us. I remember blurting out on more than one occasion, "I can't believe I'm getting paid to say these words!"

The phenomenal—and enduring—success of M*A*S*H has been analyzed and parsed in every conceivable way, and I suppose there are as many theories about it as there are theorizers. We took a lot of hits for being antimilitary, which we were not. Jamie and I were the only members of the cast to actually serve in the military, but everyone on the set appreciated the women and men who wore the uniform, whether in combat or during peacetime. What the show spoke out against most clearly was the hypocrisy that sends young people (mostly men) to fight and die to meet old men's ego-driven, dishonest, jingoistic, or megalomaniacal needs. We despised political self-promotion at the expense of others' lives. We reviled mindless authoritarianism and sought to make clear that blood is not spilled without cost. Trumpets and fanfare, stomping feet and flags unfurled can sometimes overwhelm reason, but one is ultimately left with weeping loved ones, armless, legless, mindless vets, and rows of gravestones.

Gene came closest to explaining the reason that people so identified with the show when he described M*A*S*H as "the perfect
existential situation." Most people never go to war or serve in the military, but everyone can understand the feeling of being duty-bound to
do something that, even if distasteful, needs to be done. Everyone
understands what it feels like to be away from the ones you love. And
most of us have an appreciation for the integrity it takes to do a job
to the best of your ability because others are depending on you, especially when you'd rather be back home. Whatever the reason,
M*A*S*H touched a collective nerve, and people responded in a
deeply personal manner, embracing the show in ways that made us all
the more intent on getting it right. The bonds formed in those wonderful days are just as meaningful today, more than twenty years after
the show came to an end.

After appearing on the show for a couple of years, I was walking
down the street in Green Bay, Wisconsin, having appeared on a
telethon there to help raise money for a local charity. A man saw me
and shouted, "Hey! Hi!" I said "Hi" in return, and he stepped toward
me and stuck out his hand, asking, "How the hell are you?" I laughed,
shook his hand, and said, "Fine, thanks. How the hell are you?" He
suddenly stepped back, embarrassed, and apologized, explaining "Oh
God, I'm sorry. I just realized I don't know you." I told him it was fine
and that I was flattered at his happy greeting. He began telling me
how much the show meant to him and then stopped, thought for a
minute, and asked, "How does it feel to have half a relationship
formed with millions and millions of people?"

It feels good.

People often ask if being on M*A*S*H was as much fun as it
appeared; it was more. But beyond the pure joy of the work and the
horseplay on the set, another aspect of my new job quickly became
clear: Being the new guy on an extremely popular show created a certain amount of interest from the media. Prior to this time, popular
characters on hit shows had rarely been replaced successfully. Some

of the press, anxious to exploit controversy, chose to focus on my
positions on social and political issues. I didn't see any reason to moderate them just because I was suddenly talking to millions of people
in the papers, on the radio, or on television, instead of a crowd of
demonstrators or a group in a small room in South Los Angeles. Not
that I was leading a charge for the Red Brigades, but there were some
things I felt strongly about, and, as I had discovered at the Ellsberg
event, media plus celebrity plus issues can be a volatile mix.
Sometimes it simply creates a fuss, but sometimes it actually results in
a better understanding of the issues and more attention to the positions of those whose perspective is often ignored.

In the fall of 1975, not long after I began work on the show, I got
a call from a woman named Margie Tabankin, the director of the
Youth Project. She was involved with the union democracy movement and had been referred to me by a mutual friend. She wanted to
come to the set to see about getting my help with a union issue. I said
sure.

Margie wanted me to appear at an event to raise awareness and
funds for a dissident group of steelworkers who were trying to wrest
control of the United Steelworkers Union from leadership that they
considered to be out of touch with the membership. Unions were not
new to me, since my dad had been a strong union man and one of his
brothers had been an organizer for the Teamsters during some very
tough times. As a truck driver after I was released from the Marines,
I had been a member of the Retail Clerks Union and had appreciated
the good hourly wage as well as the medical coverage that took care
of my surgery and hospitalization after a motorcycle accident. Now, I
was a member of both the Screen Actors Guild and AFTRA. But
apart from supporting the United Farm Workers' struggles, which I
thought were as much about racism as they were about labor, I really
didn't have a lot of experience in the labor movement. I certainly
didn't know anything about the current dynamics in the United
Steelworkers Union.

I got a quick tutorial, however, from this extremely intelligent woman, to whom I instantly took a liking. Her organization had worked in support of the United Mine Workers during their very bloody period, and the members believed that the nascent union democracy movement was important. The steelworkers, she felt, were one of the most promising groups at the moment and deserved support. *What the hell?* I figured. *If I can be helpful, why not?* I agreed to attend the event and meet Eddie Sadlowski, the leader of Steelworkers Strike Back, to see what was what.

After spending a little time with Oil Can Eddie, as some called him, I could see that he was a good guy: a smart, charismatic, dedicated workingman's workingman. Eddie believed that the United Steelworkers Union's I.W. Abel was out of touch with the members. He thought a more militant leadership could achieve better results for workers who were already dealing with shrinking steel production and uncaring bosses and didn't feel supported by a complaisant union leadership. Sadlowski's group was extremely diverse by design, its leadership composed of white, black, Chicano, Christian, and Jew. The event I attended was spirited and exciting with fiery speeches and powerful emotional appeals. It was the first time I heard "Joe Hill" sung in a context that highlighted its meaning. I wasn't clear just how well organized Eddie's group was, truth be told, but whatever they were up against, there really wasn't much I could do for them but show up and be supportive. What impressed me most about Eddie was his devotion to his fellow unionists and his willingness to sacrifice for the ideal of workers' rights. What embarrassed me was how much it meant to Eddie and his coworkers that "a guy from M*A*S*H" would care enough about their struggle to lend a hand. It was another lesson; both touching and disturbing, it showed just how little attention and respect the workers received.

Eddie left the event charged up with a bit more money and a sense that there were interested people on the West Coast willing to help if they could. He didn't win the union election, but he got the attention of the union leadership by doing much better than expected. He's still active in union work today. For me, the primary benefit of it was getting to know Margie, a smart, fun, fascinating, incredibly energetic and idealistic person. Her network of friends was amazing. She had been to North Vietnam during the war, shooting footage of the destruction caused by the U.S. bombing campaign (and almost ending up a victim of it). Her experience with the peace movement, along with her work in labor and so many other fronts, made her the nexus of significant progressive political and social efforts in the country, as I was to witness time and again over the years.

In late 1975, as the presidential campaign heated up, I was invited to meet a few of the candidates. At a home in Beverly Hills, I met Senator Fred Harris of Oklahoma, who was attempting to mount a campaign with relatively little money against heavy odds. Fred and his wife LaDonna, a Native American of the Comanche tribe, impressed me immediately as decent, thoughtful people who were dedicated to the kind of America that made sense to me. Fred's honest, straightforward approach was wonderfully appealing. He articulately made the case that a candidate operating on the personal level, rather than being "handled" and "packaged," could rekindle the hopes and enthusiasm of so many of the Americans who had been left behind. For starters, Fred campaigned much of the time in an RV, rather than in limousines and jets. I quickly volunteered to help in any way I could.

The next thing I knew, I was in Chicago at a big rally for Fred, hosted by Studs Turkel, the journalist, radio commentator, and proponent of the workingman and woman. An icon of people-oriented politics, Studs was a huge figure on his own, and I was thrilled to meet him. His support helped bring a lot of attention to the campaign.

Later, with some time off from work, I flew to Boston to do some campaigning before driving up to New Hampshire to help in the looming primary. It was pretty heady stuff. Fred and LaDonna were all over the state, and everyone was pitching in to do whatever they could, as the campaign seemed to be gathering momentum. As one of the few celebrities around, I was promoted from passing out leaflets to speaking to small groups and, whenever Fred and I were in the same part of the state, introducing him at increasingly larger and more enthusiastic rallies. Since Fred couldn't be everywhere, some of us were assigned to stand in for him as surrogate speakers. It was a scary proposition, but having spent time with Fred, read his position papers, and heard him speak many times, I agreed to stand in for him with somewhat larger groups.

On one memorable occasion, I was asked to stand in for Fred at an event at a high school. When I got there, I discovered that all the other candidates—Governor Jimmy Carter, Senator Birch Bayh, Congressman Mo Udall, and former ambassador Sargent Shriver—were there for a debate. Panicked, I got on the phone and begged Fred's campaign manager to find him and send him right away. There was simply no way I could represent him in a debate with all the actual candidates. Happily, Fred showed up and I got out of that one by the skin of my teeth.

The opportunity to spend some time with the candidate and to see firsthand what is required of one who seeks elective office in America was thrilling, overwhelming, and exhausting. Fred and LaDonna's openness and just-folks attitude also made it a great experience. They and the hard-working volunteers around them were an incredible group. Beyond developing deep respect for and lasting relationships with Fred and LaDonna, I made another friend during that campaign when I found myself plowing through the snows of northern New Hampshire with Jim Hightower, then the Texas Agriculture Commissioner. Jim later became a successful author, radio commentator, strategist, and political speaker.

On our trek to Berlin, New Hampshire, Jim and I encountered a phenomenon that would repeat itself on the West Coast and lead to a movie that I made some years later. A terrible odor pervaded this beautiful little lumber town near the Canadian border; it so clouded the senses that it overwhelmed the considerable beauty of the area. I asked about the cause of the smell and was quickly informed that it was "the smell of money." The odor was the by-product of chemicals used to pulverize wood in the local processing plant, providing jobs that supported the town. The assault on my senses in the midst of such beauty was truly offensive, but even more troubling was the willingness of the townspeople to accommodate and justify it as an acceptable trade-off for maintaining their livelihood.

The New Hampshire Primary didn't result in the upset that we were hoping for. A second- or even a third-place finish for Fred might have earned the attention of the media and turned his low-key, inexpensive campaign into the phenomenon we felt it deserved to be. It was a good idea, but it didn't work. Jimmy Carter took the roses and went on to win the nomination and the election. Fred and LaDonna went home, and I went back to the show.

There was one immediate advantage to the election of Jimmy Carter: My friend Margie Tabankin was quickly appointed Director of VISTA (Volunteers in Service to America), a kind of domestic Peace Corps. Margie subsequently provided many scuttlebutt-filled phone calls that gave me an insider's view of political life in Washington, D.C.

My education continued as my involvement received more public notice. Periodically, some hostile reporter or interviewer would run down the list of, to him, unrelated issues with which I'd been associated and suggest that I was a political dilettante. It seemed odd to have to defend myself for being involved in political and social issues, but it became clear over time that many people have a love/hate relationship with celebrity. Press people often search out and slavishly report the most personal details of one's life while secretly yearning to find a chink in the armor they can use to expose the shallowness and insincerity of one-who-dares-to-be-famous-when-I'm-not.

I tried to explain that the issues that concerned me didn't feel disparate at all. I'm not a pacifist, though I have great regard for those who are. I believe in the right of self-defense, be it personal or national, but I also believe in finding peaceful resolutions to disputes and oppose war except in the face of the most dire national threat. I think the Cold War mentality, born partly of fear and partly of the need to dominate, did more to destabilize the world than to make us safe. I supported the movements for equal rights by disenfranchised groups that had arisen from the civil rights era and felt that Paul Robeson, Jr. had expressed a very deep truth when he said, "If you scratch the surface of a right-winger you often find a racist." Opposition to equal rights and equal opportunity too often grows out of the fear that opportunity for "them" means something will be taken from "us." So the many causes I supported fell under the simple rubric of "people issues": support for unions and the rights of the working person, equal rights for women and minorities, protection of the environment, the right of the disadvantaged to a social safety net, the protection of the mentally ill and the physically infirm, the right of children to a loving environment free from pain and fear, reform of prisons, equal access to law for all, and an end to the death penalty.

Some of my interrogators, however, found it easier to say dilettante. But in a speech given shortly after he was elected, President Jimmy Carter combined all these concerns in a single concept that rang true. He tied America's foreign policy to a commitment to "human rights." Human rights, I thought, was it exactly: the inalienable right of every human being to live, to strive for the full realization of her potential, to be free of oppression, free of fear, and supported in claiming his inherent dignity and value. For me, it was an amplification of the basic concept that I'd learned years earlier at The House: Everyone deserves what everyone wants—love, attention, and respect.

Chapter 8
B.J. . . .

In 1977, Anita Bryant—singer, one-time beauty queen, and the virtual embodiment of the All-American Woman in her role as the national TV spokesperson for Florida orange juice—launched a vicious campaign against gays with the establishment of Save Our Children. Bryant and her organization opposed a human rights ordinance in Dade County, Florida which held that rights could not be abridged on the basis of sexual preference. Bryant's assertion that "if gays are granted rights, next we'll have to give rights to prostitutes and to people who sleep with St. Bernards" inspired a wave of hysteria about homosexual "recruitment" and accusations of child molestation. Once again, celebrity was the magnet that drew media attention, and Bryant's hateful campaign quickly caught fire.

Deeply offended, I drew up a statement on the set deploring Bryant's small-minded, hysterical campaign, and a number of the cast members signed it. Fanned by the media, her campaign turned into a crusade and spread to other states. Joined by Jerry Falwell and other hyper-Christians, she claimed that homosexuality was "against God's wishes" and that homosexuals aimed at converting children to the gay lifestyle. "Since homosexuals cannot reproduce," Bryant posited, "they must recruit and freshen their ranks."

It was as embarrassing as it was odious. Bryant's celebrity credentials inevitably focused attention on others in our industry, leading to finger-pointing and a growing witch hunt. It was sickening; it was false; it was bigotry at its worst. And it was quickly picked up by State Senator John Briggs, a right-wing California politician who introduced the Briggs Initiative, Proposition 6 on our 1978 ballot. If passed, Proposition 6 would have barred homosexuals from working as teachers in California's schools. *Don't let those fags near our kids* was its unstated but clearly intended theme. Great media fodder, Proposition 6 got much more attention than it deserved, and the gay community was quickly on the defensive. Seeing that it was important for straight people to stand up against the onslaught, I agreed to do some television appearances debating Proposition 6. This, of course, brought raised eyebrows and typically ignorant innuendo. It was a truly ugly period, with fear-mongering and hysteria reaching levels that were frightening and difficult to comprehend. To the credit of the people of our state, the proposition was soundly defeated, but the experience gave me further insight into the precarious nature of the lives of so many in our society.

A friendship formed during the Proposition 6 campaign taught me even more about how precarious life can be for some. David Mixner had been one of the chief architects of the Vietnam Moratorium, a hugely successful initiative in the movement to end that war. At the time of his very public activities, it was not known that he was gay. When David finally came out of the closet a few years later, old friends—even family members—deserted him in droves. As told in his book, *Stranger Among Friends*, the price of honesty—and of being different—in our society can be monstrous. At dinner at our house one night, David told us about a loving aunt who did not cut him off when his sexual orientation became known.

"David," she said, "I understand you suck cock."

"Yes, Aunt Helen, that's right. I do."

"Well," Aunt Helen responded with a smile, "so do I, dear. So do I."

Due to his own strong character and the understanding and love of people like Helen, David survived it all and went on to become a national leader on gay rights issues; he now works internationally on the AIDS pandemic.

The marriage of the peace and environmental movements was a natural segue during these years. Though not much was yet known about the full effect of the use of the chemical defoliant Agent Orange in Vietnam, there were growing fears that it would become a major problem in the lives of veterans on both sides of the conflict and might prove even more troublesome for future generations. (Sadly, those fears proved correct, and raise similar concerns about the use of depleted uranium weaponry today.) Concern about the spread of nuclear weapons, which ultimately led to the development of the nuclear freeze movement, also encouraged opposition to the nuclear power plants that were sprouting up around the country. A process creating waste that would remain deadly to human life for 250,000 years struck me as lunatic. To support the emerging anti-nuclear movement, I took my kids to demonstrations against the building of the Diablo Canyon Nuclear Power Plant on an earthquake fault outside San Luis Obispo, California, and to Peace Sunday and Survival Sunday concerts at the Hollywood Bowl. As the movement grew, I was occasionally asked to speak and sometimes to introduce performers or other speakers. This allowed me to maintain contact with John Denver while getting to know such committed souls as Jackson Browne, Peter, Paul and Mary, Holly Near, Bonnie Raitt, Crosby, Stills, Nash and Young, and many others.

At one Survival Sunday, I was asked to introduce Allard Lowenstein, a political figure of great renown whom I had admired for years. Architect of the Dump Johnson Movement and later a member of Congress, Allard was a legendary figure in the civil rights and antiwar movements and a stunning and inspiring speaker. I was hyped to have the chance, because it meant I'd get to meet him. But then Theo Bikel, a well-known actor and an old friend of Al's, asked if he could take my place. *Well, shit,* I thought, *there goes my chance to meet Lowenstein.* Fortunately, Al sought me out later, introduced himself, thanked me for letting Theo do my duty, and expressed appreciation for the show. He said when I was next in New York to drop into the UN Mission where he was working with then–UN Ambassador Andrew Young. Months later I did so, and was treated to one of his storied dinners with a huge crowd of family and friends. As our friendship developed, I read *Brutal Mandate*, a book Al had written about a trip to South Africa with two friends some years earlier, and thought it would make a terrific movie. He agreed to let me try to develop it, and I got CBS interested enough to pay for a script. Sadly, we never got to make the film, but it was great fun to work on it and get to know Al.

With a roughly seven-months-on/five-months-off shooting schedule on M*A*S*H, we had plenty of time to pursue our other interests. Each year, we'd check in to begin the new season in July and catch up with each other's exploits. One year, after having been so moved by people's reactions to the show, I sat down with Alan on the first day back and asked, "Are you hearing what I'm hearing out there?" He was. We talked for quite a while about the sense of responsibility that came with the outpouring of appreciation and affection people lavished on us everywhere we went.

After my third year on the show, I got word one day that someone wanted to see me. The name was one I remembered with great affection, so I quickly agreed. Jeannie was an incredibly bright young woman I had known at The House, and I was anxious to see what life had brought her way. I remembered her as surpassingly intelligent and quite attractive. I don't remember exactly what brought her to The House, but I know that we had high hopes when she left. When she came to the studio, she was just as bright and lovely as ever, and now an M.D. specializing in public health. After we caught up, she told me she had come in contact with a small refugee-aid organization that was doing very important work. Started by a group of Irish priests working in Africa, Concern had now expanded its mandate to other parts of the world. Based in Ireland, they were not yet well known in the U.S., and Jeannie was hoping I'd be willing to learn about them and perhaps help promote the organization. Someone had seen an episode in which B.J. helped a bunch of refugee kids and thought we were a match. An interesting leap, I thought, but didn't argue since her request was fairly simple. One of the priests who had started the organization, Father Michael Doheny, had made a documentary film about the plight of children in Asia. Would I be willing to take a look at it and see if I could think of a way to bring it to a wider audience?

That certainly wasn't much to ask. The film proved to be very moving, showing the gasping need in what was then known as the Third World, and the relatively simple and inexpensive ways it could be addressed. Focused on the problems faced by children, the film seemed perfect for Dinah Shore's talk show. Dinah, a lovely woman, had invited me onto her show a number of times to talk about different issues. She'd said that if I ever had something I particularly cared about, all I had to do was call. So I called. She quickly arranged a showing on her program, and an interview with Father Mick, the joyful, charming, tireless leprechaun who had made the film—or "fillum," as he pronounced it.

Mick was a delight, on the show and off. Learning where he had been and what he had seen, though, made his cheerful spirit a wonder. A member of the Holy Ghost Fathers, an order of Irish missionary priests, he had worked in Biafra during the terrible war there from 1967 to 1970 in which a million civilians, mostly women and children, died, largely from starvation. Mick rarely spoke about what he'd experienced in Biafra, but what I heard from others about these priests—running the blockades, bringing in food, treating the wounded and sick, and attempting to provide some level of human comfort in so desperate a situation—defied the imagination. Father Mick's commitment to meeting the needs of "the least among us" was an inspiration, and I like to think that Dinah's show helped bring an awareness of the work of Concern to a lot of people.

The day we did the show, some of those associated with the organization were in the audience, including Denis Garvey, a former priest, and his wife Marianne Loewe, a former nun, who ran the office of Concern America down in Santa Ana, in my old stomping grounds of Orange County. Their gratitude for this exposure for Mick's film and the work they were doing seemed a bit outsized to me. All I had done was make a phone call and show up. But their sincerity was clearly genuine, and I appreciated the absence of the slick sophistication that permeated everything in the business I worked in. For these people, the little I had done was a great gift. What mattered most to them was that the outreach and impact of their work would be magnified by this exposure. That being so, I asked what else I could do to help, a simple question that set in motion a relationship that continues today.

Their first thought was that I take part in their next event, a hunger walk in Orange County. So I did, and brought my kids along. There's something wholesome and down-home about these events. We made a day of it, walking along and talking with the other marchers, many of whom were students from local Catholic schools.

Denis explained that the organization's history with the Holy Ghost Fathers, its Irish heritage, and his and Marianne's relationship with Catholicism had created a kind of natural affinity with the Church. But they were trying to reach out to other faiths and secular communities as well, since Concern America was not and did not want to be perceived as a Catholic organization. In addition to being totally nondenominational, they strictly avoided any government money and the expectations that came with it. They gladly accepted help from any legitimate source that was willing to give it, as long as there were no strings attached. Work in the underdeveloped world was complicated enough without the pressures and biases of religious or government funders.

As I came to know the people associated with Concern America over time, I grew more and more impressed with their straightforward and unapologetic dedication. Although Denis and Marianne had left their life in the Church, they remained committed to a life of service. This work was their way to honor God, whatever that meant to them at this point. The simple clarity of their devotion to this incredibly important, selfless, deeply human work touched me then and has stayed with me.

Mick was a scamp. Every time he'd come to the U.S., Denis would bring him by to see me. He'd go on and on about his most recent adventure and then take something "for the kids." It became a tradition. On our first meeting at Dinah's show, he described the fundraising auction that Concern held in Ireland every year. "Wouldn't it be grand," he asked, "if I could bring back something from B.J. to auction off, though?" Every time I saw him after that, he'd end our conversation by saying, "Ah, Michael, the shirt of B.J.'s you gave me was a big hit at the auction; brought a lot of money for the kids, you know. We'll be after havin' another one, you know, and it'd be a grand thing if I could bring another little something this time. D'ya really need that belt to hold up your trousers?" I'd laugh, hand it over, and chase him out before he picked me naked.

Chapter 9
. . . AND BEYOND

I was blindsided in March of 1980 by a call from Peter Yarrow of Peter, Paul and Mary. I had been a huge fan of the trio for many years, inspired by their artistry as well as their personal commitment to the peace and civil rights movements, and had been thrilled to get to know them personally, primarily through Margie Tabankin. Peter was also very close to Al Lowenstein, and that mutual friendship had cemented ours. On this March evening, however, Peter was calling to tell me that Al was dead, murdered by a deranged man who had once been his friend. Peter and I wept together on the phone as we tried to work our way through the brutal pain of losing a treasured friend to such a senseless act.

Struggling to find a way to deal with the loss and somehow express my admiration for Al, I decided to produce a documentary film about him with my friends Julie Thompson and Brogan De Paor. With the able assistance of a crew of friends, *Citizen: The Political Life of Allard K. Lowenstein* used film clips to demonstrate Al's brilliance and interviews to capture his impact on the lives of family members, coworkers, friends, and admirers like author David Halberstam and Senator Ted Kennedy.

After a couple of years working with Concern America, Denis and Alex Tarbett, then Irish Concern's Executive Director, visited my home one day and asked if I would consider becoming the organization's official spokesperson. When I began to demur, they quickly reassured me that they weren't asking for a bigger commitment, but simply wanted to officially recognize what I was already doing. In the discussion that followed, I explained that I'd be more comfortable taking on the role if I could actually get out to see some of the work the organization was conducting in the field.

We decided that Concern's most pressing effort at the moment was in Southeast Asia, and that was where I would go. Nixon's "secret war" in Cambodia had so destabilized the regime of Prince Norodom Sihanouk that the country was taken over by the notorious Khmer Rouge, a murderous group of radical Communist extremists. The incredible brutality of this group, led by the criminal Pol Pot, resulted in the systematic murder of millions of people. In the late 1970s, Pol Pot and his forces were driven from power by invading troops from Vietnam, but freedom from the Khmer Rouge terror was quickly followed by general turmoil in the country, forcing hundreds of thousands of Cambodians to surge toward the border with Thailand. There they were stopped by the Thai military, effectively trapping them between the contending forces within their own country and a hostile military from the neighboring land.

The UN had set up camps astride the border and asked non-governmental organizations to help them dress the wounds of the Khmer refugees, meet other needs, and generally bring order. The term "refugee" refers to one who has fled his or her country as a result of oppression or catastrophe. Those who are chased from their homes but remain inside their country's borders are considered "displaced people" and are not entitled to the same protections under international law as are those who cross a border. That problem is being addressed today, but at the time of the Khmer exodus, the old rules were still in play. Concern immediately agreed to dispatch its volunteers to assist in the relief effort. We all agreed that this would be the best place for me to see the work Concern was doing.

Despite the horror of the atrocities committed by the Khmer Rouge, the U.S. refused to recognize the Heng Samrin government that had taken power in Cambodia once Pol Pot had been sent packing. The new Cambodian government was considered politically tainted, having been put in power by the Vietnamese. While no one in an official capacity admitted it openly, our government preferred to support Pol Pot, a genocidal maniac, rather than value anything done by the Vietnamese, who'd had the audacity to defeat us in a war.

The trip to the Thai/Cambodian border camps was an eye-opening, heartrending experience. Even the expression "life-changing" fails to convey the full reality. I described the trip in a chronicle called "Around the World in Eight Days." Too long to include here, it's available at: http://www.mikefarrell.org/Journals.html.

Those eight days were a race through a world so different from my own that it had to be swallowed in a gulp and digested slowly over time. International travel is said to be broadening; in this case, it was stupefying. Diving into a culture so entirely different from our own, I found myself in a kaleidoscopic whirl, surrounded by weapons of war and competing symbols of the old and the new. Westernized Easterners in jeans walked alongside Saffron-robed Buddhist monks, or "bonzes," most very young with shaven heads, seeking donations of food for the day. Men and women on motorcycles raced in and out between buses and trucks, while the poor pushed carts, looking to earn or scrounge a living. And, seemingly oblivious to it all, the traditional rice farmers, knee deep in mud, slogged along behind their primitive wooden plows, planting seed, depending for their very lives on the tireless ox, just as they had done through countless seasons, wars, and centuries.

In my first exposure to the refugee experience I saw thousands of sweet, shy, quiet people—many of them children—crammed together in tents too small for standing, all in need of food, medical care, psychiatric help, attention, respect, love. A psychotic blind boy shrieked at the touch of any liquid, fearing it was blood, while a catatonic woman couldn't utter a sound. Sick people sought folk medicine as Western doctors attempted to cope. Scholars, who had escaped death by discarding their eyeglasses and pretending ignorance, tried to reconstruct from memory books destroyed in a mad cultural genocide. All this and more beyond imagining was being patiently tended to by Irish volunteers, all of whom seemed to be named Mary.

The week was a mélange of mine fields, heat, warring factions, stories of slaughter, areas under strife, unimaginable pain. I walked through "No Man's Land," through small camps and giant camps, and encountered children with no parents sweetly crying, "Hello, okay, bye-bye." I saw a building afire, angry soldiers, astonishing courage, mosquito netting, women sterilized, a market in the jungle, days blurring by, a "land bridge," another plane, and, finally, home.

Returning to life as I had known it required a decompression process. The trip had come and gone so quickly that it was almost possible to believe it hadn't happened. This dynamic was abetted by my difficulty in adjusting to the dramatic difference between the realities of what I had seen in Cambodia and my own life back at home. Here I was, home, safe, without a care in the world. Yet the people I had just left were still there dealing with the pain, the heat, the need, the crushing legacy of bloody death and destruction.

At home, I held my kids extra tight and for longer than usual, until they squirmed out of my grip and ran off to play. They had important things to explore and do and learn about. How could I tell them what I'd learned about people called "refugees," about the courage and dedication of the volunteers whose tender hands, eyes, and hearts made so much difference in these wounded lives?

I wondered how we could ever shape the world into the kind of place we want it to be. It was daunting, yet there were people out there trying. Somebody had conceived of the United Nations High Commissioner for Refugees. Somebody had seen the hideous catastrophe in Cambodia/Kampuchea and designed a response to the human exodus that threatened to turn into yet another sea of death. Someone had formulated the Universal Declaration of Human Rights. Someone had believed enough in the possibility of a worldwide code of civilized behavior to postulate standards, international covenants, even laws of war. It was all dizzying. But it was also inspiring. I had no idea how to tell my kids about what I'd learned. Maybe eventually I'd figure it out. Or maybe I'd just try to show them.

* * *

After some time and much soul searching, there were other realities to deal with. As committed as we both were to Erin and Michael Josh, Judy and I finally had to face what had become more and more clear over time: Our lives were going in different directions once again. Acutely aware of how traumatic a divorce would be for the kids, we tried to put the best possible face on it, but it was hugely painful nonetheless. Telling the kids was the hardest part, and, of course, I did it all wrong. As I reflect back on it now, I realize that there probably isn't a right way to break that kind of news to a child. If there is, I certainly didn't find it.

The whole process was a wrenching, deeply painful ordeal for all involved, but Judy and I were able to work out a cooperative arrangement. I bought a house down the hill from ours and built steps and a gate, providing the kids with easy access both ways. We managed a shared custody arrangement that imposed as little insanity as possible on the kids while we worked our way through the hurt that a failed marriage inevitably brings. It wasn't a case of one being right and the other wrong; there wasn't another man or woman waiting in the wings; there was just a harsh reality that had to be faced.

It was awful. Sure as I was that the decision was right, I waffled constantly, fearing that anything that inflicted so much pain on the kids had to be a stupid mistake. More alone than I could ever remember feeling, wracked with indecision, searching for answers to the million and one questions that besieged me, I somehow managed to cling to the idea that if I could just hang on, things would ultimately work out.

The saving grace was work: being back on the set with the gang from M*A*S*H. As always, they were great: curious but respectful upon hearing how I'd spent part of the time off and sympathetic and supportive about the situation at home—or at what was no longer home. They had come to love Judy, and knew how devoted I was to the kids. But they also knew that these things happened, and, beyond being supportive, didn't intrude. I was grateful to be able to bury myself in work when on the set, and I focused on keeping things as normal as possible for the kids when I was at home.

* * *

Somewhere along the line, I suggested an idea for an episode to Burt, who was by then our Executive Producer. Upon hearing it, he said, "That sounds great. Why don't you write it?" This was the kind of open, supportive atmosphere that made M*A*S*H a creative community— and such a welcome tonic during this period in my life. After Larry Gelbart's departure, the studio had hired a number of talented writers to fill his very large shoes, and they were all very supportive. And, since ours was a safe setting for me to spread my wings, Burt also encouraged my interest in directing. With a number of directors in the company, there was little danger, as I learned the ropes, of straying too far off the mark without someone giving a gentle nudge.

Ronald Reagan was the Republican nominee against Jimmy Carter that year. Because I was embarrassed at the thought of a Reagan candidacy and unhappy with Carter, I got involved in the presidential campaign of John B. Anderson, a moderate Republican Congressman who ran as an Independent. Anderson offered an enlightened alternative to the Neanderthal Reagan and the uneven Carter, whose inspiring position on human rights had fallen on hard times with his embrace of the Shah of Iran and saber-rattling about the Soviet adventure in Afghanistan. Sadly, John Anderson's campaign, like that of Fred Harris four years earlier, went nowhere; he was yet another decent, honorable man who couldn't catch the attention of the media and, ultimately, the voters.

Reagan's victory was a shock. What I saw as obvious transparency and simplistic views apparently struck a hopeful chord in the American voter. Reagan may have been perfectly sincere with his "Morning in America" perspective, but no matter how sugarcoated his own views, the people behind him were zealots. Ed Meese and his holier-than-thou patriotism set a tone that was reflected throughout the incoming Administration. Margie Tabankin, while not happy with my support for John Anderson, called me on the set during the transition period to express her concern. She and others in the Carter

Administration were doing their best to facilitate the transition of the newly elected administration, explaining the operations of their departments and the ways of Washington to their incoming counterparts. Instead of being appreciated, however, the Carter crew was stiff-armed and treated with disdain by the Reagan people. Margie is a savvy woman who had been around enough to not be surprised by much, so the distress in her voice caught my attention. "These are not nice people," she declared.

The truth of her observation quickly became clear. Carter's human rights–based foreign policy, nominal as it had been in some instances, was quickly scrapped and replaced by a foreign policy based on "antiterrorism"—at the time, a euphemism for anti-Communism. The Soviet Union was the Evil Empire, and any unacceptable political movement, particularly in the underdeveloped world, was declared a sign of Soviet expansionism. Castro's Cuba was seen as a horrendous insult to freedom that Reagan's people couldn't wait to rectify.

Their foreign policy was best articulated by Jeane Kirkpatrick, whom Reagan appointed ambassador to the UN. Kirkpatrick insisted that the U.S. should support authoritarian regimes while opposing totalitarian ones. Pinochet in Chile and Stroessner in Paraguay were thus perfectly acceptable, despite the fact that they were clearly fascist dictators who brutally oppressed their people, while popular movements for national liberation were "communist-inspired" and targeted for extinction. Nowhere was the difference between the two approaches clearer than in Central America.

With Costa Rica, which had disbanded its army decades earlier, as the sole exception, Central America's nations were largely regarded as exploitable resources in our backyard. Guatemala—the original Banana Republic—El Salvador, Honduras, and Panama were all run by military strongmen or puppets of the U.S. government and U.S. business interests, with poverty and misery the plight of the vast majority. Those who had the audacity to object were exiled, "disappeared," tortured, or murdered. Nicaragua, of course, was a thumb in the eye of the Reaganites, who insisted that the Sandinista revolution, having thrown out the dictator Somoza, was part of a Moscow-driven attempt to subvert the Western hemisphere toward Communism.

This, then, was not a happy time for those concerned with human rights and peaceful resolutions to international problems. The U.S. military budget escalated and military advisors were dispatched to El Salvador to "safeguard democracy." Echoes of Vietnam kept reverberating.

My domestic situation smoothed out a bit during this time. The kids adapted reasonably well to the two-house situation, splitting their time between Judy and me. During one of the hiatus periods between seasons of M*A*S*H, I drove Erin, Michael Josh, and one of their friends across the U.S., up to Canada, back across to the Pacific, and then down the West Coast and home again. There were, of course, times when I thought I'd lose my mind, but we had a ball, stopping wherever and whenever the spirit moved us. Upon our return, though, I got a call from Phil, the wonderful agent who had represented me now for more than a dozen years, informing me that he was leaving the business. That was a sad day.

As we closed in on the end of our tenth season of M*A*S*H, I began to wonder what would happen next in my career. I talked to Alan about his plans, and he said that he had always thought ten years would be enough. We discussed it for a while and then, as had become our custom, gathered the entire cast to talk it over. At first, there were varied reactions: Some agreed that it was time to stop, others wanted the show to continue. But finally we all agreed to call it a day.

To put it mildly, neither CBS nor Fox was happy to get the message. They were minting money on us and had hoped that the show would go on for years. But that was exactly what worried us. None of us wanted the show to wear out its welcome, eventually becoming a one-dimensional copy of its former self. We didn't want to one day hear an executive say, "Ho hum, I think we've had enough of that," and pull the plug. We wanted to end the show while we were still on top. And we wanted to wrap it all up with an end-of-the-war episode that would give us a chance to say goodbye and thank you to each other, to the characters, and to the audience.

Once they got over the shock of losing the show, the network executives rejected our idea for the last show. "Why?" we asked.

One of the executives sat down with us and explained: "Do you remember David Janssen's show, *The Fugitive?*" Of course we did. "Well, when David decided to end the show, they wrapped it up by finding the one-armed man, remember?" Sure. "Well, ending the show that way, finding the one-armed man, killed the show in syndication. Everyone knew how it would end, so they didn't turn it on. So you see, we can't do that here. It'll kill the syndication."

We all sat there and stared at him in silence, stunned by this reasoning.

"It might surprise you to hear this," I then observed dryly, "but most people already know the Korean War ended."

These guys could be amazingly obtuse. But as it happened, we worked out a compromise. The executives asked us to consider doing a limited number of episodes for a shortened eleventh year. We agreed, if we could do the end-of-the-war show as the final episode. They partially agreed, though not to a final episode. They gave us a two-hour movie that would end the war and the show as we wanted. (It would also, of course, allow the network to withhold the two-hour special from syndication, thus avoiding their dreaded *Fugitive* problem.)

Chapter 10
REVOLUCÍON!

During the hiatus before the eleventh season, I began to explore the idea of another trip for Concern America, now a stand-alone group independent of Irish Concern. Their volunteers in Honduras were working with a flood of peasants from El Salvador coming into camps across the Honduran border as the fighting in their country increased. What the Reagan Administration had identified as yet another Soviet/Cuban–inspired Communist insurgency was instead, according to many who had been there, a homegrown civil war, sprouting from decades of exploitation of the poor by wealthy landowners who controlled the government, the military, the economy, and most of the country.

In the early spring of 1982, Denis and Marianne arranged a much-needed four-wheel-drive pickup truck for Mesa Grande, one of the largest camps for Salvadoran refugees in Honduras near the border with El Salvador. They needed medical supplies delivered to Tegucigalpa, loaded onto the truck, and driven to the camp. This offered the opportunity to see that operation, meet the volunteers, and get a sense of what was going on in the region, so I said I'd do it. If I could leave soon, they said, Dr. Davida Coady, my guide and traveling partner from the Thai/Cambodian border camps, would be able to go with me.

They said I could use the truck to visit other camps and even venture into Nicaragua if I had the time. Before leaving, I called Margie Tabankin, who was now running the Arca Foundation, a small philanthropic organization in Washington, D.C., to let her know. She immediately said, "Can I go?" That was great by me. A day later, she called, saying LaDonna Harris wanted to go, too. So in mid-April, Margie, LaDonna, Davida, and I met at the Houston airport for a connecting flight to Tegucigalpa. While waiting to board, we met Father Frank, a Catholic priest from a Houston parish whose congregation had been sending supplies to the camps and who wanted to see for himself what was going on down there. He quickly became part of our little band.

Given the tensions in the area, we were told to expect a hostile reception from the Honduran military and, perhaps, U.S. government personnel. Beyond hosting UNHCR camps and thousands of Salvadoran refugees, Honduras was the staging area for the war being waged by the Contras, the anti-Sandinista force sponsored by the Reagan Administration and run by the CIA. There was so much U.S. money, personnel, and equipment in the country that it became known as the U.S.S. Honduras. At its helm was U.S. Ambassador John Negroponte, whose blind eye and deaf ear to the murderous Battalion 316's death squads and unswerving support of the brutal leadership of General Gustavo Álvarez Martínez would later be rewarded by George W. Bush with appointments as U.S. representative to the United Nations, U.S. ambassador to Iraq, and, finally, America's first Director of National Intelligence.

On the flight, Davida told us what to expect in the camps. She also made sure that Margie, LaDonna, and Frank understood all the "don'ts" she had given me in Thailand: Don't eat uncooked food; don't drink anything but bottled water unless it has been boiled or treated; don't use ice cubes unless they were made from safe water; don't use local water to brush your teeth; don't get water in your mouth when you bathe or shower. And don't run afoul of the military. Torture was commonplace.

Entering Honduran airspace, the pilot announced that a hostage situation at the Teguce airport meant we'd be setting down in San Pedro Sula, in northern Honduras, until it was resolved. Davida, who'd been through this before, said these delays could be lengthy and that we should consider going on by cab. Not an auspicious beginning, but what the hell?

It soon became clear that indeed the plane wouldn't be departing that night. The airport was a welter of confusion. Outside the terminal, with no cab big enough to take us and our gear, we took two. We loaded some of our stuff all over one cab and flagged down a second for the rest of the gear and ourselves. Then we tore through the Honduran night, over the mountains toward Teguce, with a driver who must have learned the job in Italy. He raced along the narrow two-lane highway, passing anything that loomed up before us, regardless of whether we were going up a hill, down a hill, around a blind corner, or by the edge of a cliff. His one concession to anyone coming the other way was to lean on his horn. It was so terrifying that it became funny. Margie and LaDonna shrieked, either with laughter or fear, for most of the ride.

We arrived in Teguce quite late, and Davida directed the driver to the home of the people with the pickup. Even in the dark, we could see that Teguce was a good-sized city set into a bowl of surrounding mountains. Our target was in what must have been a neighborhood of professionals, as nice homes lined the way. An orange Toyota pickup truck marked our place. Just down the road, a lot of vehicles gathered by a large, well-lit two-story house with what appeared to be guards posted in front. This, we later learned, was the home of the general who headed Honduran military intelligence.

The husband and wife who welcomed us were both doctors, friends of Concern America. If they were nervous about attracting the notice of the guards down the street as we unloaded everything, they didn't show it. It's hard to know what risks they ran by accommodating us, but they were very gracious and their hospitality was greatly appreciated. I was directed to a room that was plain and spare; there was a tiled shower, a rotating ceiling fan to keep the warm, close air circulating, and a bed. I slept, grateful.

We awoke with the early-morning light, and, after some peeled fruit and juice, thanked our hosts, stashed everything in the back of the truck, and piled in. The truck was an extended cab with a back seat, so there was room for the five of us. As I love to drive and am good at it—and because I'm a control freak—I took the wheel.

Teguce is an old city surrounded by hills, with narrow streets, crumbling buildings, and tiled roofs. There were people everywhere, some walking, others selling fruit and vegetables at the side of the road. Smoky vehicles competed with trucks, buses, and motor scooters, all of them racing through and around the people. Except for the difference in ethnicity, it was very reminiscent of the cities I'd seen in Southeast Asia. Here, too, the many serious-looking uniformed men in jeeps, trucks, and other military vehicles conveyed a sense that war was not far away.

Once out of the city, Honduras was lush and covered with tropical growth, but not as much as I'd expected. Heading west, I was struck by the industry of those walking beside the road. Men wearing straw hats and carrying machetes moved along purposefully, often followed by women in gay colors balancing impressive loads on their heads. One of the few visible signs of modern influence on the people we passed was the plastic tubs in which many of their items were being carried.

We were a pretty congenial group, enjoying the ride and getting to know each other. We shared a common perspective on the political situation, both here and in the States. Davida had the most knowledge and experience in this part of the world, so we paid attention to her. Father Frank, a bright man, probably in his forties, was very disturbed by what he had learned from immigrants who had ventured north and sought help from his church. Led here by his faith, he wanted a clear sense of the situation so that he could properly guide his congregation in their response.

We aimed for the town of San Marcos, above which was the Mesa Grande camp. As we headed into the beautiful mountainous reaches, signs of settlement became more scarce and military checkpoints more serious. We were stopped a number of times and asked to produce documents. At the last checkpoint before San Marcos, things got a bit ugly. Stopped by a barricade, we were all told to get out of the truck. As we did, a squad of very young soldiers with very big automatic weapons surrounded our little group and pointed them at us.

The officer in charge was unpleasant and asked a lot of questions. Davida responded patiently, and Frank, who also spoke Spanish, offered a few thoughts in a pleasant tone. But things didn't seem to be going well. I told Davida to ask the officer to have his men put up their weapons, but she said it wasn't a good idea to challenge him. He demanded to know why we were bringing medicine and supplies to the refugee camp. When she explained that Concern America sent us to deliver supplies to the volunteers in the camp, he wanted to know why so many of us were needed for this. She assured him that the rest of us—including the wife of a U.S. senator—were there to see first-hand that the Honduran government was doing everything in its power to make sure that the people in the refugee camps were being well cared for. After considerable debate, she apparently convinced him that we were not arming the guerrillas. He opened a few of our boxes to check the supplies, then suddenly gave a dismissive gesture and walked away. At this point the young kids with the big guns backed off, the barricade lifted, we all got into the truck and resumed breathing. Thank you, Davida!

Even with the drama, we were able to find San Marcos by early afternoon and went directly to the house of Father Earl Gallagher, a much beloved New Yorker who had been dealing with the spiritual needs of the people here for years. Known as "Bedo," Gallagher is a charming man with sparkling eyes, a glorious wit, and a pronounced New York accent. He thanked us, saying he wished more Americans would come to see what was happening here.

"We just ran into an officer down the road who would argue that point," I countered.

"Oh, they think we're Communists, you know," he laughed. "Anyone who says the poor should be treated with dignity is a Communist."

Later, with a little prodding from Davida, Bedo told us about the Rio Lempa massacre. The previous year, just beyond the hills west of us, he had seen hundreds of fleeing Salvadoran refugees slaughtered by the pursuing Salvadoran army as they tried to find safety in Honduras. "When you see helicopters—American helicopters—dropping bombs and machine-gunning unarmed women, children, and old people trying to scramble to safety across a river, it isn't hard to figure out which side you're on."

Gallagher's commitment to these people was remarkable. His parish, such as it was, spread for miles around, and he walked or rode a donkey through the mountains bringing the Word to some of the world's poorest. When he couldn't make it into an area for a while, he sent *Delegados* ("Delegates of the Word") to carry on in his stead. These lay preachers came out of the base communities, composed of deeply religious people who practiced and taught a Christianity founded on social justice and honoring the dignity of the poor. Not ordained, they didn't offer the sacraments, but simply ministered, preached, and educated the people in the Gospel of Jesus.

Bedo noted that almost every home, no matter how rude the structure, featured two artifacts: a crucifix or picture of Jesus and a photo of John F. Kennedy. How ironic that these folks revered a former leader of our country as a symbol of hope even as the present one created such horror in their lives. As we prepared to make our way up the hill to the camp, Bedo left us with one final observation: "The wellspring of the Salvadoran revolution isn't Communism; it's poverty."

The dirt road up to Mesa Grande was steep, rutted, and narrow. Grinding our four-wheeler up the trail, we were confronted by a jeep on its way down. I pulled over as far I could to allow him to pass, but the driver didn't acknowledge us with either a wave or a glance. Davida said it was the American representative for the area, either from the embassy or seconded to the UNHCR. She explained that he was hostile to the refugees and generally an asshole.

Reaching the top of the mesa, the camp was suddenly before us. Rows of tents stretching into the distance sporting the UN-supplied blue plastic canvas roofs took me right back to the Thai/Cambodian border. Here again were thousands of people—fifteen to twenty thousand, we learned—whose survival depended on the outstretched hand of caring people from across the world, all working under the aegis of the United Nations High Commissioner for Refugees. Locating the tents of the Concern America volunteers, we pulled up to deliver our goods.

Rob, Bobbie, Diane, Ed, and Sally—the Concern America volunteers—were bright young Americans who brought to mind the fresh-faced Irish volunteers in the Thai/Cambodian camps. As we unloaded our supplies, two *campesinos* took one of the heavy suitcases full of medicine and headed off down the road. Davida assured me with a nod that they would take good care of it. This meant, I assumed, that the medicine was needed on the other side of the border, where health care was almost nonexistent. We'd heard of a lone American doctor who was dealing with the needs of those who either couldn't get across the border or had chosen to hide in the mountains of El Salvador. Hopefully the suitcase would get to him. Everything else went into the "pharmacy" tent, and we put our personal gear in the volunteers' tents.

A quick tour of the camp showed us the same spare living conditions I had seen in the Asian camps. Concern America's assignment here was handling the nutritional needs of the refugees and developing a sanitary system for the camp. Both were critical because refugees traditionally arrive in various stages of malnutrition and ill health. Many had been wounded, and some were victims of torture. The wounded had been dropped off by the truckload after being collected from small Honduran villages. Having been pursued by the Salvadoran military, they were now targets of the Honduran military, making this camp their only place of refuge. The first job of the aid workers was to set up tents, gather blankets or extra clothing to compensate for the colder temperatures up here, and provide water, which was not readily available.

Children and pregnant and lactating women are always the first concern when setting up a refugee camp. Some of these kids exhibited signs of severe psychological distress and near-starvation. A few of them clung to any adult with whom they felt comfortable. Others became hysterical at any unfamiliar face.

Things had settled down a bit in the months since the first refugees arrived, we learned, though the population continued to grow. In addition to feeding them, the volunteers were teaching these people how to cook with earthen stoves and explaining the importance of boiling water. About half of their children were dying before they reached five years of age. Since most of these deaths were due to preventable diseases, primarily water-borne parasites, the education provided could have a dramatic impact.

The people were sweet, friendly, polite, and obviously very appreciative of the shelter. We saw immediately, as Bedo had suggested, that most of them were women, children, and the elderly. There were very few middle-aged men and not many male teens. The men had either been killed, imprisoned, or had chosen to remain in the mountains of El Salvador, some attempting to maintain their villages and others choosing to fight. One of the volunteers said there were increasing signs of depression among elderly refugees, many of whom feared that they'd never see home again.

In the *cocina*, or mess tent, we enjoyed a good meal of rice, beans, and fried plantain, topped off with some clean water, then made our way back to the tents. The night quickly became very dark and very cold, so we huddled inside and quizzed the kids for a while about what brought them to this life. When time came to hit the sack, I was offered a choice between a hammock and a cot. The hammock sounded interesting, but I was warned that sleeping in one is a learned art. I decided to try it anyway and quickly appreciated the voice of experience. First, I could hardly get in the damned thing, and then once in, I couldn't get over the feeling that I'd fall out any time I moved. I moved and discovered I was right. Soon I was in my sleeping bag on the cot and remembering why I wanted the hammock: Army cots aren't long enough for me. When I rolled over, I discovered that they're also noisy. Every move I made caused the wooden frame to squawk and, I was sure, kept my tent-mates awake.

Embarrassed, I did my best to lie still, but it was impossible. Roll, squawk. Roll, squawk. I briefly considered trying the tent floor, but then remembered that someone had said something about snakes. In all, it was a horrible night, for me and for everyone within squawking distance.

Dawn came, thank God, announced by a rooster. They actually do crow at dawn. The camp was quickly aboil with work and I wanted to see the children's art that had been mentioned. Because many of the kids were reserved, some quite manic, and others acting out in different ways, they were given art supplies to draw them out, quite literally. The results were heartrending: rude images of soldiers firing into huts, helicopters dropping bombs on homes, dead bodies—things kids just shouldn't know about.

I asked Davida about the guy we saw leaving as we came up. Though charged with overseeing the care of the refugees, she said he was openly distrustful of their relationship to the guerrillas fighting in El Salvador. This, of course, mirrored the view of the Salvadoran military, by whom the people had been attacked, massacred, and, in the case of these folks, driven out of their country. Talk about a rock and a hard place.

After a full tour of Mesa Grande, we took our leave, impressed with the dedication of the volunteers, but depressed at the state of their charges. Heading south, we found our way to a remote cluster of buildings housing Alas de Socorro, or "Wings of Help," an air ambulance service operated by a group of Christian missionaries. They also schlepped volunteers in and out of the most remote camps, and our next stop qualified. Pulling up, my first thought was, *Where are the planes? Where is the airstrip?* Inside a garage, though, we found a small red plane that looked like an old Piper Cub. A concrete pad extended out from the garage/hangar. But still, *Where is the airstrip?*

A man came out and pushed open a gate in the fence separating the yard from a pasture. I thought: *Oh no. This can't be . . .* A man of few words, he smiled, climbed in, cranked up the engine and taxied it out onto the pasture. Leaving the plane idling, he came back and said to leave whatever we could spare in the hangar or the truck, to cut down the weight. While we did, he'd "taxi down a ways to chase the cows off."

I couldn't believe it. He was going to take off from a cow pasture? A cow pasture? With cows on it? It wasn't even flat, for God's sake!

Imagine my surprise, then, to find myself going along like it all made sense—pull jacket out of bag, stash bag in truck, walk into cow pasture, watch little red plane come back after chasing off cows. I'd lost my mind.

We squeezed in, my compatriots in the back, me up front with the pilot asking a bunch of dumb questions just to hear myself talk. "No problems," he said. "We do this all the time." "Nope," in response to another question, "they don't like the sound of the engine, and the propeller scares them away." We bumped our way down the pasture, gaining speed as we jounced and bounced over rocks and dirt clods that must, I was sure, have created problems for the landing gear. "Not so far," he smiled, and we lifted off.

The lush green, forested mountains of Honduras are amazingly beautiful from the air. A convenience for us, this air ambulance service made a huge difference in the lives of poor people who would otherwise be S.O.L. The pilots committed to a number of weeks or months down here, leaving their families back in the States. It was their way of practicing their faith. Pretty damned impressive.

After about an hour, our pilot pointed ahead to a brown spot in the green. As we got closer, I saw that the top of a hill had been cut off, probably by a bulldozer. There was no sign of life anywhere nearby, but this was where we were going to land. Oh boy. It just kept getting better!

We buzzed the "field" once to make sure there were no boulders, trenches, or other impediments, then we looped around and began to settle down, heading in from the west. The spot wasn't long or level enough for a regular landing, he said, so we'd come in on the low end and use the incline to help stop us. That was more than I needed to know. Coming down, he pointed to a valley off to our right where the camp peeked through the trees. "Directly behind us now," he announced, "is El Salvador. The camp sits virtually on the border." Okay, but what had my attention was the fact that we were landing on a tabletop. There was a sheer cliff below the flattened area we were approaching, and one at the other end, too. Coming in too fast or taxiing too long might just be a problem.

I took a deep breath as we hit the dirt right beyond the cliff edge. The engine reversed with a roar, out pilot braked sharply, and we skidded to a dramatic stop. All in a day's work. A jeep pulled in off the road. I remembered to breathe as Ellen, the Concern America volunteer here, welcomed us to Colomoncagua. When we climbed down, our pilot reminded us that we needed to be back in no more than two hours to avoid taking off in the dark. Good thought. Landing lights were in short supply.

Winding down the road into the camps, Ellen told us it was possible to drive here from Teguce, but that the trip could be torturous, taking most of a day even when the roads were not washed out, so we were wise to get the Flying Doctors to bring us. I thought I'd try driving next time. Ellen, we learned, had established the Mesa Grande camp, only coming here when that one was adequately staffed.

Nearing the entrance to Colo, she told us about the suffering these people had endured from the Salvadoran military, a now familiar story. An unofficial yet real part of her job was to protect them from further abuse at the hands of the Honduran military, who maintained an oppressive presence here because of the proximity to the border. The military claimed that guerrillas came into the camps for rest and medical care before heading back into the hotly contested Morazan Province to fight again. None of it was true, Ellen insisted, but the military presence at the camps created a very tense situation.

The camp's name was borrowed from a nearby town. Colomoncagua was actually six or seven camps linked together and was home to about 6,000 refugees. In the main camp, the kids were what we noticed first, shy as we jumped down from the jeep and then quickly warming to our presence. With Ellen's coaxing, they were soon running circles around us, laughing and wanting to have their pictures taken. Quickly using up a roll of film, I unwrapped another. When I looked for a trash can, Ellen smiled and held out her hand, explaining that there wasn't much use for trash cans here. Instead, she took the empty film box, put a pebble inside, and gave it to one of the kids, who was delighted with the new toy. I felt like a dope, but she laughed it off.

As in the previous camp, Concern America was in charge of nutrition and sanitation, but poached into other areas as the need arose. Education was one of the main interests of the refugee leaders. Most here were illiterate, yet keenly aware of the importance of education, especially for their children. Ellen showed us a large, one-room log structure with a blackboard and rough-hewn benches. The people had built this school by themselves because the UNHCR had other priorities.

Colomoncagua was greener and shadier than what we had seen at Mesa Grande, but the plight of the people was the same. The kids were laughing and having fun today, but given the opportunity, they'd be just as likely to create the pictures of horror we had seen at Mesa Grande. The depression of the elderly, the trauma of those whose villages had been torched or families massacred, the malnutrition and disease, the anxiety created by not knowing what the future held—all were prevalent here as well, amplified by the suspicion and hostility of the Honduran army. Yet we were received with grace, kindness, and unfailing appreciation.

Colomoncagua was well organized and largely self-sufficient. Shoes, clothing, pottery, hammocks, and woven items were made in workshops and then sold in the U.S. by Concern America, the money earned coming back to the people.

Ellen was very impressive. Her willingness to leave a life of comfort and come here to feed the hungry, bind the wounds, heal the tortured souls, and nurture the children left me feeling more than a bit guilty. It suddenly seemed shallow to drop in, look it over, say "tut-

tut," then hop into a plane and fly away with an American passport in my pocket and a comfortable home where I could forget about all this if I chose to.

As night approached, Ellen loaded us into the jeep, navigated the climb, and dropped us at the plane. Perhaps sensing my guilt and confusion, she said that we all had a part to play in this tragedy. Our responsibility, she believed, was to find a way to tell people back home what was really happening here.

Maybe it was the cumulative effect of what we were experiencing. Maybe it was the distance, the feeling of utter separation, the sense of vulnerability that surrounded the place. Maybe it was just plain guilt. But it was hard to leave Colomoncagua.

When we got to the plane, the pilot said there was a slight problem. *Oh good*, I thought. *What now?* Because the strip was so short, he'd planned to take off downhill, using the incline to our advantage. "Uh-huh." But he was afraid he still couldn't get up enough speed to take off with all five of us on board. "Uh-huh. So what do we do?" Well, there was a longer strip down in a valley a few miles away. He could take two or three of us down there, drop them off, come back for the rest, and then we'd all fly off together from the second runway. Well, we didn't want to walk, so Margie, LaDonna, and Frank would go first and Davida and I would wait, hoping he'd come back.

The four of them loaded in, the pilot cranked it up, revved the hell out of the engine, popped the brakes, and rolled away down the incline with the engine screaming. The plane accelerated right to the end of the dirt strip and immediately dropped from sight. *Holy shit!* I stood frozen, wanting to run to the cliff edge, but hoping for a sound. Then, finally, I heard the faint buzz of the plane's engine pulling through the air, and up it came, into our line of sight, before turning away to the north. *Jesus . . .*

Twenty minutes later the little red plane plopped down in a cloud of dust, and we clambered aboard. As we raced to the edge, catapulted off and fell, I told him how much it had scared me to see them disappear from sight a few minutes earlier. He shrugged as if it was just another day—which I suppose it was.

Before long we landed on a grass strip in a deep, thickly wooded valley. Taxiing to the spot where the others waited, I spotted a crumbling wall on which was painted, *Revolución*.

After yet another sphincter-tightening takeoff, this time barely clearing a cluster of tall trees at the end of the strip, the flight back was a delight. I even enjoyed buzzing the pasture to chase off the cows. Then, with thanks to our pilot-of-few-words, we loaded into our good old, solid, on-the-ground truck and headed north toward Copan, near the Guatemalan border, where we would stay before venturing up into the mountains to El Tesoro, a camp for refugees from the killing fields of Guatemala.

In Copan, we happened on a wonderful fiesta. Music played in the square and candles, flares, and fireworks lit up the night. People strolled, children ran and played, and war seemed far away. We stopped in a church for a while and heard a *Delegado* preach the mysteries of the Gospel, his deep, rich voice rebounding off the walls. Despite the language barrier, his faith and passion shone through.

The next day we headed up into the mountains toward El Tesoro on a road that I was sure only goats could navigate. Thank God for four-wheel drive. We bounced over gully-sized ruts and navigated around rocks I knew would turn the truck over if I made a single mistake. As we climbed into the heights, the road narrowing and the drop beside it deepening, I was crowing to myself about this superb job of conquering impossible terrain when we suddenly came up behind a bus. A broken-down clunker, full of passengers and belching smoke, had somehow . . . *Well, shit.* I'm sure glad I hadn't been crowing out loud.

By the time we got to El Tesoro, it was nearly dark. Cynthia, the Concern America volunteer, was a registered nurse whose duties ranged from treating wounds and dealing with malnutrition and other illnesses to overseeing the camp's sanitation programs. She also taught health promotion techniques to those who were planning to return to the areas under strife in Guatemala. El Tesoro was much smaller than the camps we'd already seen, providing shelter to about 2,500 people. Many of the Guatemalans who had been targeted by their country's military were Mayan Indians. By the time the Carter Administration cut off military aid because of ongoing human rights violations, it was generally conceded that well over 100,000 had been killed.

Cynthia introduced us around. Beyond the horror stories of their experience at home and the hostility these folks felt from the Honduran military's regular sweeps through their camp, I was most impressed by their vivid sense of humor and the sound of guitars playing and people singing. These people seemed to be in a better place psychologically than those we had met in Mesa Grande and Colomoncagua. I don't know if that's a fair assessment, but I was impressed by the smiles and the music.

Because we needed time for Nicaragua, the next day we did a quick tour, then said our goodbyes and took off. Bouncing crazily down the road to Copan, exhaustion, nervous tension, and the crazy ride began to tickle us. As we hit the worst stretch of road, LaDonna announced in a loud voice that she had to pee, which made everyone laugh even harder. Fighting the wheel, I was asking if she wanted me to pull over just as we hit a rock that threw us all into the air. A brief, shocked silence was broken when she yelled, "Not anymore!"

Later, as the others slept, I had a great talk with Father Frank. He loved Liberation Theology, a movement that grew out of the Latin American Catholic Church in the 1960s. Foreswearing the idea that faith for the impoverished meant meekly accepting one's plight, causing no trouble and awaiting a heavenly reward, Liberation Theology urged engagement in the world, demanding human advancement and social justice. It promoted a "preferential option for the poor" and spread through base communities that studied scripture and saw Jesus as a revolutionary intent on liberating people from poverty and oppression. Because some of their social analysis paralleled Kant, Hegel, and Marx in honoring the dignity of the poor, they were quickly denounced as Communists and attacked by the powers-that-be. Two members of the Sandinista leadership in Nicaragua, both Catholic priests, were proponents of this movement. Frank's explanation brought it vividly to life. Had I been aware of this kind of Catholicism some years ago, I said, as we drove through the Honduran night, I might have been more interested in staying with the Church.

Military checkpoints grew more frequent as we neared the Nicaraguan border in the morning light, but most of them just waved us past. At the border, however, our papers were seriously examined by a grim-faced Honduran officer who found it suspicious that Americans were venturing into Nicaragua for any reason, but he eventually let us through. On the Nicaraguan side, a couple of young kids in Sandinista uniforms smiled and welcomed us with a wave, causing a huge burst of relieved laughter in the truck. The difference was quite seductive. But not far down the road, we were flagged down as we approached the Rio Coco. A Sandinista soldier, warning us of a collapsed bridge, directed us off the road and down into the river basin where a number of workmen had shoveled dirt and laid sandbags into the water to allow travelers to ford the river. A couple of old trucks struggled across with some coaching from the workers, then it was our turn. I thought the passengers should follow on foot after I drove the truck across, but it was all for one and one for all. Besides, Margie said, if they stayed in the truck, they wouldn't have to get their feet wet. We hoped. Happily, the four-wheeler lived up to its promise and we made it across, climbed the bank, and it was on to Managua. Later we learned that the bridge had been dynamited the night before by the Contras in their first major act of war against the Sandinista government.

The road to Managua took us through lush countryside and small villages, many bearing scars of the war. Walls without bullet holes were rare. Managua itself had been badly damaged by an earthquake in the early 1970s, and President Anastasio Somoza Debayle's refusal to fund the necessary repairs contributed to his estrangement from the people and eventual defeat by the Sandinistas. Though intimidated by Somoza's Guardia Nacional, the people finally grew sick of the looting and supported the revolution.

Managua greeted us with its slums. Carts, animals, trucks, and children lined the road into the center of the city, which was dirty, noisy, full of crumbling buildings, and bustling with people. From all outward appearances, the revolution was popular. Music poured from radios and nearby places of business. We rode around until finally spotting the Intercontinental Hotel, which seemed to be thriving. The hotel's grand lobby was filled with a very cosmopolitan crowd, including many Americans and a lot of international press.

As we checked in, some of the press approached us and wanted my view of the situation here, but having just arrived, I said I had none. It was clear that we'd stumbled into a hub of energy in a country that was the focus of much attention—most of it negative—from the U.S.

Davida went to find an American friend we were hoping to meet, and the rest of us put our gear away and tried to catch our breath.

When the day cooled into evening, Margie, LaDonna, and I walked down into the square. Here, again, we found a vivid sense of life and hope in the people. *Viva la revolución!* The smell of food in vendor's carts, the swell of Latin music, the excitement everywhere around was intoxicating, almost overwhelming, given the pace at which we'd been moving. After drinking in the feeling of freedom and the bubble of enthusiasm that seemed to spring from every corner, we headed back for a night's sleep.

The next day was one of listening and looking. The Sandinistas were as optimistic about the future as they were critical of Reagan's attempts to interfere with their revolution, an attitude that was echoed everywhere. It was clear that they had a huge task ahead. Rebuilding a badly damaged infrastructure while establishing a working government would be mammoth undertakings for a wealthy country in a supportive world. Unfortunately, the Nicaraguan banks had been looted by the Somoza family, now living in comfort in Paraguay under the protection of General Alfredo Stroessner and his thugs. And the Sandinistas were living under the crushing thumb of Big Brother from the north—Ronald Reagan and his band of anti-Communist zealots.

In the afternoon, we joined a demonstration in front of the American Embassy downtown. People from different parts of the U.S. were there declaring that Reagan should let these people decide for themselves what kind of government they wanted. One of the pro-testers, Jane Olson from Pasadena, California, introduced herself. Years later Jane became a close friend as we worked with Stanley Sheinbaum to establish the California Committee of Human Rights Watch, eventually becoming its co-chairs.

Later, Margie and I accompanied Davida and her friend to dinner with a Sandinista official, where we listened to a long and ultimately exhausting dissertation on *Socialismo* and the value of the revolution. Without questioning the Sandinistas' right to form the government they thought appropriate for their country, Margie and I wanted to know more about what they were doing for the people and hear their responses to the Reagan Administration's charges against them. They'd been accused, for example, of mistreating the indigenous pop-ulations, particularly the Miskito Indians on the country's east coast. But Davida's friend was more interested in lauding the *revolución* and expressing solidarity with everything this guy had to say than in allow-ing any controversy into the room. We did learn that the government planned literacy courses for the largely illiterate population, and redistribution of some large landholdings that would give the poor an opportunity to be landowners. While I had no problem with that and no idea why the Reagan people were so exercised about it, the tri-umphalism in all this talk was a bit much. It eventually became such an exercise in smoke-blowing that the two of us excused ourselves and grabbed a cab back to the hotel. Pulling away, Margie let out a long breath, exclaiming, "It's enough to turn you into a right-winger!"

Davida came by later, upset about my rudeness to our host. I hadn't meant to be rude, I said, but neither did I want to be schooled in *Sandinismo*. These people had every right to arrange their lives as they chose. But if I couldn't ask questions, even tough questions, to get the answers I needed to make the case for leaving the Sandinistas alone, I wasn't sure what the point was of coming down here. I understood the desire to support this government, but couldn't do so unquestioningly. I could get Socialist theory from a book. I wanted to know that people's lives were being improved and that the government wasn't discriminating—for example, against the Miskito Indians. And I didn't appreciate having my questions shoved aside and buried in a mountain of *solidarity* bullshit. In the end, Davida and I agreed to disagree.

With a plane to catch, we were soon off again. Davida had people to see in Nicaragua and more work in the camps, so we said our goodbyes and took off. The river-fording process was easier the second time with a temporary crossing in place. After exchanging friendly waves with the young Sandinistas guarding their side of the border, we were back into the U.S.S. Honduras. Grabbing a meal at a Tegucigalpa hotel, we speculated about who was CIA and who was military intelligence as American men in civilian clothes and military haircuts engaged in earnest plotting at tables nearby.

The flight to Houston allowed time for a bit of sleep and some discussion. We were uniformly impressed with the volunteers, outraged at the plight of the refugees, and furious that the Salvadoran army, killing families and razing villages, was being lauded as a U.S. ally and armed, trained, and maintained with our tax dollars. As for the Sandinistas, they should be given the chance to run their country without Uncle Sam pushing them around.

Back in Houston, we suddenly—and oddly, after having been so intimately entwined—went our separate ways.

Again, coming home required a decompression period. As troubling as the plight of the people in the Thai/Cambodian camps had been, that was a disaster to which U.S. actions had contributed, yet it was not directly of our making. This, on the other hand, was a huge, ugly, bleeding sore born of political and strategic decisions made right here. I had to do something. But what?

Chapter 11
GOODBYE AND HELLO

I n life, things sometimes overlap in ways that are hard to comprehend, so you try to roll with the punches. With far too little time to think about what I'd just seen, I was reminded of a commitment I had earlier made to the network: to attend CBS's yearly affiliates meeting, where owners and managers of the network's affiliated stations are plied with food and wine and regaled with promises that the next television season will be even better than the last. Along with the new shows they preview, the network likes to have stars from some of their popular shows on hand to be introduced and mingle a bit. It's not a bad thing to do. A free trip and star treatment can be a lark. But on the heels of such an intense experience, I felt as if I was in a time warp—maybe a reality warp.

But my commitment to the network turned out to be one of those little decisions that becomes life-altering. I flew to San Francisco, put on my duds, and went to the appointed destination—the Fairmont Hotel. Making my way to the celebrity party, I was very much a lost soul, not wanting to get into meaningless conversations with people I didn't really know or much care to talk to.

Hoping for a friendly face, I found one when I spotted Shelley Fabares, the woman I had thought so lovely when we'd worked together a dozen years earlier on *The Interns*. I'd seen her a few times since, but only in passing. After she finished talking to someone, I touched her shoulder. When she turned and gave me a lovely smile, I said, "We don't really know each other very well, but I want you to know that every time I see you I get a really nice feeling." She responded very sweetly, without being either silly or flirtatious, and seemed to be touched. Given the circumstances, her warmth and simplicity were just what I needed. We talked until the CBS shepherds had us line up to be introduced to the assembled multitude, and then, put in alphabetical order, found ourselves together again. She was excited about only one thing this particular evening: Walter Cronkite was supposed to be there, and she was very hopeful she'd get to meet him.

We were at separate tables during the dinner and show, but as we left I caught her and asked if she'd gotten her wish. She hadn't. I offered to help her look for Cronkite but we had no luck. I really didn't want to let her go, and as we stepped outside a cable car was pulling up, so I impulsively asked if she'd like to take a ride. After a moment's hesitation, she agreed.

For the next couple of hours I embarrassed myself completely by pouring out my guts to this person I barely knew. A sympathetic ear seemed to pull the plug on all of the tension, pain, confusion, and anger that was roiling in me from the trip. I know there was a lot she didn't fully understand. How could she? But she was patient and sweet and brave enough to try and take it all in. We walked along Fisherman's Wharf and stopped for a drink. When I finally shut up, I heard about her current relationship, some about the man himself but mostly about his two wonderful girls, whom she adored. We walked and talked and walked, somehow got to the hotel, and said goodnight.

The next morning the CBS people were arranging cars to the airport, and fate—or CBS—put us together again. On the plane back to L.A., we talked more. She told me about a problem with the writers on *One Day at a Time* and more about the doctor she was seeing and his daughters. She was terrific, but clearly involved, so I invited her to bring her fellow to a meeting the following week where I'd be showing some slides and talking about the trip—if she could stand it. She said they had plans, but asked me to let her know if I ever did it again.

Back at home the days and nights were full—full of my kids, full of concern about the gathering storm in Central America, full of opportunities to talk to groups about the situation down there. Margie and I were on the phone a lot as she steered the Arca Foundation toward support for efforts to expose the truth about the brutal underside of the Reagan policies. What we'd seen came vividly back into focus when a call from Concern America brought news that Cynthia, the nurse we had met at El Tesoro, had been kidnapped by the Honduran military. All that was known was that she'd been taken into custody along with Dr. Oscar Giron, a Guatemalan doctor, as the two were traveling between refugee camps.

A series of calls from aid organizations, the UN, and members of the U.S. Congress brought pressure on the Honduran government, but the episode still ended in tragedy. Cynthia soon turned up and reported from the U.S. Embassy that she and Dr. Giron had been stopped by a military unit, roughed up, and separated. She'd been brutalized and abused, but released. Dr. Giron's body was found shortly thereafter.

I took Cynthia to Washington in the hope that her experience would open some eyes. Predictably, the only ones willing to meet us were those, like Senator Chris Dodd, who were already outraged at what Reagan's people were doing in the region. Chris, John Kerry, Tom Harkin, Ed Feighan, and a few other frustrated legislators were trying heroically to find ways to restrain the Administration, while their colleagues, caught up in the anti-Communist hysteria, were willfully blind and deaf. We finally got a meeting with Thomas Enders, Reagan's Assistant Secretary of State for Latin American Affairs. Upon hearing about the brutal treatment of Cynthia and Dr. Giron, Enders offered what seemed an utterly insincere expression of regret, coupled with a rueful plea that we understand the difficult situation the Honduran military was facing. The situation was difficult indeed, we responded, but not for the military, and we provided him with additional examples of how the refugees, mostly women and children, were treated by the Honduran authorities. But we had to understand, he insisted, that they "are the families and friends of the guerrillas." It was not a successful meeting.

Margie and I kept trying to steer information to people who could be helpful in unmasking the horror of Reagan's Central American policies. Little by little we saw a movement develop to stop what clearly had the potential to become another Vietnam.

Back at M*A*S*H, we did our best to maintain equilibrium as we counted down each episode and each day of the final season. Even though it was our idea, we all dreaded saying goodbye to what had come to mean so much. Alan was hard at work writing what eventually became *Goodbye, Farewell and Amen*, the final movie that would wrap up this extraordinary adventure. We continued to goof, make practical jokes, play volley-glove, laugh, and do the best work we knew how to do, always painfully aware that every step brought us closer to that final, heart-wrenching moment.

A couple of months into the season I was asked to speak to another gathering about the trip to Central America. Remembering her request, I called Shelley and left a message inviting her to come and bring her fellow. A few days later I got a message in return, asking if it would be all right if she were to bring her sister instead. *Indeed,* I thought to myself, *it would!*

Shelley and her sister Smokey showed up, and when it was over I asked if they'd join me for a cup of coffee. (I don't drink the stuff, but didn't want to let them go.) I was hoping there was significance in the doctor's absence, but didn't know how to ask. Talking later, I remembered Shelley's comment about a problem with the writers on *One Day at a Time* and asked if she ever got the situation worked out. Misunderstanding the question, she said, "Oh, we're not seeing each other anymore." Delighted, but not knowing how to cover the embarrassing moment, I was graceless enough to say, "Oh, I was talking about your problem at work." Now having embarrassed her, I felt like a complete idiot. But I got the information I was hoping for, so it wasn't a total loss.

A couple of weeks later, I asked her out to dinner. I picked her up. As we walked to my car, she looked up and stopped for a moment, then quietly began, "Star light, star bright, first star I've seen tonight . . ." I was a goner, this time for real.

Toward the end of the show, I was contacted by Joe Ingle, a minister of the Church of Christ from Nashville, Tennessee, who was at that time running the Southern Coalition on Jails and Prisons. Working against the death penalty, he had heard I opposed it and asked if I'd give him a few minutes. We were at "the ranch" the day he showed up, which was quite a schlep, but it didn't stop him. The Twentieth Century Fox ranch was a sprawling tract of undeveloped land in the Santa Monica Mountains off Malibu Canyon. Many of the exterior shots for Fox's movies and TV shows were done there, including Robert Altman's feature, *M*A*S*H*. While they had duplicated much of the compound on Stage Nine at the studio, we used the ranch for any shots that called for a grander sweep or that included big equipment or helicopters.

The word "minister" always brings with it some expectations for me—scholarly reserve, patient, dignified balance, careful deliberation, and faith. Joe had faith, all right, but he was pissed. Younger than I, he was thin and bespectacled, with an unruly shock of black hair. And he was ready to do battle for the Lord. While at Union Theological Seminary in West Harlem during the time of the Attica Prison slaughter, he spent his off hours working at the Bronx House of Detention, where he formed strong views about our nation's criminal justice system and the use of the death penalty.

After state killing had largely fallen into disuse in the late 1960s, the U.S. Supreme Court held, in the *Furman* decision of 1972, that, as it had been practiced in this country, the death penalty was "cruel and unusual punishment" and thus unconstitutional. In 1976, in *Gregg vs. Georgia*, it was reinstated with the proviso that certain safeguards were required to make it meet constitutional muster. When I met Joe, only a couple of executions had taken place: Gary Gilmore died before a firing squad in Utah in 1977 in a case often thought of as state-assisted suicide, and John Spenkelink was executed in Florida in 1979, the first "involuntary" execution since the *Gregg* decision. Joe had been Spenkelink's spiritual advisor, and he was furious at the injustice of the case. He was determined to spread the word that the death machine was cranking up for a blood bath in this country and wanted my help.

Shooting *Goodbye, Farewell and Amen* was a deeply emotional experience for all of us. At every step along the way, I kept thinking, *This is the last time I'll be here.* The sense of loss was palpable. You know the feeling: *This is the right thing. This is the right thing. I know this is the right thing, but God it hurts!* At one point, Burt, who was directing, observed, "This is the only time I've ever had to tell actors to not cry so much."

But we got through it—got through it wonderfully, if I do say so myself—and went back for the last few half-hour episodes. Seeing our relationship grow, the cast took Shelley in as one of us and generously made her a part of it all.

The last episode we shot involved striking the camp, and one of the story points was burying a time capsule containing evidence of our stay. Caught up in the idea, we buried a real time capsule on the lot, complete with souvenirs from the show and each of the characters, thinking that this secret, once uncovered, might someday have great significance. (As it turned out, the studio commissary was expanded a year or so later, some workmen dug it up, thought nothing much of it, and threw it away.)

Literally hundreds of reporters and camera crews were on the set for the last day of filming, recording our every move. Loretta and I each carried a box of tissue to wipe away tears that came regularly, and Alan, Jamie, Harry, David, and Bill, after initially laughing at us, later had to borrow from our supply. Jamie had the last words in the scene, and then Burt yelled, "Cut! That's a wrap!" And it was over.

But it'll never truly be over. The mayhem on the set was followed by a press conference, an extraordinary salute from Fox, CBS, and other notables, and many more tears.

We all gathered for the screening of the movie and wept again, and then all of America embraced the showing in a manner never seen before or since. Truly something. A splendid, rich, powerful, and deeply personal connection was made during those wonderful years, one that continues today. It was certainly the most important professional experience I'll ever have—and one of my most important personal experiences as well.

The show over, we all went about our business. Alan did a movie. Loretta went back to the stage. Stiers went off to conduct a symphony. Harry, Jamie, and Bill began to think about doing a sequel. And I went to El Salvador.

Chapter 12
SALVADOR

In the year since our trip to Honduras, violence in the region had escalated dramatically. The Reagan Administration poured money and U.S. military advisors into El Salvador to support the fight against the insurgency there, while at the same time building up the Contras, the anti-Sandinista force in Nicaragua. Both the Salvadoran military and the Contras were roundly condemned for human rights violations, some of them astonishingly brutal. A struggle had developed in Congress between those who opposed these campaigns and those who argued that they were necessary to protect us from the Communist menace. Congress finally decided that money could not be sent to El Salvador unless Reagan certified that improvements were being made in the behavior of the forces he was arming. Simply put, the human rights violations had to stop. Despite that intention, however, and against all the evidence, Reagan certified that the human rights situation had improved.

Margie wangled me an invitation to be part of a delegation from the Commission on U.S./Central American Relations, to observe the human rights situation firsthand. The group included members of Congress, writers, human rights experts, educators, and clergy. We spent a couple of days in D.C. being briefed before flying south. Margie's friend Janet Shenk, author of *El Salvador, the Face of Revolution* and scholar at the North American Congress on Latin America, served as our guide and translator. One of the primary issues of the day was the call for dialogue between all parties in the conflict, meaning substantive discussions between the Salvadoran government and military high command on one side and the guerrillas and popular organizations on the other. That idea was utterly unacceptable to the Reagan Administration and those in power in El Salvador since it represented a tacit admission that something was wrong with the way things were being done and suggested the possibility of compromise.

Landing in El Salvador and being bused into San Salvador early in 1983 was an eerie experience. Ita Ford, Jean Donovan, Dorothy Kazel, and Maura Clarke—four American churchwomen—had been headed for this airport when they were stopped by the military, dragged off the road, raped and murdered a little over two years earlier. Mutilated bodies were regularly displayed on the highway as a warning to those who called for change in El Salvador. "Body dumps" became part of the lexicon, reported by human rights researchers and verified by American newscasters but hotly denied by Reagan Administration officials as propaganda, exaggeration and lies. Ray Bonner, a *New York Times* reporter, had exposed the massacre of 900 peasants at El Mozote, a village in Morazán Province, by the American-trained Atlacatl Battalion of the Salvadoran army. Bonner was then accused by the Reagan gang of being a Communist sympathizer, so the *Times* caved in and removed him from reporting on Central America. Among those attacking Bonner and others while denying the massacres were State Department stooge Thomas Enders and a lethal right-wing hatchet-man named Elliott Abrams, who was later convicted of lying to Congress about the Iran/Contra scandal, resurrected through pardon by Bush I and, appallingly, appointed to the National Security Council by Bush II. A documentary I had narrated some months earlier, *El Salvador, Another Vietnam*, detailed evidence of the horrors experienced by those in the camps we had visited a year earlier—horrors denied by Abrams, Enders, and their ilk in the Administration. It all made for a nervous entry into the city.

The slums that greeted us in the outskirts of San Salvador seemed even denser and more heavily populated than what we had seen in Nicaragua the year before. Once inside the city, though, we drove through a section of large, well-kept homes, mostly hidden behind high walls, the gate to each boasting a machine gun–toting guard. The social hierarchy couldn't have been clearer.

Once checked into the El Camino Hotel, we caucused, met some of those who would be showing us around, and were told to assume there were listening devices in our meeting rooms. We had been allowed into the country because it was in the interests of the Salvadoran government to maintain good relations with the U.S., but since our mission was viewed as hostile to those very interests, we should never assume goodwill. It was deemed unlikely that we would be in any danger, but we should stay alert, stick with the group, accept no invitations to private meetings, and not wander off alone.

Our days and nights were filled with meeting everyone who would see us, including representatives of the American Embassy, peasant groups, labor organizations, landowners, educators, religious leaders, farmers, human rights organizations, workers, and even the heads of the military. Here was my first contact with Americas Watch (later to become Human Rights Watch, the world's largest American-based human rights organization), meeting David Holiday and later Jemera Rone, who made themselves very unpopular by investigating violations of human rights.

The city was alive, jammed with people, cars, trucks, and buses. It was sometimes easy to forget that there was a war going on, but the sightings of Jeep Cherokees with smoked windows, known to be used by the death squads, was a reminder that all was not as it might momentarily appear.

Traveling into the countryside removed any doubt. Military checkpoints were everywhere, and we were regarded with suspicion. On one occasion, we pulled off the road in an area with downed power poles that showed signs of a recent firefight. We were out of the van taking photos when a truck pulled up, a number of men in the back. Only the driver was in uniform, but all were armed. Our guide quickly herded us back to our vehicle and away.

On one of our first nights in the country, we were invited to a party at the home of the Chargé d'Affaires, second-in-command at the American Embassy. There we were introduced to a high-ranking member of ARENA, the right-wing party thought by many to be the "legitimate" face of the death-squads. He complained of the terrible lies about his group—and particularly his leader, Roberto D'Aubuisson—told by the Communists intent on taking over his country. It was odd to have this conversation in the home of an officer of the American Embassy, particularly in view of the fact that many believed D'Aubuisson had ordered the killing of Archbishop Oscar Romero less than two years earlier. D'Aubuisson was the reputed leader of the White Warriors Union, also known as the White Hand, a death squad whose slogan was *Be Patriotic, Kill a Priest*. He is reported to have said publicly, "Jesuit priests are the worst scum of all."

Archbishop Rivera y Damas was a dignified man walking a political tightrope. Many of the priests in his authority were accused of having sympathy for, if not affiliation with, the guerrillas. But despite the influence of Liberation Theology in the region, the Catholic hierarchy was staunchly anti-Communist and had long ago made peace with the existing social order. After Archbishop Romero's murder, however, reality could no longer be avoided and Rivera y Damas found himself in a tough spot, trying to negotiate a middle ground. His neutral stance didn't please those victimized by the military and terrorized by the death squads. But his willingness to house the Independent Human Rights Commission in his building and support the Madres, a group of women who had lost children to the violence and were fearless about demonstrating their opposition to the army, were clearly attempts at balance.

Maria Julia Hernandez ran Tutela Legal, the legal assistance office of the Archdiocese. A student of philosophy and law at the University of Central America, she had worked closely with the martyred Archbishop Romero. She filed thousands of complaints with courts that ignored them all because of fear or corruption. Her work was the definition of heroism and would be of great value to the UN investigation many years later.

* * *

General José Guillermo García, best known for his view that "all peasants are potential subversives," fended off our questions about massacres by claiming Communists threatened his nation and insisting
we should thank his army for protecting our own southern border
from their menace. The idea of a mad crowd of Salvadoran guerrillas
invading Texas on their way to take over Washington was bizarre
enough to make me laugh out loud, but I bit it back. We had no better luck with General Eugenio Vides Casanova, head of the dreaded
Treasury Police, who verbally attacked one of our group for a question
about torture chambers in his headquarters. Both men retired to the
U.S. and were later denounced by the UN Truth Commission. Sued
in federal court, a jury in West Palm Beach, Florida found them liable
for torture and other human rights abuses on July 23, 2002, and
ordered them to pay $54.6 million in damages for complicity in the
murders of the churchwomen and others.

One of our most impressive meetings was at the University of
Central America. Viewed by the military as a hotbed of radicalism
and Communism, UCA had been regularly raided during openly
repressive periods, but now, with everything under scrutiny, was only
surveilled, infiltrated, intimidated and periodically "inspected." It
was run by an extraordinary group of Jesuits who were keenly intelligent, politically sophisticated, and utterly despised by those in
power. They walked a delicate line by speaking frankly with groups
like ours (though asking that we not record them or use direct
quotes), while officially maintaining a rigidly neutral posture on the
conflict in the country. One of them said of the recent electoral
sham, "Elections are icing on the cake of democracy. Without the
cake, however, the icing has little value." Probably because of the
power of the Church, they were able to survive in this atmosphere—
at least for the time being. Six years later, all six (Ignacio Ellacuría,
Segundo Montes, Amando López, Joaquín López y López, Juan
Ramón Moreno, and Ignacio Martín-Baró), along with their cook

and a maid, Elba Ramos and Celina Ramos, were murdered by the Salvadoran army.

In suburban encampments and a few areas inside the city, we met tragic figures: poor, mostly illiterate, desperate people, full of stories of the army's brutal sweeps, horrifying torture, the death squad murder of loved ones, and the separation of families. They were helped by the Catholic Church, the Green Cross, and Concern America, but the military, customs police, treasury police, and national guard raided the encampments periodically looking for subversives. Those taken away were never seen again.

The constant exposure to suffering took its toll. At one of the camps, I became so sickened that I thought I'd either explode in rage or break down in tears, so I told the others I'd meet them at the truck. Heading across the open dirt compound my head was down, eyes on the ground so I wouldn't have to gaze into any more stricken faces. Nearing a withered tree in the center of the compound, I noticed a small boy standing silently, looking at me. I didn't want to see him, wanted to walk past as if he wasn't there. But there he was. As I got closer, I saw that he was holding a rubber ball. His face was sober, clearly without expectation. At a spot about ten feet from him, I realized I couldn't just walk by, so stopped and looked at him. He returned my gaze. After a moment, I held out my hands and he tossed me the ball. I caught it, held it for a beat, and tossed it back to him. He caught it and threw it back to me. Before I could toss it back, a number of children ran out from somewhere on the periphery and lined up beside him, squealing, laughing, and jumping up and down. I tossed the ball to the first of them, who caught it and tossed it back, laughing. I repeated it with each of them, but before I got very far down the line, I realized I was laughing and jumping up and down too.

Everywhere we went the divisions were clear. Landowners said the threat was Communism; the workers in their fields feared murder by the military and death squads. Generals said they fought to protect their land, while a young soldier said he was dragged from his village and forced into service. One woman opened her blouse to show where her breasts had been hacked off by soldiers whom she had dared to ask about the whereabouts of her son.

A few of us met with some of the political prisoners at Mariona Prison, the first American delegation to do so. Dirty and forbidding, the place was an old, crumbling fortress. Down an unlit passageway in a dingy cell we squatted by a man in his forties or fifties. He was quite dignified, despite the dirt, scraggly beard, and shapeless clothing, greeting us cordially, thanking us for coming. He had a rich, deep speaking voice that reminded me of the *Delegados*, but he told his story in the monotone many victims of trauma use to distance themselves from the horror they describe. He had been picked up by armed men in civilian clothes and taken to a secret place where he was tortured for the names of his coconspirators. Having none, he was helpless in the face of their sadism. He opened his shirt and showed us the scars where acid had been poured on his chest. "Why were you the target of these torturers?" we asked. He said he thought it was because he was president of the teacher's union.

A few weeks after I got home, Margie called to say that a congressional committee was going to hold public hearings about military aid to El Salvador and they wanted me to testify on behalf of our delegation.

It was thrilling, if intimidating, to be asked to testify before Congress. Given the politics of the situation, this was right on the firing line, and they hoped celebrity would encourage the press to cover the hearing. As I walked into the room that day, it was clear that we didn't have much to worry about in that department. Cameras were everywhere. The place was a bit churchlike: lots of wood, no stained glass, but flags, uniforms, and other icons of power. The pews for the communicants faced an elevated bench on which sat the row of priests, all white men in suits and ties instead of robes. Very imposing.

The committee first heard from some who supported the

Administration's policy, then from representatives of aid groups working in the region. Policy apologists were welcomed warmly; the aid-
types, compassionate fools that they were, less so. By the time I was
called, it was pretty clear that those opposed to killing Commies were
in for a roasting. I made my way to the dock—at least it felt like the
dock—and introduced myself as the cameras clicked. The faces
above me were tense and unnerving, but the outrage I still felt helped
me push past the nerves and give my statement (the full text is at
www.mikefarrell.org/speeches/house.html). I told of the misery of the
refugees, the plight of the peasants, the brutality of the military, the
corruption of the government, the complicity of the Reagan
Administration, and the courage and self-sacrifice of the humanitarian volunteers we had met along the way.

Afterward, I was thanked by those open to my point of view and
attacked by the Reagan supporters. Henry Hyde, a bright, articulate,
very right-wing Reagan loyalist, was particularly irate, questioning my
testimony, my reasons for going, my motive for testifying, and my relationship with the refugees. We yammered a bit. Given the heat of his
attack, I figure I must have scored some points.

When they finished with me, the next speaker, a slim man with
thinning brown hair, thanked me as he went by to take the hot seat.
He was, I soon discovered, Dr. Charlie Clements, Air Force Academy
graduate, pilot during the Vietnam War, and mysterious American
doctor who had worked with the poor in the mountains of El
Salvador. It was Charlie to whom the suitcase of medicines that had
walked away from us in Mesa Grande was likely delivered. He was
roundly denounced in the room and his patriotism challenged, but his
military history and the incredible courage of the campaign he single-
handedly carried out on behalf of the poor in El Salvador was more
than ample defense for what they threw at him.

Charlie soon became a friend. He continued to be a thorn in the
side of the Reagan Administration during its tenure and has maintained
his commitment to serving the poor and working for peace to this day.

* * *

Back at home, I caught up with my kids and pursued an increasingly delightful relationship with Shelley. Everyone was full of questions about what I'd seen and done, and I found that talking helped me sort out my feelings about the increasingly bifurcated life I was living. I was the same guy I'd always been, but the opportunities presenting themselves were way beyond anything I'd ever anticipated. Since I had the access that came with being a celebrity, it seemed I had a responsibility to do what I could. It wasn't a bad thing, I guess; it was just a lot to deal with.

I came to realize that the special place in people's hearts that M*A*S*H occupied offered those of us lucky enough to be part of the show a unique entrée. It was the chance to be an ambassador of sorts, someone welcomed across the board: from the rudest huts in the underdeveloped world to the greatest mansions in the richest countries. It wasn't universal, of course, but the feeling of openness and possibility was a constant surprise.

A call from Joe Ingle introduced me to yet another world. Per our discussion on the set, he had arranged a pass for us to visit death row at Tennessee State Prison, and then he wanted me to come to a meeting in Chicago where he would make a pitch for his organization. I flew to Nashville and we drove out to the imposing eighty-year-old facility. Though I'd been in prisons before, I'd never been on death row and found the idea a bit spooky. The guards treated Joe with respect and me with friendliness and curiosity. We left our IDs with the man behind the double-thick bulletproof glass and worked our way into the facility through a series of gates, each one clanging shut behind us with a claustrophobic finality. What if something happened? We've all seen the movies and heard the horror stories. My thoughts on capital punishment were clear, but the gory media exploitation of horrible murders committed by sadistic fiends conjured images of fang-toothed, child-eating monsters.

Death row was in a small building across the yard from the main facility. The cells were back-to-back, butted up against one another, creating a row of cells in the center with open space between the bars and the outer wall for a walkway on either side. This allowed us to say hello to each inmate as we walked up one side, around, and down the other. It was like every other part of every other prison, except that these men had been convicted of the worst crimes and were awaiting death.

Most of them were black, and all of them seemed poor and ill-educated. Though some didn't look up from whatever they were doing, most were happy to see Joe and, when he introduced me, were knocked out that someone they had seen on television had come to visit. I was very touched by how human these guys were. Their loneliness, their gratitude for our presence, was so loaded with pain that it was hard to take. Some were too embarrassed to meet my eyes, instead pointing out things in their cells or talking about me to Joe, while others were quick with questions—most about Hot Lips, then the others from the show. A few were simple, quiet, deeply and touchingly sweet in expressing their thanks for my time. One man gave me a crucifix he had glued together out of matchsticks. It still sits in my room.

Many of the men reached through the bars and clasped my hands. We talked about mundane things and simply shared a bit of time. As I moved away from each one and on to the next, there was always the unstated reality: I could leave and they could not. They had done terrible things, of course, and I had not. But that couldn't have been the sum total of their existence, could it? Many of them had children, mothers, fathers, wives, brothers, and sisters. They had felt things and hoped for things and wondered about things just as I had. Some had experienced lives filled with such misery and pain as to be beyond imagining. And while I could go home, this was their home until the day they would be taken into another room and killed.

We went into the death chamber, not far from the cells we'd just left. It was a room with a cement floor and bare cement walls—and an electric chair. Bright yellow, it sat on a little platform, a kind of ghastly throne with wires, and straps for the arms and legs. A little metal skullcap hung on a hook behind.

Driving away later, I tried to give voice to some of what I was feeling. Joe was quiet, letting me get it out. Then, still quietly, he expressed his own fury. He reminded me of the practitioners of Liberation Theology in Central America whose Christ was an active and unyielding champion of the poor and oppressed, and whose loving embrace refused to discriminate against the sinner, chastising only those who would cast the first stone.

Chicago was a curious experience after death row. In a very ritzy penthouse in a very posh building, I introduced Joe to a very wealthy crowd gathered by a sympathetic friend and watched him try to bridge the gap. This simple, decent Southern minister made a mighty effort to reach across the divide and bring the reality of death row into a room whose furnishings cost more than it would take to run his organization for a year. I don't know how successful he was that night, but I could hear God cheering in the roar of the wind just outside.

At home, show business and reality collided as I was offered a part in a movie for television about the murder of the four American churchwomen in El Salvador. Written and produced by the award-winning writer David W. Rintels and directed by the equally esteemed Joe Sargent, *Choices of the Heart* was a courageous project given the political mood at the time. It starred Melissa Gilbert and other actors who opposed U.S. involvement in Central America, including Martin Sheen, Helen Hunt, and Peter Horton. I was thrilled to be asked to play Robert White, U.S. ambassador to El Salvador at the time of the murders, a hero who was openly critical of the Salvadoran government and the Reagan policies. Now president of the Center for International Policy, his is one of the most influential voices for sanity in U.S.–Latin American affairs. We all felt the film would reach a different and far broader audience than we ever could with news stories, protests, or testimonies before Congress.

With the same thought in mind, Shelley costarred with me later that year in a picture for CBS about the lingering impact of their war on returned Vietnam veterans. Titled *Memorial Day*, it was one of the earliest exposures of what came to be known as Delayed (or Post-

Traumatic) Stress Syndrome, a phenomenon that has wreaked havoc in the lives of many servicemen and women and their families. I proudly coproduced the picture, which was again directed by Joe Sargent, beautifully written by Michael Bortman, and featured a young performer who has since become a great friend and a beloved champion of the disadvantaged: Danny Glover.

In early 1984, Margie arranged another trip to El Salvador, this one sponsored by the Arca Foundation and the Center for Development Policy. I signed on immediately, as did Shelley. René Auberjonois joined us, along with Bill Ford, whose sister Ita Ford was one of the murdered nuns.

The killing of the churchwomen had remained a hotly contested issue in the U.S. The Reagan people tried everything they could think of to keep the responsibility for the murders from tainting support for their policies. Five low-ranking National Guardsmen were finally brought to trial in 1984, convicted of the rape and murder of the four women, and sentenced to thirty years in prison. Few believed the case was truly solved by what was clearly a show trial of a few scapegoats, but, as with Iraq today, the higher-ups were very crafty.

Landing in El Salvador, we found the situation to be even worse than a year earlier. Armed men at the airport looked us all over very carefully, clearly not pleased at our presence. Going through the passport process, I noted a list on the counter in front of me. I couldn't make out many of the names at a single quick glance, but I did see Bill Ford's. He was in a different line and I couldn't get his attention. He made it through all right, but was very interested to hear about the list. It was unlikely that they had missed him. Maybe he was someone they were simply keeping an eye on . . . ? Given the political climate here, it certainly didn't seem a good thing.

The heat was intense and the air thick, but that was the least of our worries. After dinner that night, walking back to our hotel from a nearby restaurant, we passed a darkened building beside which a group of men were quickly moving gear from one of the Jeep Cherokees we had come to associate with death squads to a waiting truck. They were in military boots and partial uniforms. Everything about the scene spelled trouble, so we held our breath and kept walking.

On the way to one meeting, we were pulled over by the military, ordered out of our van at gunpoint, and told to produce our documents. Having been through this before, I wasn't overly alarmed. Broad daylight on a well-traveled road didn't seem the optimum place to kill a group of American citizens. But once the tense process was completed and we were safely back in the van, it became clear that some of our company—including Shelley and our friend René— had been terrified. I felt stupid for not having reassured them earlier, but upon reflection I realized that theirs might have been the proper reaction after all. It doesn't pay to get too comfortable in a place like this.

General Garcia the gargoyle had been replaced by General Blandon, a smiling salesman whose looks and apparent gentility made him the antithesis of his predecessor. I'm sure Blandon's pleasant demeanor, polished English, and sugared blandishments were much more palatable for visiting congressmen looking for reassurance than Garcia's snarling condemnation of "Communist" peasants. I was embarrassed at the end of the meeting when General Blandon asked to have his picture taken with me. I found it impossible, given the chumminess of his approach, to say no, but squirmed at the thought of this picture being used for personal PR, as I'm sure it was.

The hideaways of the displaced people were heartbreaking, an orphanage in the middle of the city the worst. Stories there verified reports from human rights investigators about the escalating war: helicopter-assisted assaults on villages, the slaughter of unarmed civilians and the use of anti-personnel weapons like cluster bombs, all financed by U.S. taxpayers. We heard from witnesses to the massacre at Rio Sumpul, similar to the Rio Lempa horror Father Gallagher had described. The report of a pregnant woman sliced open with a bayonet, the fetus removed and the severed head of her husband stuffed into its place was horrifying and infuriating.

Given an opportunity to get out into the country, we flew with a few of the others into Morazán Province, where some of the most intense fighting was taking place. Once down, Shelley and I got a ride to San Francisco Gotera, where we were slipped into the rectory of a church by a friendly priest. An Irishman who had been there for years, he regaled us with stories about the spirit of the people, whom he loved dearly. Everything he said came out with a laugh, as if it were all a big cosmic joke.

One day a man had knocked on his door, the priest told us, requesting help for a woman in distress. He went with the man to a small, poor home where a young woman waited stoically. She had been pulled from a bus by soldiers, searched, slashed with a bayonet, and left for dead. Somehow, she survived and was taken in by this man and his family. Removing the rags they had placed on her back to stop the bleeding, the priest found a deep gash running from shoulder to hip. "And they expected," he boomed, "me to fix it!" So? "So I did," he laughed again. "Never done it before, you know, but they had a needle and some thread. So I had them give her a big drink, had a gulp meself, and went to work. I had the señora, the lady of the house, pull the skin together and sewed her right up! Had to keep talking the whole time so as not to think too much about what I was doing, you know. The poor thing never flinched. And I didn't do a half bad job, if I do say so." He roared with laughter. Shelley and I were alternately stunned, sickened, shocked, and knocked out by this guy, by the story, by this reality. "And you know," he continued, "she never cried, never whimpered, never let out a peep. What a woman." What a woman indeed. And what a man. What a fucking world.

We spent that night in a small bed in a cramped, dirty room. None of this, I should quickly add, was easy for Shelley. It was certainly not the life she was used to, nor, dare I say, the life she had dreamed of. Yet here she was, this sweet, beautiful woman, running afoul of her own government, putting herself at risk in a country at war, spending the night hiding behind a church in a conflict zone with a crazy priest spinning stories of tragedy and heroism, and, to top it off, trying to get to sleep by counting the spiders on the wall. How lucky can a guy get?

Early the next morning, our host tiptoed in to wake us. Signaling for quiet, he beckoned us to the window and drew back the ragged curtain just far enough for us to see what looked like a battalion of soldiers forming up in the square. "Getting ready for one of their sweeps," he said. "Don't go outside." As if we needed the warning.

After the soldiers finally moved off, we thanked the priest for what he was doing, received his blessing, and took off for the spot where we were to be picked up. The plane was gone, so we got a bus for the long ride back to San Salvador.

Having made the rounds, our group split up. Shelley had to head home for work and others back to Washington. The rest of us took a short flight to Managua, Nicaragua. Not much had changed since my last trip. But at the Intercontinental Hotel we found new interest from the rest of the world. The place bustled with reporters, businesspeople, tourists, diplomats, legislators, women and men in uniform, and, doubtless, spies.

We had meetings in Managua, too, but the difference from El Salvador was night and day. Here there were dinners and laughs, with no concern about death squads. We met Daniel Ortega, the primary leader of the five-man Sandinista junta, who would become the nation's president in its first free election a few months later. We enjoyed a lively dinner with the radical poet Rosario Murillo, Ortega's attractive and effervescent wife. We met the beautiful Nora Astorga, who had been dubbed by *Time Magazine* "the Mata Hari of the Sandinista Revolution" for luring a notorious National Guard torturer, General "The Dog" Vega, to a spot where he was to be kidnapped. The kidnapping attempt had failed, however, and Vega was killed as he fought to escape. A respected lawyer, Astorga later served as Nicaragua's ambassador to the United Nations before succumbing, at a very young age, to leukemia. We also heard the passionate political poetry of Ernesto Cardinale, Sandinista minister and Catholic priest.

While some of this was interesting and fun, I found much of it repetitive, self-congratulatory, and ultimately exhausting. I thought it important that this political experiment be given the chance to work for the benefit of the Nicaraguan people, and I was embarrassed and offended by U.S. efforts to undermine it before it got off the starting blocks. But I didn't think we should shut our eyes to the possibility that the Sandinistas might be capable of some of their own dirty tricks, as well. If we truly supported self-determination and human rights, they had to apply across the board.

On a trip to the countryside to meet with workers, growers, and religious and community leaders, we stopped in Matagalpa for lunch with a group of coffee growers in the courtyard of Noel Bolt-Rivera. Señor Bolt was unable to meet with us, but his wife graciously provided a meal while her husband's colleagues told us of the difficulties created by U.S. economic and military pressures. In spite of everything, they said, they were much better off under the new revolutionary government than they had been under Somoza. Because of their support for the new government, though, they were threatened and harassed by the Contras. They urged us to carry back the message that the Contras were not heroic defenders of democracy, as Mr. Reagan claimed, but were, in fact, terrorizing the countryside in an attempt to undermine the good that was being done.

The next day some of us loaded into an antique Sikorsky helicopter, clearly a hand-me-down from the Russians or the Cubans, and flew out toward the east coast to look at a Miskito Indian resettlement camp. The Indians on the Atlantic coast were an independent lot. Largely ignored by Somoza, they had developed no particular sense of nationhood and weren't generally supporters of the revolution. Some of the Miskito Indians, under the leadership of Steadman

Fagoth, had been recruited by the Contras to wage a guerrilla campaign of their own, creating both governance and public-relations
problems for Managua. In spite of Reagan's attempts to paint the
Sandinistas as vicious murderers who had forced themselves on the
people, human rights investigators found that the Contras themselves
had been the primary source of terror in the region, decimating villages, destroying rural cooperatives, raping, and killing. Their intention was to establish an area of control in Nicaragua from which they
could, with the overt support of U.S. troops, overthrow the Sandinistas.

The purpose of our flight in the rickety helicopter was to check
out Tasba Pri, one of the Miskito Indian relocation camps. The
Sandinistas claimed that the Miskitos had been moved to protect
them from harassment and intimidation by Fagoth and the Contras,
but some human rights workers feared it was more about control than
protection.

After a couple of hours in the air, we landed in an area secured by
a squad of Sandinista soldiers, young teenagers who greeted us with
smiles. Clambering into the back of a truck, we were driven some
miles through the jungle to a well-laid-out facility of small, prefabri-
cated houses in a clearing. Many of the houses had gardens, and all
were well kept. The residents were quiet but pleasant, and some of
them spoke English, the apparent legacy of the seventeenth- and
eighteenth-century pirates who roamed the Atlantic Coast.

Those to whom we spoke described raids, firefights, and ongoing
intimidation by Fagoth and the Contras, because of which many of
them were grateful for the protection of the Sandinistas. All was not
entirely positive, however. The forced resettlement was done peremp-
torily, without much notice and little discussion, leaving many of the
Miskito people bitter and resentful. It wasn't clear to me whether
those who were dissatisfied were free to return to their original
homes, or what was left of them. The decision and move seem to
have been done bureaucratically, demonstrating both the best and
worst aspects of the Sandinista approach. Doubtless there was a genuine concern for the welfare of these people, but the decision was

clearly influenced by political considerations. It's hard to know which took precedence.

I had promised my kids a souvenir, so I picked up something that, given their current fascination with combat, Bruce Lee, and super-heroes, best represented the experience of Nicaragua. I bought them each a machete. Because I'd learned to travel light and generally limited my gear to carry-ons, I stowed the pair of three-foot knives across each other in an X in the hang-up bag with my requisite suit for more formal meetings. Given the primitive state of technology in Managua, they went unnoticed at the airport, and I forgot about them as we flew north. In Miami, René and I raced through a casual customs check—nothing to declare—to make the connection for an early flight to Los Angeles that hadn't yet left the gate. Approaching security, I suddenly remembered the crossed machetes in my hang-up bag. Eager to get home early, I decided to go for it and just give the damned things up if I couldn't explain them satisfactorily. Tossing the bags onto the conveyor belt, I quickly passed through the metal detector and waited, wondering if I'd be arrested or simply forced to give up what were clearly dangerous weapons. To my amazement, the person at the monitor didn't say a word. I grabbed the bags and dashed to the gate and onto the plane. Try that today.

Chapter 13
BORDERS

A t home, things were popping. Reagan was forced to eat months of denials of any connection with the Contras when the U.S. was caught mining Nicaragua's harbors, a flagrant breach of international law. The Sandinistas were suing us in the World Court and likely to prevail, so in a staggering demonstration of arrogance the president's people refused to submit to the jurisdiction of the court. They (actually *we*) were further embarrassed when heavy-handed U.S. meddling in the Nicaraguan election was exposed. Then came the revelation of a fake story about MIG fighter planes in Nicaragua, and the discovery of a CIA assassinations manual in the hands of the Contras. The Great Communicator outdid himself in the face of it all, calling the Contras "freedom fighters" and claiming the CIA manual "never mentions assassination," that the term "neutralizing" simply meant saying "to the fellow who's sitting there in the office, 'You're not in the office anymore.'"

Two months later, I learned that Señor Noel Bolt-Rivera, the Matagalpa coffee grower whose hospitality we'd enjoyed, had been murdered by the Contras. His severed head was left to be discovered by his wife and colleagues, a none-too-subtle warning of what could be expected for those who chose to work with the Sandinista government.

This being an election year, I spoke, debated, and wrote on Central America policy, believing that if people truly understood the facts we could stop these insane misadventures and let the Nicaraguans make their own decisions—even their own mistakes. We formed the Committee of Concern, primarily from the Hollywood community, to educate and inform. Robert Foxworth and Elizabeth Montgomery, courageous and outspoken leaders on the issue, hosted Daniel Ortega at an event in their home. All this, of course, was grist for the right-wing rumor mills.

Having met Patti Davis, Reagan's daughter, I asked if she'd have lunch with me. I hoped that if I could successfully convey to her the reality of what I'd seen on the ground, there might be a chance that it could be communicated to her father in a way he'd understand. As I told her what was happening in Central America, the misery that was being created by his policies, she grasped it immediately and shared my frustration. I had to say that from what I had personally seen, her father was either a bald-faced liar or he had been terribly misinformed by those around him. Though estranged from her family at the time, Patti said that part of her sadness came from the fact that her father was utterly insulated by his advisors. She thought he was speaking from genuine belief, but it was based on the information he was allowed, which was very limited. While not a complete surprise, it was terrifying to think that we had a leader who was at once so trusted and yet so utterly cut off from reality.

On the work front, most of the ideas pitched in my direction were a variation on "B.J. goes home" and not very interesting. Having done what I still consider the best TV show to ever grace the airwaves, I really didn't see the point in ripping it off. So I looked for projects to produce, discussed the future with Shelley, and played with my kids.

Then along came David Susskind with an idea that knocked me back on my heels—a one-man show on JFK. Frank Perry was interested in directing and they wanted me to play Kennedy! I was flabbergasted. JFK had been one of my heroes and I had long fantasized about one day playing him. But now? In a one-man show? Susskind was a well-known and controversial figure in television. We met for lunch, and he literally wouldn't take no for an answer. I was flattered to be courted so passionately by a respected figure, and I gave him a tentative yes, with a hedge. If he'd arrange a speech coach and give me time to develop the accent, I'd be thrilled to do it.

I worked for weeks with David Alan Stern, a wonderful dialect coach, alternating between being sure I'd never get it and feeling right on the edge of success. After a couple of months, I was on a soundstage in New York with the wonderful Frank Perry living out one of my dreams. Susskind couldn't possibly have been more supportive, a true gentleman from start to finish. The show aired on PBS, and the kind words I heard from old Kennedy stalwarts at a screening brought tears to my eyes.

New Year's Eve, a holiday I've never been fond of, became my lucky day that year when Shelley and I were married in her aunt Nanette Fabray's garden. As I tell her regularly, now more than twenty years later, I'm the luckiest man in the world.

It's tough taking on the job of stepparent. My kids had come to like Shelley a great deal, but we all knew their fondest hope was that their mom and dad would somehow get back together. Shelley and I were clear with them and tried to include them in everything. And Judy had developed a relationship with Joe Bratcher, a mutual friend and partner in her developing writing career. Even so, our marriage was tough for Erin and Mike. Shelley, bless her, went out of her way to embrace and support them, giving them space and believing that in time they'd come to accept it. Judy and Joe also worked hard from their end to help the kids through the transition.

In the spring of 1985, I got a call from a psychologist who was concerned about the anti-Soviet saber-rattling coming out of the White House. He wanted to put together a "track-two" delegation—people to people—to meet with counterparts in Soviet society. His hope was to put to rest some of the fears each had about the other. I was intrigued by the idea, but didn't know this fellow and wasn't sure how seriously to take him. When he said Dennis Weaver and his wife Gerry had agreed to go, I warmed to the idea. I didn't know Dennis personally, but liked what I knew about him. He was a thoughtful and decent guy, from what I'd heard, and was concerned about the state of the world.

I called Dennis and we had a good conversation, although there was a brief hiccup. I told him that what had piqued my interest was learning that he was committed to going. He said, "Well, that's what I was told. When I heard you were going, I thought it must be a good group." Once we got that little detail straightened out, we decided to sign up for the trip and I started gathering information about political prisoners from a friend at Amnesty International.

Shortly before we left, I was given a contact number for Edgar Chamorro, a former Contra leader who had grown disenchanted. Amazingly, he was very open. For days, at the end of April and the beginning of May when I should have been prepping for the U.S.S.R., I spent hours on the phone with Chamorro, getting powerful information about the CIA's complicity in the horror generated by the Contras, and passed it on to members of Congress and the human rights groups I'd been working with. (See "Chamorro Notes" at www.mikefarrell.org/publications/chamorro.html.)

Everyone had fantasies about the trip, but none of us really knew what we'd find. Many worried about danger, while others wondered how much our views had been poisoned by the anti-Soviet rhetoric we'd been bathed in for so long. One way or another, we were about to find out.

When the day came, our pals Tom and Claire Callaway took us to the L.A. airport for the first leg of what was a phenomenal, frustrating, infuriating, eye-opening, and often hilarious two-week adventure. (For a thorough account, see "To Russia with 'Unconditional Love'" at www.mikefarrell.org/Journals.html.) We met our Soviet counterparts, listened, discussed, argued, dodged surveillance, sneaked around with dissidents, learned history, and saw many glorious and sad aspects of contemporary life in the Soviet Union. These were the early days of Perestroika, and Gorbachev's changes were embraced by some and resisted by others. The food was terrible, vegetables almost nonexistent, the water scary. But the bread was good, and the ice cream wonderful. Shelley laughed about surviving on a diet of champagne and ice cream.

Hiding unacceptable items from the very intimidating border police was an adventure, and pressing an arrogant bureaucrat for answers about some of Amnesty's "prisoners of conscience" was kind of fun. But the welcome we got from the people, their openness to our presence, the beauty of the region's highly prized heritage, the courage of their religious communities, the social stratification in a "classless society," the open and vigorous debate—all of it was challenging and enlightening.

Shelley and I formed a lifelong friendship with Dennis and Gerry Weaver, and with another fellow traveler, the truly unique, utterly captivating and irrepressible Dr. Hunter "Patch" Adams, about whom my partner and I sort of made a movie years later.

Returning to the U.S., I sent pictures and information off to friends at Amnesty International and began telling audiences and friends that people in the Soviet Union really didn't have horns and tails. We sent a gift to Senator Paul Simon. A Democrat from Illinois, Paul was a great senator, a wonderful guy, and a good friend. Very dignified, straight-laced, in some ways old-fashioned, he always wore bow ties. Shelley and I bought him a red one at a department store in Moscow and asked him to wear it on the Senate floor one day while saying a special hello to Jesse Helms for us.

In mid-1985, Marvin Minoff, an independent producer, broached the idea of partnering on some projects. Marvin is married to Bonnie Franklin, Shelley's friend and the star of *One Day at a Time*, and we decided to kick the idea around a bit.

Our discussions bore fruit and Farrell/Minoff Productions is now in its twenty-second year, but only because Marvin is exceptionally patient. I was quickly pulled away to chair the Committee of Concern for Central America and drawn into yet another aspect of that struggle.

Beyond the debate over our military involvement in the region, the war in El Salvador was increasing the number of undocumented aliens coming here after making their way out of Central America, through Mexico, and across our southern border. International treaties require the receiving nation to provide sanctuary for refugees fleeing violence, but the Reagan Administration wouldn't admit that the Salvadoran government was murdering its people. They maintained these were simply economic refugees looking for work and ordered the Border Patrol to round them up and send them back. In the West, the job fell under the watchful eye and heavy hand of Harold Ezell, the Reagan-appointed Western Regional Commissioner for the Immigration and Naturalization Service (INS). Ezell's harsh views on immigration and refugees were expressed in many ways over the years, but their sting was felt most sharply by Salvadorans, tens of thousands of whom were sent back to the slaughter.

While making him a hero of right-wing bigots, Ezell's action gave rise to the Sanctuary Movement, a reprise of the Underground Railroad of antislavery days. Growing out of the religious, civil liberties, and refugee rights communities, the Sanctuary Movement offered shelter to Salvadoran and Guatemalan refugees because of the oppression they suffered at home and the fate that might befall them if sent back. Refugees who had been detained were given legal assistance, while others were moved via underground railroad to different parts of the country. In the Southwest, in particular, many were given sanctuary in churches. The most famous was the Southside Presbyterian Church in Tucson, Arizona, where the Reverend John Fife and a Quaker named Jim Corbett had organized to assist those making their way across the desert. Along with two priests, three nuns, and other locals, they were indicted by the U.S. government for their trouble. The Committee of Concern helped raise their profile by lending our presence, debating the issue and drawing media attention. Along with others, I appeared before the City Council asking that Los Angeles declare itself a city of sanctuary, and flew to Tucson and Phoenix to appear with Reverend Fife, Jim Corbett, and others to help raise funds for their defense.

The next morning we went to Tucson's Southside Church for a press conference. When the Reverend Fife opened the doors to let us in, we found a Salvadoran man, covered with dirt and exhausted from his trek, asleep on the floor before us.

Frustrated upon returning home to find the racist anti-Sanctuary campaign endorsed by Ezell in a hateful editorial in a local paper, I responded, pointing out the laws and traditions at which he was thumbing his nose. (See "Response to Harold Ezell," www.mikefarrell.org/publications/ezell.html.)

As an ironic counterpoint, I was contacted about a situation in El Salvador: A wounded guerrilla had been captured and was being denied medical treatment in prison. A *comandante* of one of the five guerrilla "tendencies" making up the Farabundo Marti Liberation Front (FMLN), Nidia Diaz was a significant prisoner, her capture considered a win for the army. A group of physicians on a medical rights mission examined her, determining that a bullet wound in her arm was causing the loss of the use of her thumb. The problem was reparable, they felt, but only if surgery was performed very soon. The Salvadoran army refused to allow it. Again, we contacted members of Congress and human rights groups, pressuring El Salvador's leaders to meet their responsibility under international law and ensure that the necessary procedure was done.

The debate caused significant problems between San Salvador and D.C. Salvadoran officials claimed that no doctor in the country would perform the surgery. The truth was that the repression by the military was so complete that anyone assisting the enemy, wounded or not, would be considered a traitor and face dire consequences. It was finally resolved when Medical Aid for El Salvador found an American doctor willing to fly down and do the surgery if the U.S. could get the Salvadorans to agree. It's hard to know whose arms were twisted and how hard, but an agreement was struck.

Medical Aid asked me to go as an observer. Amnesty International asked, too, wanting a first-person account of what transpired. Shelley gave her blessing and I met the doctor, a very pleasant—even jovial—

neurosurgeon from Los Angeles, and his wife, a nurse-anesthetist, at the airport and we headed south. Neither seemed in the least nervous about what we were getting into and I wasn't sure if I should find that reassuring or not. On the flight, Dr. S., who got a big kick out of the fact that I'd played a surgeon on M*A*S*H, had a great time showing me pictures of the operation he anticipated and regaling me with O.R. stories. They both seemed more enthused about being with a TV star than concerned about what awaited us. Some of this optimism began to take the edge off my private fears and let me hope that the government-to-government cooperation that led to the deal would somehow make this trip different.

In San Salvador, we were taken under guard to a prison in the city. The officer in charge brought us into a compound with cells in tiers five or six flights high opening onto a common space where guards watched. The prisoner was happy to see us. Proud, dark-haired, probably in her thirties, she was clearly a powerful woman, having maintained her sense of humor in very difficult circumstances. Dr. S. examined her, going to pains to include me in the discussion of the wound, her symptoms, and his sense of what was amiss. He then asked her permission to do the surgery, which she granted. It was a gesture of respect that did not go unnoticed. She was a prisoner to them, but to him she was a proud and independent woman. After this, our guard—who had never been out of earshot—took us back. We were escorted to the hotel and told to await word, which would probably come that night.

It was well after midnight when we got the call. Picked up in military jeeps and flanked by stone-faced, machine gun–bearing soldiers, we were taken to a hospital somewhere in the city. It was an eerie ride, everything about it implying a potential attack at any moment. We entered the hospital through the back entrance and, still under guard, were brought by freight elevator to where a surgery had been set up. The patient was on a gurney, with lights and the necessary equipment around her. Having delivered us, the soldiers left, and we were suddenly confronted with a problem. Dr. S. had assumed there would be surgical nurses to assist him, but the moment we arrived, all the Salvadorans who had prepared her simply walked out. His wife, there to administer and monitor the anesthetic, would be completely occupied and unable to provide any other assistance during surgery.

At that point, Dr. S turned to me and said, "Go scrub up and put on a gown and gloves."

Fearing that I had heard him correctly, I panicked and said, "Doc, you've got to be kidding." He wasn't. "But I'm not a real doctor," I protested. "All that stuff we did on the show was fake: fake blood, fake wounds, fake everything."

He smiled, and said, "You understand the process; you know sterile procedure. Without another pair of hands, I can't do this, so get scrubbed."

I was flabbergasted. Now the pictures he had shown me, the care he had taken to include me in everything, suddenly made sense. He had clearly sussed out the situation and thought through all the possibilities. But he had more confidence in me than I had in myself. There really wasn't time to argue. My mind racing, I said that it was important that the patient, who was lying there waiting for us to quit talking and get to work, be told that I wasn't a doctor. I wanted her to know that she had the option of waiting for another opportunity, rather than having an amateur take part in the procedure. Dr. S. and his wife explained it to her in Spanish, and she laughed and said (they told me), "In the mountains, those who can, do."

So I went into the scrub room and did all the things I'd done hundreds of times before for what felt like the first time, all the while telling myself not to pass out or vomit when the cutting started. Mrs. S. helped me with the gown, cap, and gloves, and soon everyone was ready. Sort of. But the doc never hesitated. He told me to listen carefully and to mirror his actions. If he moved tissue aside in one direction, he wanted me to do that same in the other. Otherwise, I should simply do as I was told.

We'd been warned that because of guerrilla attacks to the electrical grids, the hospital sometimes lost its power. If that happened, we should hold everything in place until the auxiliary generator kicked in. And, of course, that's exactly what happened. The patient had only been given a local anesthetic, and when the power failed, she laughed and cheered the *muchachos*. I wasn't all that happy about their timing.

Nonetheless, we went forward. The first cut was what worried me most, but there it was. And it was amazing. The forearm tissue separated, we dealt with the blood and moved into another world. Once through the initial steps, I found the entire process fascinating. Did you know that the fatty layer below the skin is yellow and looks like bad oatmeal or curdled Jell-O? The bullet had apparently damaged a nerve. Her fingers were fine, as we'd seen, but the thumb was useless, limiting her ability to use the hand. Once inside the arm, we traced the route of the bullet while the doc looked for a point of contact with the nerve, perhaps damage to the sheath, but couldn't find anything. After probing for a while, he decided to go to the second option.

Opening the back of the woman's hand, Dr. S. said we would cut one of the two tendons connected to the forefinger and reroute it, making it the new thumb tendon. Though at first I mainly helped by holding things, here he had me sever the tendon, tunnel through some tissue, and attach it to the other! After some incredibly delicate, utterly fascinating work, we stitched the tendon, and the job was done. We cleaned everything, sewed up the wounds, bandaged and reassured "our" patient, accepted her groggy thanks, and exchanged congratulations. Then we passed word to those outside that they could come get their prisoner.

There was a good deal of press attention the next day about the M*A*S*H doctor's role in the surgery, though I'm not sure just how word got out. I took the opportunity to condemn the repression and lack of humanitarian assistance in the country.

Before leaving, I took Dr. S. and his wife to Bethania, the church-supported encampment just outside the city that housed so many displaced and orphaned children. The situation for these poor kids had not improved since my last time here, and it was a difficult and discouraging visit. The entire encampment smelled of urine and rot from open ditches serving as toilets. A foul stream cutting through the camp was the sole source of water for cooking, drinking, and bathing. Dr. and Mrs. S. were devastated.

Once home, there was a flurry of attention, but it died down pretty quickly. A network morning show, *Today* or *Good Morning America*, invited me for an appearance, but let me know they'd also have to have someone from the "other side."

"What other side is that?" I asked.

"Well, you know, the Reagan Administration; we've got to give equal time to both sides."

"You mean you want us to debate the right to humanitarian assistance? I thought that was pretty well resolved some years back with the Geneva Conventions."

Needless to say, the idea was quickly scrapped.

Seven years later, Nidia Diaz used her now-working hand to sign the peace treaty ending the civil war in El Salvador. Today she is a member of the Constituent Assembly, El Salvador's Congress.

Chapter 14
ANASTASIO, AUGUSTO, DOMINICK AND EUGENE

S ettled back at home, Farrell/Minoff Productions was born. Because there was still interest in my doing another television series, we explored the possibility of setting up at one of the studios in town, and we eventually secured a housekeeping deal at Disney, including a nice set of offices and an allowance for an assistant. Marvin hired a secretary, and I brought along Nancy Cluss, who had started out working as a nanny for the kids when I was doing M*A*S*H and gradually took over arranging my life. Nan was a true flower child, as sweet and loving a person as ever wore sandals. She had a knack for organizing, a head for figures, an ability to comprehend developing technologies, and an understanding of psychology that could have taken her anywhere she wanted to go. Fortunately for me, she didn't want to go anywhere until many years later when she fell in love and went off to live on a farm in Idaho. Disney was not her favorite place. Nor, as it happened, was it mine.

Marvin and I met with all the appropriate people at the studio. Michael Eisner welcomed us very graciously and immediately began talking about a television series. I made clear my lack of enthusiasm for the idea, but that was obviously the reason for his interest. We had some ideas of our own, including the possibility of developing some movies for him. "Fine," he said, "you just keep saying no until we wear you down."

Our year at Disney was frustrating. Everything we tried met resistance. We pitched them a terrific idea for a western but were told it wouldn't work because "Michael doesn't like dust." Marvin had a longtime relationship with Bruce Joel Rubin, a wonderful guy and an

Academy Award–winning writer for *Ghost*. We brought Disney a great story by Bruce, set in the jungles of South America, but were told it wouldn't work because "Michael doesn't like green." Trying to anticipate what else Michael didn't like became an arduous process.

The relationship with Disney died after one year. Apparently my disinterest in a series was another one of the things Michael didn't like. But I had other things to do. Margie, whom Marvin dubbed my "political wife," put together another human rights trip, this one to Paraguay and Chile. Back to Washington for the briefing sessions, I was delighted to find that our delegation was to be led by Robert White, the ambassador I had played in the movie about the four churchwomen. Bob had been the ambassador to Paraguay before moving to El Salvador, and his knowledge of the Latin American political scene was extraordinary. Our group also included Janet Shenk, the talented scholar, author, and translator; Smith Bagley, one of the heirs to the Reynolds Tobacco fortune and the angel behind the Arca Foundation; and his wife Elizabeth Frawley, lawyer, political activist, and later Clinton's ambassador to Portugal.

General Alfredo Stroessner was the typical South American dictator. A military man who took over Paraguay in a 1954 coup d'état, he was a cruel and repressive leader in the Somoza/Pinochet mode favored by Jean Kirkpatrick and the Reagan gang. Stroessner's worldview was best illustrated by the fact that he granted Somoza and his family asylum after their defeat by the Sandinistas in Nicaragua. Having taken power violently, Stroessner maintained it the same way, telling his Paraguayan subjects that the absence of democracy is the price to be paid for peace and political stability. (Think Patriot Act.)

After a very long flight and a change of planes in Lima, Peru, we set down in Asunción, Paraguay, where we found a neat, orderly society without even a hint of revolutionary activity. Just beneath the placid surface, however, we were soon exposed to a pall of fear fed by thirty-two years of state-of-siege governance, repression, preventive detention, systematic torture, and widespread corruption of unbelievable proportions, all justified by virulent anti-Communist rhetoric.

Through Bob White's connections, we were introduced to those members of Paraguayan society who were actively struggling toward democracy. Our guide, an enormously courageous young man who had already been imprisoned and tortured for his "antisocial" tendencies, said our visit would certainly not escape the notice of the authorities. When we asked if he was putting himself in danger by accompanying us, he simply shrugged, insisting it was worth the risk to see that the world knew the truth. He then taught us to listen for the tattoo that, though subtle, was everywhere: tapped out on automobile horns, whistled, spoken, sung. It was a beat, a rhythm, a tune that said: *He will fall.*

In the countryside, we met with indigenous people who had staked a claim of ownership to unused land long ago taken from them by the state. Weaponless but insistent, they dared the government to challenge their right to return. We went to the gates of a prison, ancient and filthy, and were denied the promised entry because of our concern about human rights. In the city we met with homeless, impoverished *campesinos* "squatting" on privately held land, demanding their right to shelter and a life of dignity. To protect them from a return visit by police goons who had set upon them, we sat with doctors and nurses, representatives of a medical rights group demonstrating for equitable wages and benefits for those working in the public sector. In a shantytown a child caught my eye and I pulled out a Hacky Sack I was carrying and taught him the game—keep the sack in the air without touching it with your hands. Because soccer is a popular pastime there, he caught on quickly. As I walked away, he was in the middle of a circle, joyfully teaching other kids to play.

In a very nice home in a lovely section of the city, we heard from upper-middle-class men and women who were passionately committed to the return of democracy. All of these Paraguayans stirred us as they echoed the belief, *He will fall,* and yearned for the return of the leaders of the persecuted political opposition, Domingo Laino and Miguel Saguier, one now in exile, the other in prison.

On our last day, we visited Radio Nanduti, the country's only independent station. Radio Nanduti had regularly suffered jammed broadcasts, sabotaged equipment, and raids by government goons. We held a press conference there summarizing the findings of our trip and offering a broad condemnation of Stroessner's repression, but later learned that the entire broadcast had been jammed, a parting gesture of contempt from the authorities. To their frustration, however, tapes of the broadcast were being circulated.

Our quick flight over the Andes was breathtaking. Chile, as was clear from the bus ride into Santiago, is amazingly like California. The land, the crops, the climate all felt like home. Santiago, though, was more like a beautiful and grand European city. Yet here we were in the heart of the anti-Communist cauldron. General Augusto Pinochet Ugarte's murderous thirteen-year-old regime was a gift from Richard Nixon, Henry Kissinger, and the CIA, and it was hard not to be shamed by the knowledge.

We stayed in a lovely hotel across the square from La Moneda, the presidential palace that had been bombed during the U.S.-supported 1973 coup that killed President Salvador Allende and brought about Pinochet's rule. The coup itself has been called the bloodiest in twentieth-century South American history, claiming more than 3,000 lives. But that was only the beginning of a regime that ruled by terror and quickly became infamous for the murder, torture, and "disappearing" of thousands of its opponents.

Ten years before we arrived, Orlando Letelier, a former Allende ambassador, and his American assistant Ronni Moffett, were murdered in Washington, D.C., by a car bomb. The act was attributed to DINA (Direccion de Intelligencia Nacional), the brutal Chilean version of its ally, our CIA. The director, Colonel Manuel Contreras, a notorious torturer, was famous for saying to anyone brave enough to quarrel with his tactics, "Gentlemen, I am the law, and . . ." pointing to his pistol, "this is the judicial system."

Once again, Bob White's connections to the human rights community provided access to the dissident groups that still existed.

Unlike in Stroessner's Paraguay, we had some official meetings, since Pinochet was still trying to maintain the appearance of popular rule. Prior to the 1973 coup, Chile had enjoyed a 140-year history of democratic governance in which all sectors, including the Communist party, participated openly.

Though many dissidents chose not to meet with us, some were courageous enough to do so. The wife of an admiral who had opposed the coup and was killed for his impertinence invited us to her apartment. She was quite lovely and well-spoken, the bitterness of her experience barely breaking through as she described the cowardice of so many of the fellow officers who turned away from her husband and his comrades who refused to join in Chile's overthrow.

Less willing to hide their anger were the leaders of the *poblaciones*, or shantytowns, large slum areas populated by impoverished workers and families who were furious at the repression. Through strikes and other forms of civil unrest, they bravely expressed their demands for better working and living conditions, all of which were regularly met with brutal military responses.

In our meetings with intellectuals and educators, we heard proud recitations of Chile's democratic history, denunciations of Pinochet's monstrous tactics, and angry indictments of U.S. complicity in their country's grievous state. One participant cited the now infamous order of Richard Nixon to the CIA's Richard Helms to squeeze the country "until it screamed."

Absent any official political opposition, the Roman Catholic Church had assumed the role of moral critic, openly denouncing government repression. Cardinal Silva, a much beloved leader of the church, told us that "the mentality of this government is war with Marxism" and that "anyone who doesn't think as the government does is a Marxist." The Vicariate of Solidarity, a Catholic Church human rights organization, had recently been denounced as Communist, as has its leader, Cardinal Juan Francisco Fresno, the Archbishop of Santiago.

As our bus pulled into the compound of the U.S. Embassy, Janet said I should expect to be challenged about the surgery on Nidia Diaz, the Salvadoran guerrilla *comandante*. Apparently, the story had been passed around, but twisted until it was almost unrecognizable. In the version told here, it was her trigger finger that had been injured and, ignoring the protests of the Salvadoran people, I had rushed to her aid rather than repairing the damage done to thousands of small children maimed by guerrilla landmines. Other claims were made about my notorious Communist sympathies and other treasonous activities. Anticipating a pretty hostile reception, Janet asked if I'd like to skip the meeting. I had no desire to skip the meeting, but didn't want to create a problem for the rest of the group, so left the decision to them. We soon entered the building together.

The meeting went off without a hitch, as it turned out, with only one elliptical reference to "a story circulating about an adventure you apparently had in El Salvador." I responded that "story" was exactly the right word and that, if anyone cared to hear what had actually happened, I'd be happy to set the record straight. No one chose to go further, and the subject was dropped (though the fabricated version still reappears from time to time in right-wing rags).

During a meeting with a government functionary in charge of investigating claims of human rights violations, Margie and I inadvertently caught each others' eyes after enduring about fifteen minutes of artless platitudes and bald-faced lies, and suddenly broke into a fit of uncontrollable giggling. We were embarrassed to be so impolite, but he was so profoundly self-important and so plainly full of shit that we finally had to excuse ourselves and stagger out of his office into the street to stand there hooting, tears streaming from our eyes.

Later we met with an incredibly calm and dignified woman, Estella Reyes Ortiz, who told us of the disappearance of her father, a Communist Party member and advisor to the Allende government. From the time of his disappearance nearly ten years earlier, she had pursued every legal avenue available in an attempt to discover what had happened. Only a month and a half earlier, a courageous Chilean judge (one of very few) had charged forty high-ranking men with responsibility in the case. Without allowing any investigation, however, the Chilean Supreme Court had immediately provided all forty with a general amnesty, foreclosing any possibility of Señora Ortiz learning the truth.

In addition to her father's disappearance, the woman had also lost her husband to the rampage of oppression and violence in her country. A lawyer and a Communist, he had been working with the Vicariate of Solidarity to expose a secret organization whose goal was to destroy all Communists. After walking his daughter to school one day a year earlier, he was taken off the street by armed men in civilian clothes. The next day his headless body was one of four found on the city's streets.

"I'm convinced he was killed because he represented living proof that Communists and Christians can work together and agree," she told us. She faced the ongoing difficulty of explaining all of this to her daughter, "especially the meaning of the word 'decapitation,' which was everywhere in the news."

We left that meeting as we left the country: wounded, yet inspired by those we had met and learned from, sobered by the task of explaining what we had seen and heard to those back home.

Years later, the satisfaction of learning of General Pinochet's detention in London and subsequent legal travails at home was tempered by hearing from those who rose to his defense, determined to deny his—and by extension *their*—complicity in the horrors that were committed in the name of anti-Communism. Out of respect for those we met and the thousands who suffered, here are just three forms of torture that are acknowledged to have been used on military men who objected to the coup against Allende:

1. An open oil drum filled with urine and excrement was employed to submerge the head of the man being interrogated, to the point of asphyxiation, every time he refused to answer a question or confess to any crime of which he was accused.

2. The prisoners were hung naked, head downward, from a gymnastics bar and struck repeatedly on the scrotum and at the root of the testicles.

3. The prisoners were forced to drag themselves naked through a "pool" full of hammer-broken rocks over which was hung, at a height of about one foot, a strong steel net to keep them from standing. They were made to crawl between the net and the rocks several times during the interrogations.

Back in Los Angeles, we met with Juan Mendez from Americas Watch. Tortured during the reign of terror in Argentina, Juan, a lawyer, became a respected champion of human rights. His encouragement stirred the beginnings of what became the California Committee of Human Rights Watch. Jane Olson, whom I'd met in Nicaragua, had been working with Reverend George Regas, Rabbi Leonard Beerman, and Harold Willens against the development of nuclear weapons. Stanley Sheinbaum, who had organized the campaign for Daniel Ellsberg, was, with his wife Betty, deeply involved in virtually every major civil and human rights issue since the early days of the Vietnam War. Dedicated to making America live up to its principles, this group inspired many to emulate its efforts.

The Committee of Concern for Central America put together a series of town meetings coordinated by Donald "Buddha" Miller, Jackson Browne's manager. Featuring the talents of Jackson, Bonnie Raitt, and Peter, Paul and Mary, the meetings attracted media and crowds across the country. And we had a ball. Robert Foxworth, Diane Ladd, Martin Sheen, Howard Hesseman, Edward Asner, Michael Douglas, René Auberjonois, and I spoke to huge gatherings in L.A., Chicago, Atlanta, Washington, D.C., and New York. We were joined by Studs Terkel in Chicago, Julian Bond and Andrew Young in Atlanta, former CIA agent David MacMichael and former Reagan consular officer Wayne Smith in Washington. In Atlanta we were invited to the

Carter Center, where former President Jimmy Carter expressed support and lamented the cruel and shortsighted policies of his successor.

Though it's impossible to quantify the impact of the movement, many in Central America believe our combined efforts stopped a Vietnam-style military involvement in El Salvador and stripped away the façade of respectability shielding the Contras in Nicaragua.

Through all this, I still had to make a living. I showed Marvin a story I had always loved but hadn't been able to get moving. It came in over the transom, among the thousands of letters I received during the M*A*S*H years, from a young ex-Marine who wanted to be a writer but couldn't get anyone to read his stuff. Though his first story didn't work as a film, I encouraged him to keep writing. A few months later, his second story, a tale of orphaned fraternal twin brothers, captivated me. One was brain damaged and quite simple while the other was a brilliant, highly motivated medical student faced with the dilemma of what to do about his brother if he got the prized internship he sought and had to leave him. It was *Dominick and Eugene*. I loved everything about it. Marvin did, too.

Motivated again, I called Sean Penn, whom I had met years earlier through his father, Leo, a director on *The Interns*. Sean loved it and wanted to play Nicky, the brain-damaged twin. He said that Orion Pictures was interested in working with him and that he'd like to show it to them. It really does happen that way sometimes.

Meetings were set up, and before we knew it we had a deal to develop a script. Making a movie is a long and arduous process. It had been nine years since Bill Blinn, who originally selected me for the role in *The Interns*, and I optioned the story from Danny Porfirio in the late '70s. Bill graciously opted out when Marvin and I decided to make a run at it.

Corey Blechman, who scripted the award-winning television drama *Bill* for Mickey Rooney, wrote the first draft. It got some of what we wanted, but still lacked the grittiness in the brothers' lives. Sean then wanted to rewrite it himself. If we liked what he wrote, we had a deal. If not, we were out nothing (except probably our star). Sean left to spend some time with his then-wife Madonna, and when we next heard from him, he had rewritten the story completely, as promised. But while Sean's version had the grit, it lost much of Nicky's innocence and the simple beauty of the brothers' dilemma, becoming a darker story. Realizing that we might lose our star, Marvin and I gritted our teeth and told him his version didn't work for us and we wanted Corey to try again. Sean wasn't interested in the direction we were going, so, as feared, we lost him—and, we thought, probably our deal with the studio.

But Orion stayed with us. Mike Medavoy and Jon Sheinberg still believed in the picture, felt confident we'd find another actor, and gave us the go-ahead to revise the script. We were thrilled. Corey improved the screenplay, but still not to our satisfaction. We sent the new draft to the studio and got a call to come to the office. Medavoy, Orion's West Coast partner, greeted us by saying, "Come on in, the boys are here." In the next room, we were greeted by Arthur Krim, Eric Pleskow, and Bill Greenberg, the other three heads of the studio. All congratulated us, extolled the virtues of our script and hailed it as the next *Marty*, a classic they had made years earlier.

The next half hour was an experience never to be repeated. The four kept raving about the script and I kept thanking them but insisting that, as good as it was, it still needed work. Medavoy said he had sent it to Milos Forman, the brilliant, academy award–winning director of *One Flew Over the Cuckoo's Nest* and *Amadeus*. Thrilled, but worried, we said we intended to produce the picture and expected to be making those decisions. But nothing would dampen their enthusiasm. They were ecstatic!

Waiting for the elevator after the meeting, I was floating. Marvin, with years of experience as an agent and producer, turned to me and asked: "Do you know how many times producers of a picture get to meet with the four heads of the studio?"

"No," I responded, "how many?"

"None!" he said emphatically. "And when the four heads of the studio are telling you how much they love your script, DON'T ARGUE!"

Much of the next year was devoted to putting *Dominick and Eugene* together. During a gap in the preparation, Marvin produced and I directed a little TV movie for CBS called *Run Till You Fall,* a sweet story written by Dan Wilcox, one of the writer/producers in M*A*S*H's later years. It starred my old M*A*S*H sidekick Jamie Farr, my beloved Shelley Fabares, and a youngster named Freddy Savage who went on to become a star in his own right.

D&E, as we came to think of it, was blessed from the beginning. Marvin and I fell in love with Robert Young, a sweet, passionate, enormously talented director. Bob brought in Alvin Sargent, one of the premier writers in the business and an incredibly generous, intelligent, and insightful man, to finish the rewrite, and we went to work looking for our actors. With Alvin's help, the script was now so good that we had to fight them off, including some rather big names, but Bob, Marvin, and I had the luxury of taking our time to find just the right people.

And then Tom Hulce walked into the office. Tom, a brilliant actor who had starred in *Amadeus,* was simply perfect, and we all saw it. Having him clearly in mind helped us agree that Ray Liotta, who had charmed us all when we met, was not only right for the part but that the two worked as fraternal twins. As we were agreeing to offer the part of Gino to Ray, who had gotten raves for the only movie he had done thus far, Jonathan Demme's *Something Wild,* I decided that I ought to do my homework first. I hadn't seen the Demme film, so I arranged for a copy to watch at home. Ray was so nuts and so powerful in the picture that he scared the hell out of me, scared me so much that I decided I had to meet with him again. It was clear he had the power to be the protective brother, but I needed to be reassured that he could play the gentle side of Gino as well. Marvin, Bob, and I met with him again, and I laughingly apologized, saying the rage he brought to the character in *Something Wild* had so frightened me that I wanted to make sure the other side of him was available, too. Ray was wonderful. He laughed and said he understood. He talked about him-self and his life in such an open and utterly guileless manner that my concerns were put to rest and I was once again completely charmed.

We met a number of lovely and talented actresses, both in New York and Los Angeles, for the part of Gino's romantic interest, but I kept insisting that Jamie Lee Curtis was the one. I had seen her on a talk show and found her to be captivating. Smart, sexy, gorgeous, she just hadn't yet had the career opportunity, as far as I was aware, to put it all together. And after we met a number of candidates, I'm happy to say we all agreed that Jamie was the one.

We shot the picture in Pittsburgh, Pennsylvania, mostly down in the Southside area, where we were welcomed like family. Not many pictures had been done there at that point, and locals came to the set to watch and say hello, bringing cookies, cakes, and goodies for the cast and crew. It was a fabulous experience. We used wonderful actors, some from New York, some from L.A., and some we found locally, and filled the featured roles with great talents like Bill Cobbs, David Strathairn, and Todd Graff.

The experience is full of special memories for me, but I'll mention only a couple. We needed a baby for a very important role and wanted to cast twins in order to accommodate sleeping, feeding, and shooting schedules. As we were about to proceed, we learned that Pennsylvania had a law against children under six working. It was well intended, of course, arising from a desire to keep children from being exploited, but if adhered to strictly, it meant we simply couldn't shoot here. In researching the law and trying to figure a way out of the dilemma, I learned that the man now in charge of the state's labor ministry happened to be someone I had met when involved in a polit-ical campaign years earlier. After a single phone call, Minister of Labor Harris Wofford came to see us in Pittsburgh. He understood the situation immediately and arranged for a special permit to allow us to hire the local twins. One of the founding spirits of the Peace Corps, Harris later became a U.S. senator from Pennsylvania and now leads a national effort on behalf of America's youth.

Then the legal department from the studio called to say we couldn't use the name of our primary character. Their research revealed that there was a real Domenico Luciano in Pittsburgh, and they informed us that we would have to change Nicky's name.

"That's absurd!" I said. "We can't change Nicky's name! That's Nicky's name!" We'd been living with it for years, and it was simply impossible to consider changing it.

"Well, sorry," replied the legal eagle, "but that's the way it is." They wouldn't use a character name if someone living in the area actually had that name because they could be sued.

I couldn't believe it. I argued, but he was adamant. I argued some more. He got snide, and I got really pissed. I hung up and stewed and fretted and talked to Marvin about it, and then we stewed and fretted together. That was Nicky's name, for Christ's sake. What the hell were they talking about?

Then I got an idea and called the lawyer back. "What if I got the real Domenico Luciano to say it was okay?"

He was nonplussed and stalled for a moment, then said, "He'll never do it."

"But what if he did? Would that make it okay for us to use the name?"

"He'd have to sign an affidavit to that effect, but he'll never do it."

"I'll get back to you," I said and hung up.

I looked up Mr. Luciano, who had a small pizza place out on the north side of Pittsburgh, got in my car, and drove out there. It was a little storefront place with just a few tables. I walked in and asked for Mr. Luciano. The young man I was talking to said, "Hey, aren't you that guy from M*A*S*H?" I said I was. He introduced himself as Mr. Luciano's son, and I knew we were going to be okay. He got all excited as I explained the situation, then went into the back and brought out his dad, a sweet older man who didn't speak much English. The young guy explained everything in Italian and pointed to me and nodded. Then Mr. Luciano looked at me, and soon they both were nodding and smiling. Before long the deal was done, and we were all sitting down and having spaghetti.

Before we started shooting, we took Tom to a dentist to see about getting a steel cap glued onto the face of one of his front teeth. The idea of Nicky having a cheap steel tooth had struck us all as a good way to depict the brothers' situation in a single stroke. As we were explaining to the dentist what we wanted, he said the way they usually put a cap on a tooth is to grind it down and cement it on permanently. Tom, who had been rehearsing with Ray and getting into the character, immediately said, "Okay, let's do that." Marvin and I quickly said, "No, no, Tom, that's not necessary," but he thought it would be a great idea and help him get into character. It could be repaired later, couldn't it? Tom was a truly incredible actor and a wonderful guy who, it seemed, would do almost anything to further the reality of the character and the situation. In this instance we prevailed, convincing him that much as we loved the picture, we didn't think it was worth ruining one of his teeth; the facing would be plenty realistic. (It fell off once, by the way, during a shot. Tom looked at me and said, "See, I told ya'!")

After we had shot for a week or two and were in love with the dailies we were seeing, Marvin and I stopped by Ray's apartment to say hello. When he opened the door to let us in, he seemed very uncomfortable, rather stiff and formal, nothing like the easygoing Ray on the set. After a couple of minutes of oddly strained conversation, we said we had just dropped by to tell him how thrilled we were with everything and to thank him for the work he was doing. In an instant you could see the tension go out of him like an untied balloon. Then he laughed and confessed that he feared we had come over to tell him we didn't like what he was doing and fire him. The insecurity of actors . . .

Jamie did wonderful work in the picture, and we kept trying to find more for her to do. The story was fairly clearly laid out, however, with the primary relationship being between the brothers, so it wasn't easy. Late one night Bob came up with an idea that knocked us out.

It was a beautiful coda to her character's relationship with Gino that involved her simply sitting on the curb outside their apartment, alone, quietly weeping. She did it wonderfully, blowing us all away. Unfortunately, when we cut the picture together, it just didn't fit—didn't "drive the story forward," to use Bob's phrase. We all hated to lose it, and I fear it hurt her feelings to have it left out. But try as we did, we couldn't justify leaving it in. The face—and in this case the beautiful scene—remained on the cutting room floor.

Bob, Marvin, and I had agreed early on that no major decision would be made without all three of us in agreement. The original end of the picture had Gino leaving his brother behind as he drove off to his prized internship, then, unable to do it, returning to get him so the two could go off together. I loved it. Somewhere during the filming, though, Marvin made the point that Nicky's growth would be much more clearly demonstrated if Gino did not come back, but rather was able to go off without him, trusting that his brother would be okay. I hated it. As we worked our way toward the shooting of that final scene, the momentum began to go against me, with Bob, Marvin, and even Alvin now in agreement that the boys should part. I fought, bitched, moaned, argued, and did everything but hold my breath until I turned blue, believing it was urgently important that the two stay together. And then at some point, I got it. They were right. As painful as it would be, Nicky's ability to send his brother off and be okay was dramatically powerful and thematically right. When the day came and we shot that goodbye scene, I wept through every take. And to this day, I can't watch the film—or for that matter talk about it at any length—without the tears.

It was a wonderful experience to make that picture, and I'm as proud of it as anything I've been associated with. If you haven't already seen it, go rent it.

I'd had my motorcycle brought out to Pennsylvania on one of the equipment trucks early in the shoot for the occasional weekend excursion, and when we wrapped, I decided to celebrate the end of filming by riding home. It was my first true cross-country motorcycle ride and the beginning of what has become a series of such adventures in different parts of the world. But that's a different story.

While Bob was editing the picture, I got to spend more time with Shelley and the kids, who were sprouting. Shelley was fair, clear, and straightforward with the kids, and we had pretty well worked our way through the inevitable period of adjustment. On one early occasion, when Shelley asked Mike to perform a household chore, he replied, "You know, since you married my dad, I feel like I've joined the Marines." But through her loving touch, the kids' forbearance, and increased communication and cooperation with Judy and Joe—who had married the year after Shelley and I—we continued to find our way along. Shuttling between two homes, each with its own set of personalities and rules, is a monstrous requirement for kids of divorce. After finding ourselves struggling to deal with the rigors of modern multi-marriage society and discovering a mutual willingness to put concern for the kids' welfare first, Judy, Joe, Shelley, and I agreed to a process quite unusual at the time: family therapy sessions involving both couples and the kids. Working together with a counselor, we were all able to air and deal with our problems in a safe and ultimately healing atmosphere. Given the histories involved, it was quite a strain at first, but our mutual commitment to the kids' welfare got us over the bumps and helped us work our way, over time, into what has become a close, mutually supportive and loving extended family.

One thing that did not get easier was the ever-increasing strain that Shelley and her sister Smokey were experiencing as a result of the steady mental deterioration of their mother, Elsa. What had begun as odd and seemingly eccentric behavior had become noticeably worse over time. No one seemed able to understand or explain it. After years of struggling to find an answer, with an increasingly troubled, frightened, and uncooperative Elsa making things ever more difficult, Shelley finally found a doctor who said that her mother had "multi-infarct dementia and probable Alzheimer's." Since little was known at the time about what to do for the condition, his only additional words were: "Good luck."

Shelley and Smokey struggled valiantly to comfort their mother and get her what help was available, but the process is brutal, degrading, and irreversible. The strain on the caregivers increases exponentially as the victim becomes lost to herself and to them. While I could do little but stand by and offer support, Shelley and Smokey were heroic.

In the fall, Margie finally decided she'd had enough of Washington and made good on her periodic threat to move to the West Coast. For us it was as though we had a new member of the family; for her it was panic time because she had no idea what she'd do out here. But in a few months she landed typically on her feet in a powerful spot in the middle of Hollywood's political world as Executive Director of the Hollywood Women's Political Committee (HWPC). From there she has gone on to great success and remains a wonderful friend, touchstone, and "political wife."

Once we had *D&E* together, things began to fall apart. Despite the big talk and all their loudly proclaimed support, despite the wonderful responses the picture got at test screenings, Orion blinked. They failed to give us the release we needed, changed the number of screens it would be shown on, opened it in areas where there had been no advance publicity, and generally fucked up what should have been a big hit. It hurt when Dustin Hoffman and Tom Cruise explored similar themes in *Rain Man* the same year, but those are the chances you take. If Orion had lived up to its promises, the world would have fallen in love with Nicky and Gino. Nevertheless, *Dominick and Eugene* will always be a classic for me.

Chapter 15

PROMISED LAND

On a trip to Washington to gather support from congressional members willing to take a stand on Central America, I met in Richmond, Virginia with Marie Deans, who had worked with Joe Ingle at the Southern Coalition on Jails and Prisons. Marie was now running the Virginia Coalition on Jails and Prisons, and needed help.

A soft-spoken, deeply spiritual woman, Marie was an advocate for the men on Virginia's death row. Offering counseling, advice, a willing ear and any help she could provide, she would not rest until the condemned had fully realized everything guaranteed by law or by God. The fact that she was asking for help—unusual for her—either meant time was running out or that there was something particularly meaningful about the case. This time it was both.

She took me to meet Joe Giarratano, an inmate with whom she'd been working for years. His appeals had about run out and he could soon die. As we drove toward the border with North Carolina, near which sat Mecklenberg Correctional Center and Virginia's death row, Marie explained that Giarratano had been convicted of the murder of two women—and the rape of one of them—with whom he shared a Norfolk, Virginia apartment in 1979. He had confessed, and even attempted suicide before his trial.

When she first met Giarratano, he was a twenty-six-year-old near-zombie from the Thorazine given as a result of the suicide attempt. After a few visits, she convinced him to get off the medication. Learning that he had waived his appeals at the suggestion of his mother, an act assuring his quick execution, she pressed him to reinstate them. Responding to her concern, he did.

Over time, Marie found Giarratano to be a sweet young man, equipped with a supple and open mind yet tortured by what he had done. He took an offered book and, a halting reader at first, soon demonstrated a keen if untapped intelligence. His eventual admission of a horrifically abusive childhood that left him a hopeless drug addict and alcoholic at the age of eleven explained his mother's support for a quick execution.

Leaving home, he had eventually found work as a waterman on the Virginia coast. The damage done by the abuse at home and the drugs and alcohol left him vulnerable to blackouts, and it was in one of these, he said, that he had raped and murdered.

Sometimes working, often not, Joe lived in an apartment in Norfolk with Toni Kline and her teenaged daughter Michelle. Without suggesting that they were prostitutes, he said men were always in and out of the apartment and drugs and alcohol were plentiful. One morning in February of 1979, he came out of a blackout to find himself in hell. Blood was everywhere, both women were dead, and he, the only one around, must have done it.

Horrified, he ran. But then, tortured by what he knew, he turned himself in, quickly putting his name to five separate confessions. After a quick trial, he was sentenced to death.

Working with the men on death row was both a calling and a way to deal with what Marie saw as a terrible social wrong. Seeing the value in those the state had dehumanized was as natural to her as breathing. Despite the contempt many felt for the inmates, Marie's simple decency and fundamental honesty won her some admirers, even a few converts. A documentary about her work inspired a German woman to provide funds for an investigation of Joe's background. If there was no history of violence, Marie might be able to get the death sentence reduced to life imprisonement.

Marie hired a retired police officer to go through Joe's past. When he called to report, she asked if they could argue that Joe was not a "future danger."

"Well, first things first," the investigator replied. "What about the fact that he's innocent?"

The five confessions had been coaxed out by the police, and his story didn't actually match the facts at the scene. Each time the police went to the prosecutor with a confession, another discrepancy had to be dealt with, another hole needed to be plugged: The murder weapon Joe described didn't square with the damage shown in the autopsy report. The stab wounds indicated a right-handed assailant; Joe was left-handed. The murder weapon was never found, though Joe said he had tossed it in the backyard. The driver's license of another man was found at the scene, along with bloody bootprints, hair, and fingerprints that did not match Giarratano. Marie arranged for experts on confabulated confessions to interview Joe and examine the evidence. Their conclusion: The confessions were false.

Joe had no memory of the crime. Awakening from a blackout and finding his friends dead, believing himself evil and worthless, he assumed he had done it. But had he? The investigator, and later Marie herself, came to believe he had not.

Joe proved to be more difficult to convince. Having made the initial leap, it took him quite awhile to come around to the possibility that someone else could have raped Michelle, killed both women, and left while he was passed out on the couch. But he agreed that the new evidence, including the discovery that the police were searching for another man when Joe turned himself in, should be tested in court.

However, things aren't that simple in Virginia. The state's "twenty-one-day rule" says no new evidence can be admitted more than three weeks after a verdict is rendered. Having gone down the road to the electric chair without questioning his own guilt for years, Joe was unable to get a court to hear this new information.

Marie worked every conceivable angle, browbeating attorney friends into doing pro bono work. But Virginia's attorney general was unmoved, rejecting every new motion on technical grounds, and Joe's time was running out.

Stirred by Marie's challenges, Joe read prodigiously and over time developed a remarkable comprehension of law and philosophy. In addition to acting as a key member of his own defense team, he helped eventually file lawsuits on behalf of fellow prisoners. One of those cases, *Giarratano vs. Murray*, became a legal landmark in the protection of death row prisoners' rights. When the largest death row escape in Virginia's history took place during that period, Joe, who could have gone with the six who left, not only stayed behind, but saved the life of a guard who had been held hostage. A subsequent lawsuit filed by the ACLU's Prison Project—ably aided by Joe—exposed miserable conditions and staff brutality, and resulted in the firing of the Mecklenberg prison's entire administration.

Marie believed Joe's only hope lay with Virginia's governor. The sole African-American governor in the U.S., Douglas Wilder was a studiously moderate Democrat not given to bucking the political tide. But enough attention to the case, she hoped, might get him to do the right thing despite the popularity of the death penalty in the state.

Mecklenberg was newer than Tennessee State Prison but the procedures were the same. After giving up our IDs, a series of locking checkpoints with electronically operated gates on either end created the claustrophobic effect of going ever deeper into the bowels of a submarine. On more than one occasion, Marie had been harassed by guards who closed the gate behind her and "forgot" to open the other, leaving her alone and vulnerable between the two.

Reaching the building that housed death row, we were ushered into a cage within a cage, literally a box with bars all around as well as above and below. Joe was brought down to meet us, shackles on his ankles, connected by a hobble-chain, and manacles on his wrists locked by a short chain to yet another around his waist. Once in the box, the guards locked us all in and reached through the bars to unlock the wrist manacles. He was still a young man, probably mid-thirties by now, maybe 5'9", hefty, with dark hair. He seemed somewhat shy and spoke with a slight hesitation, possibly a bit of a stammer, but was very appreciative of all Marie had done for him. Had he changed his mind? He said he was still a bit jumbled about it. Having believed for so long that he was guilty, it had taken some serious adjustment to look at another possibility. The new evidence definitely had him on the fence. He couldn't swear that he didn't do it because he didn't remember anything, but he agreed that a new trial was the right thing to do.

The visit went by quickly and soon the guard informed us that our time was up. Joe thanked me for coming and said that he appreciated anything I could to do to help Marie. I had the sense that he wasn't as concerned about my helping Marie help him, but rather helping her in *all* of her work. The clank of locks, clang of doors, chink of chains, and shuffle of feet provided the background music as he returned to his cell and we were led out into the yard and back into the world.

Later, I found myself thinking about Joe a lot. He certainly didn't seem the typical con, but it's hard to know. He didn't plead, and I didn't get the feeling he was hustling me. But this was a big one to get drawn into. After reading the material, I decided to compose a letter to Governor Wilder and circulate it to see if I could get people whose names would mean something to sign on. Hopefully, the attention would make the governor take note of the situation.

At home, *Coach*, a pilot Shelley had done for ABC, was picked up for the new season. She'd loved working with Craig T. Nelson, Jerry Van Dyke (who never fails to make me laugh), Bill Fagerbakke, and Clare Carey on the pilot and thought the show's creator, Barry Kemp, was a wonderful man and an extraordinary talent. It was thrilling to see her so happy. This business can be so cruel. With actors who are stars one moment unable to get arrested the next, there is a tendency to fear that our last job will be just that: our last. That fear sometimes leads to bad decisions, but Shelley had been patient and turned down things that didn't seem right. It appeared to have paid off.

* * *

As my letter about Joe circulated and endorsers began signing on, I was asked to be part of a human rights delegation to the Middle East, again put together by the Arca Foundation. It would be led by Ron Young, former Middle East Representative for the American Friends Service Committee and now Director of the U.S. Interreligious Committee for Peace in the Middle East. As in the past, the delegation included some with extensive experience in the region and others involved in promoting peace and human rights issues. Smith and Elizabeth Frawley Bagley were among the group members, as well as my friend Janet Shenk, who had taken Margie's position at Arca.

Peace and security in the Middle East hung on the issue of Israel and the Palestinians and had been a bitterly painful problem for years, with huge political ramifications in the States. The establishment of the Jewish State in 1948 was a highly controversial victory for a people whose legacy of statelessness and centuries of victimization, culminating in the Holocaust, had left deep psychological scars. Created by splitting a land inhabited by Palestinian Arabs for centuries, Israel's presence aggravated long-held antagonism and left the region in a state of constant tension. Determination, support from abroad, and military and technological advances have made Israel a powerful force, yet a peaceful resolution with its neighbors has been extremely difficult to achieve.

Despite a treaty with Egypt, and later with Jordan, a technical state of war still exists between Israel and many of her Arab neighbors, and the status of millions of Palestinian refugees remains unresolved. Israel's occupation of the West Bank and Gaza Strip since the 1967 War further fuels the tension. The Israeli right, coming to power under Menachem Begin, aggravated tensions with heavy-handed policies in the Occupied Territories: closing schools, sealing off villages, humiliating searches, imprisonment without charges. There were accusations of torture. The Palestinians responded with a form of rebellion known as an "Intifada," including a general strike, protests, market closings, etc. Debate has continued to rage within

Israel itself and in the U.S., particularly among the Jewish community, and our trip was likely to provoke controversy.

In early June we gathered at JFK and flew directly to Israel's Lod Airport. We were told not to have our passports stamped because an Israeli stamp would deny us entry into some of the Arab countries. Used to dealing with this issue, the Israeli immigration officers cooperated.

The land of the Bible has an impact all its own. The widespread use of a white stone in construction gives a unique glow to everything. I experienced mixed feelings as I walked around Jerusalem after we arrived. Certainly a holy land, it was just as clearly a land of huge tensions and great strain. In spite of the obvious military presence, people walked briskly and went about their business easily in cars and on buses. In our hotel, those who could stay awake heard a brief lecture describing the current "political map" of Israel. It was extremely complex. The "Green Line" meant to divide territorial Israel from the West Bank and the Gaza Strip had been breached. Israeli troops in those areas had created the "Occupied Territories." Israeli-approved "settlements" had sprung up throughout the territories with the encouragement and support of the government, with Jews, often armed, taking up residence in what Palestinians saw as their land. Deeply resented, the settlements were lightning rods for the violent expression of ever-increasing tension between the two people.

Our first morning included a visit to Yad Vashem, the memorial to the victims of the Holocaust. It was a deeply moving experience. No matter how many stories one hears or reads about the horrors of the Holocaust, nothing can prepare you for the physical evidence of that experience. Photographs, writings, artifacts bring one close to paralysis with a sense of shame for having been alive and unaware or unable to do anything about what was happening. It was overwhelming to come face-to-face with the evil of which men are capable, yet urgently important to recognize that the capacity exists in all of us.

We next met a very attractive woman, Dr. Sidra Ezrahi of Hebrew University, who offered a psychosocial overview of local culture.

According to Dr. Ezrahi, there were two schools of Jewish thought at play in the politics of Israel, both informed by the Holocaust and both under the slogan "Never again." In the first view, the horror of the Holocaust has sensitized Jews to the dangers of totalitarianism and tyranny to the degree that the state of Israel should be militant in protecting the rights and beliefs of all, ensuring that what happened to their people will never again be allowed to happen to anyone. Holders of the second view believe that because of the suffering of Jewish people in the past, the state of Israel should be impervious to criticism for doing what is deemed necessary in its own defense. This view is popular among the right-wing and the ultra-orthodox.

Ron took us to a small school where Israeli and Arab kids were brought together in an attempt to break the cycle of fear and hatred between them. He explained that just as the Arab kids have been taught to hate and fear Jews intent on destroying them, Jewish kids are learning the same in reverse. It would take time and a concerted effort to correct this mutual fear and loathing.

Meeting with members of the Knesset (Israel's parliament) brought us both of the viewpoints described by Dr. Ezrahi. Though I found more to sympathize with in the position of those who would make peace, I couldn't deny the passion and dedication of the hawks. It was nonetheless a bit disturbing to realize that some take the "chosen by God" position quite literally. As we left the meeting, I was approached by a settler who identified himself as an American member of Gush Emunim (Bloc of the Faithful), a radical right-wing ultranationalist sect. He said that he enjoyed M*A*S*H, which he could pick up on Jordanian television from his position near the border, but that he hated my support for those who would compromise one foot of Judea and Samaria (the West Bank), which he believed was granted to the Jews by God. Many of the most passionate settlers, I discovered, were deeply religious Orthodox Jewish Americans. Some were followers of Rabbi Moshe Levinger, an opponent of any peace settlement with Arabs, whom he considered "dogs." Others followed Rabbi Meir Kahane, American-born leader of a radical rightist group called Kach, which advocates "transfer," the forcible expulsion of Arabs from the Occupied Territories.

Later in the afternoon, we met with the American Consul General, who echoed the Reagan Administration's support for Israeli policies. Reagan had dropped any mention of Palestinian rights or self-determination, referring to Palestinians almost exclusively as refugees or terrorists and insisting that he would not recognize the PLO until it renounced terror and recognized Israel's right to exist. The Consul General even spoke favorably of naming Jerusalem the capital of Israel, an extremely inflammatory step, since the resolution of its status remains the subject of intense international and religious concern.

That evening we dined in Jerusalem with representatives of the Palestinian community who expressed indignation at their helplessness in the face of Israeli control. The oppression of Palestinians by the Israel Defense Forces (IDF) was outrageously cruel and inhumane, they said. With the "Iron Fist" or "bone-breaking" policy, the IDF was to take hold of stone-throwing protesters, including children, and break their arms or legs as immediate punishment. Other allegations included using rubber bullets in riot control, plowing up Palestinian farmers' olive trees, destroying the family home of anyone arrested for crimes against Israel, closure of their universities, and torture of those in custody.

The next morning we took a bus to the Gaza Strip, guided by two representatives of the U.S. branch of Save the Children. At the IDF checkpoint we broke into two groups in minivans and added representatives of UNRWA, the United Nations Relief and Works Agency formed to provide emergency aid—education, health care, and social services—to the Palestinian refugees. Since it was working in the Palestinian community, UNRWA was regularly accused of anti-Israeli/pro-Palestinian bias, though they steadfastly denied the charge.

The Gaza Strip was wrested from Egyptian control during the 1967 War and has remained in Israeli hands since that time. It houses over a million people in about six cities and eight refugee camps in a space approximately eleven kilometers—about six and a half miles—wide and forty kilometers—about twenty-four miles—long. Driving through it exposed Third World squalor and poverty on a level that jarred the senses of those of us just coming from a clean hotel and the relative modernity on the other side of the line.

Though denounced as a terrorist by the Israelis and the U.S. and thus an unacceptable negotiating partner, Yasser Arafat was clearly the most popular Palestinian leader and would easily win a popular election. The knot remains, however, since Arafat and the PLO refused to renounce their vow to drive the Jews into the sea and accept the State of Israel.

Our first stop was the UNRWA Health Center, where we heard from their director and a staff doctor. Describing their work and the plight of the people they served, one could see their fury at the treatment their charges received at the hands of the military government and the IDF. Driving on through Gaza City and into Khan Yunis Camp, the crowded conditions, crumbling buildings, and palpable tension took their toll. In Khan Yunis, we stopped at a demolished home beside which an old woman sat beneath canvas stretched over poles to protect against the sun. Partially paralyzed, she was the custodian for three grandchildren whose parents were in detention. The pile of rubble beside her dramatized the IDF policy of bulldozing or dynamiting homes, either to expand the roadways for military vehicles, or to punish those who had family members in the resistance. We met a teacher whose colleagues had been beaten in front of their students earlier that day. We were handed the remains of tear gas canisters that carried the markings of their Pennsylvania manufacturer. It became harder and harder to draw a breath.

In Rafah Camp, situated along the border with Egypt's Sinai Desert, we met with a cross-section of the Palestinian community: lawyers, doctors, the head of the Palestinian Red Crescent Society (the Islamic Red Cross), educators, the leader of a women's organization, a representative of the Near East Council of Churches, and various refugee camp officers. Their quiet outrage had more power than screaming and pointing fingers. I felt shame that there was so little we could do. The point of the Intifada, explained one, was to show the world that Palestinians were a people with legitimate national aspirations, an organized society with representative leadership. They wanted to make the occupation costly, morally and economically, and were doing so by relying on themselves rather than those outside. They wanted to attract the attention—and intervention—of international arbiters by confronting, without the use of weapons, the Middle East's biggest military power. Like everyone else, they wanted attention—and respect.

Before we left, a group of very young people told us of nets full of stones dropped by Israeli helicopters during demonstrations. They gave us a document that was simultaneously a cry for justice, a plea for fairness, and an indictment of the Israeli occupation—written in blood.

At Shifa Hospital we saw X-rays of skulls and other body parts penetrated by rubber bullets that the Israelis claimed were a humane, nonlethal response to rock throwing. As one doctor showed us, they were actually lead bullets with a rubber coating.

A child in one bed had casts on an arm and a leg. He had been in a demonstration, had thrown a rock, and was set upon by soldiers who broke his arm. And the leg? Days later, he was at home while another demonstration took place. Soldiers chasing the children came into his home and, seeing him with his arm in a cast, decided he had been one of the stone throwers and broke his leg.

Out of Gaza and into the West Bank, we drove through ancient Hebron, one of the oldest continuously inhabited cities in the world. Rabbi Moshe Levenger's community lived here, regularly expressing disdain for their Arab neighbors. On a hill above the city sat an incredible sight: a large walled compound of modern apartments. Having seen the rudimentary Israeli settlements in Gaza, I expected more of the same, but this was astonishing: a modern community, set apart from the city, that exclusively housed Jewish settlers. And as we headed back toward the Green Line, more of these huge modern settlements loomed on the hills.

The next day, we toured the Old City, an intoxicating experience for one raised on Bible stories. It's bewildering to stand near the empty stalls where Palestinian craftspeople would normally hawk their wares and realize you're on the Via Dolorosa where Christ is said to have carried his cross. To go inside a huge structure and find Golgotha, where the crucifixion occurred, is numbing.

Law in the Service of Man and the Council for Peace and Security are two Israeli groups working to establish peace with justice for the Palestinian people. A meeting with them offered hope. Later, though, Dr. Novick, Special Advisor to Foreign Minister Shimon Peres, said the Labor Party saw the Intifada heightening fears and increasing support for harsher measures by the IDF. He said a return to the pre-1967 borders as mandated in UN Resolutions 242 and 338 was out of the question, allowing that only as much as sixty-five percent of the Occupied Territories might eventually be returned to the Palestinians. These meetings reinforced our awareness of the blood knot connecting these people, locking them in a struggle for survival, groping for purchase, unable or unwilling to step back and consider the possibility of mutual accord.

That evening we flew to Cairo to meet Dr. Osama Al Baz, Special Advisor to President Hosni Mubarak. Though we were quite late, Dr. Al Baz was courteous and thoughtful, if very direct. A Palestinian state, he said, was an absolute requirement and steps must soon be taken toward its establishment. The important thing, he emphasized, was movement. Whether tied to Jordan for a few years or a transitional state supervised by an international presence, concrete progress was imperative.

The next morning we were on our way to Jordan. No grass grew on this trip! In Amman, we were transferred to a military helicopter provided by King Hussein and flown to Petra, a nearly 3,000-year-old city carved into the rose-colored sandstone of the Jordanian desert. Once situated, we left the hotel for the mile-long walk through a narrow gorge whose high, steep walls displayed a man-made aqueduct, one of the many relics of the Nabataean culture that developed the city. Coming out of the gorge into the opening of the valley, we were greeted by a huge structure in the opposite wall. "The Treasury" is one of a series of ornate tombs carefully carved into the walls of this astonishing place. Once covering hundreds of square miles and housing a population of over 30,000, Petra was a thriving center of trade at the hub of caravan routes a century before Jesus. Today it's an archaeological marvel, an Old Testament ghost town boasting living quarters and structures carved into the sandstone hills. An awe-inspiring sight, it was at once a relief from the intensity of the past few days and a profoundly moving reminder of the impermanence of our situation on Earth.

Returning to Amman, we met for dinner with representatives of the PLO who had been deported by the Israelis, and Rami Khouri of the *Jordan Times*. Khouri's view of the Middle East as a powder-keg was sobering. The Palestinians living in Jordan were a major source of pressure on King Hussein, whom he described as a highly intelligent, skilled, and moderate man faced with the nearly impossible task of maintaining a productive relationship with the U.S. and conducting ongoing negotiations with the Israelis, while simultaneously keeping the restive Palestinians mollified.

In the morning, we left by bus for Damascus, Syria. An hour out of Amman, we stopped at Jerash, once a majestic Roman city and still the site of some of the most well-preserved ruins in the region. Arches, columns, and temples surrounded by walls and partial structures dated back over 2,000 years. Many ancient cities are built upon even more ancient ruins of preceding civilizations. Under Jerash were the ruins of destroyed settlements of Bronze and Neolithic Age communities, all drawn to this valley irrigated by a beautiful stream. Walking the ancient stone street in the shadow of huge columns, I marveled at cuts in the stone beneath my feet made by the wheels of chariots thousands of years ago.

* * *

Foreign Minister Farouk al-Sharaa was not subtle. Syria was in the Soviet embrace and probably Israel's primary foe in the region. Their contest over the Golan Heights was decided by Israel's seizure of the area in the 1967 War and codified by a Separation of Forces Agreement in 1974. Al-Sharaa, a handsome man with a bitter cast to his mouth and angry eyes, was the most outspokenly anti-Israeli official I had yet encountered, referring to the country as "the Zionist entity." When asked if Syria would support a two-state solution to the Palestinian problem, Al-Sharaa hinted that they might but would not say so officially because the Israelis would "take advantage" of it. Syria would support an international conference on the subject only if Israel would agree to withdraw to the pre-1967 borders, a position that means the return of the Golan Heights.

Vice President Abdul Halim Kaddam was more politic. Most things are negotiable, he maintained, with the exception of land and national independence. He talked of Syria's advances and held out hope for a peace agreement. He wished for "objectivity" from the U.S., if not neutrality, and cautioned that Jordan could not, by itself, resolve anything. A peace agreement between Jordan and Israel that did not include Syria might even increase tensions.

During a gathering at the home of David Ransome, the American Chargé d'Affaires, we got word that a hoped-for meeting with George Habash was possible if we'd come right away. After racing through Damascus' drizzly streets, we descended dark stairs to the offices of the Popular Front for the Liberation of Palestine (PFLP). Dr. George Habash, a large man with thick, graying dark hair and mustache, ushered us into an office festooned with pictures, flags, and banners of Palestine and his many campaigns. Though there were weapons around, there was no sense of threat.

Dr. Habash and his family were forced from their home in the 1948 war that established the state of Israel, and he has worked since that time to right the wrongs committed against the Palestinians. Involved for years with Gamal Abdel Nasser in the pan-Arabist United Arab Republic (UAR), he helped establish the more radical

PFLP after the Israeli successes in the 1967 War. At its helm ever since, he had plotted, planned and carried out airline highjackings, kidnappings, and other acts of terrorism against Israel. For all that, Habash treated us well and was surprisingly open. If not amiable, he was certainly straightforward. To our surprise, he said he was now willing to support a true peace agreement with Israel in exchange for the establishment of a state of Palestine. He was not happy, arguably would never be, with the power and success of the Israeli state, but he was willing to live with it in exchange for a fair settlement. When asked what he would do if the peace process was not successful, he said he would continue to work for justice for the Palestinian people. "By what means?" one of our group inquired. Echoing Malcom X, he replied, "By any means necessary."

(Years later, those words came up again in a very different context. At the Sheinbaum home in Los Angeles, an official from the Israeli consulate cited the meeting, quoted Habash, and said his "by any means necessary" threat justified the hard line his Likud party was then taking. Astonished at the assertion, I challenged him, saying I had been there when the remark was made. Habash had responded to a hypothetical question. He did not urge violence. It was not a threat and it was unfair to misuse his words for political advantage.)

The next morning, we flew back to Amman. In contrast to the antiquity of Egypt and Syria, Amman is very much a modern Arab metropolis. It reflected King Hussein's dedication to raising the living standard of his people and his determination to make Jordan a meaningful player in the modern world.

Unlike the Israeli emphasis on security, virtually all Arab officials were focused on solving the Israeli/Palestinian problem, with most agreeing that the answer was a separate Palestinian state or entity. While the Israeli position made sense from the perspective of a people who were, or believed they were, under attack, it also perpetuated the very conditions that exacerbated the resentment responsible for the problem.

Jordan's Foreign Minister Taher al Masri was instructive on this point. He insisted that the principle of self-determination was a right of all Palestinians, and that UN Resolutions 242 and 338, the fundamental premises for solving this riddle, did not address the root question of Palestinian identity. The U.S. refused to make reference to a Palestinian people, offering only to discuss the "political future" of the refugees without recognizing them as an identifiable group with a legitimate demand for statehood. For al Masri—and for Jordan—the principle of self-determination was paramount.

Adnan Abu Odeh, advisor to King Hussein, thought a peace agreement was in the long-term best interests of Israel, Jordan, and the Palestinians. The question of Jerusalem, he insisted, could be solved relatively easily once it was separated out. For reasons of "history, religion and prestige," he said, it could not belong to one group or state. If the walled city was internationalized, the Israelis could have West Jerusalem and everything west of it, the Arabs East Jerusalem and the land to its east. The U.S., if it chose, could have one embassy in West Jerusalem and one in East Jerusalem.

Jordan's Crown Prince Hassan was quite remarkable. Younger than his brother, heavier and balding, he spoke eloquently and knowledgeably about the history and situation of the region. He was sadly prophetic: "We should not lose hope for an international conference. The alternative is conflict, and the conflict is likely to involve fundamentalism, whether Muslim, Jewish, or whatever. Fundamentalism is confrontational, and centrism cannot survive in confrontationalism." The Jordanians, he said, "could be the only party in the process talking about people. [Secretary of State George P.] Schultz says one thing in Israel, and then before coming here he says, "the three no's." Hassan suggested a bipartisan commission to examine the issue from the point of view of the people of the Occupied Territories, an urgent need that had yet to be met.

At a dinner sponsored by Jordan's World Affairs Council, business and academic leaders expressed the fear that the "transfer" (forced evacuation) of all Palestinians from the Occupied Territories was inevitable and would destabilize Jordan.

A woman told a story with profound implications for today. After a young man had been killed by soldiers in the West Bank, an ad in the local newspaper said that the family of the deceased would be at home at a specified time and date—to receive *congratulations*.

The next morning, we took a bus to the border, across the storied Jordan River, through the rigorous Israeli security check, the West Bank, and into Israel. Back in our hotel, we met with more Israelis and Palestinians dedicated to ending the occupation. We all yearned to believe that a solution was possible, but agreed that there was little hope of resolution without the even-handed involvement of the world community, led by the U.S. And that, given the politics at home, remained highly problematic. Back in the U.S., I wrote out some brief observations ("Middle East Trip, June '88," see www.mike-farrell.org/Journals/middleeast.html). How tragic to realize that although they are from a trip to the region nearly twenty years ago, so many of these points still apply.

In December, with the Reagan Administration lacking the courage to do it, Stanley Sheinbaum led a delegation of five American Jews to meet Yasser Arafat in Stockholm, Sweden, and persuaded him to publicly renounce violence and accept the state of Israel. Arafat did, a dramatic step he then followed with a more fulsome statement before the UN, where he not only renounced violence and accepted Israel but also accepted UN Resolutions 242 and 338. This laid the groundwork for the Oslo Accords. It was an incredibly courageous thing for Stanley to do, and the reaction was predictable. He was lauded internationally and became the subject of terrible attacks and threats of death from certain corners at home. I was very proud to call him friend.

Chapter 16
FATHER

I watched proudly as Mike graduated from high school. With all the potential anyone could ever hope to possess, he wasn't yet clear about his direction, so decided to work for a year rather than go straight to college. Having missed college myself, I was of two minds about it. If he went on to school, he'd be the first in my family to do so. But having only an intellectual sense of what college would actually mean in a young person's life, I didn't press, feeling it might be better for him to take the time to think about it.

On the career front, I got a role in an interesting and potentially controversial picture dealing with incest and murder. A true story, *A Deadly Silence* had to be handled carefully. A high school girl hired a fellow student to murder her father, who had been sexually abusing her for years, dicey material for 1988. On the set, the author was very protective of her work, while the network folks were nervous about how it would be received by the press. John Patterson, a laid-back guy with whom I would later work on *Providence*, directed. The producer, Robert Greenwald, was a man I admired and would end up working very closely with against the Iraq War some years later.

Meanwhile, our letter to Governor Wilder had gathered an impressive list of endorsers, and Marie arranged a press conference in Richmond to announce the campaign to save Joe Giarratano from the electric chair. We presented our case and carried the letter, a petition, and endorsements from local figures to the governor's office. Although we were not invited to meet with the governor, we got a lot of press. In the following months, I bounced back and forth to meetings and press conferences in Virginia, and continued to meet with Joe. The better I got to know him, the more I liked and believed in him. As he saw it, going to prison probably saved his life. There's little question that the thoughtful, well-read young man he had become would never have surfaced without meeting Marie. He was a living demonstration that rehabilitation was possible. The irony, of course, was that all the state wanted to do was kill him.

Ultimately, we managed to break beyond Virginia's borders to national, then international notice. Initially limited to rallies, petitions, benefits, radio and TV talk shows and press conferences, a swelling tide of support for justice in the case from politicians, celebrities, newspaper columnists, and international figures eventually led to a meeting with the governor's legal advisor.

In early 1989, the California Committee of Human Rights Watch came into being. Stanley and Betty Sheinbaum, Jane Olson, Rabbi Beerman, and I, along with other friends, acted as a local board of directors. Ellen Lutz, a lawyer with expertise in international law and coauthor of a book on torture, was our first director. Jane, a prime mover in the campaign to end the nuclear arms race, and Stanley were our co-chairs.

Around this same time, I came in contact with the Cult Awareness Network (CAN) in Chicago. As the name suggests, CAN was trying to provide good, clear information—and with it hope—for victims and family members of the Moonies, Scientology, Rajneesh, and other cults. Having had only a modicum of contact with these kinds of groups, I was impressed with the effort CAN made to distinguish destructive cults from other organizations that, while perhaps eccentric, don't destroy personalities, exploit weakness for sexual or financial advantage, imprison people, or otherwise smother lives. A small group on a tight budget, CAN helped cult victims and their families, offered referrals to therapists and self-help organizations, educated the media, and sometimes brought matters to the authorities.

Initially contacting them for a film project, I became fascinated by their work. The care taken by CAN's Executive Director, Cynthia Kisser, particularly impressed me. Given our society's commitment to freedom of speech and association, CAN faced an uphill struggle in getting people to see the danger in mind-controlling cults. Many simply don't believe that individuals or groups have developed the ability to seduce young, lonely, troubled, or naïve "seekers" into giving up their autonomy and ensnaring themselves in a world where they become tools of the leader or guru and are abused financially, sexually, or otherwise. CAN seemed like a good organization to help.

In the spring of 1989 I got a call from Bill Dale, who had been commissioned by the National Council of Churches to make a documentary film about Liberation Theology and the situation of people of faith in the war in El Salvador. Bill knew of my experience there and asked me to host the film. I was excited to go back and decided to bring my kids. So much of my time and attention had gone to El Salvador that Mike and Erin were curious about it and I thought it would be good for them to see how others live in our world. My friend Tom Callaway agreed to come along to keep an eye on the kids in case anything untoward happened.

Things went south—pun intended—the minute we landed. No baggage. What a pain in the ass to get somewhere, particularly somewhere hot and humid, and be without a change of clothing. "Sorry," was all anyone could say. "Maybe tomorrow." Maybe? Unable to get any help, we shrugged and headed for the city with Gene Palumbo, an old friend and freelance reporter who was our guide.

Rolling down the same highway where a few years earlier bodies were being left boldly on display, Gene gave Tom and the kids a sense of the place. In the four years since my last visit, little had changed. Passing the slums and moving into the city, armed guards still posted in front of the residences of the wealthy, I asked Gene about a Chevy wagon with smoked glass that had been behind us for a while. "Yeah," he said, "I've been watching them." Erin and Mike had heard stories about the death squads and got a bit nervous, but Gene laughed it off. "Nothing to worry about. It's probably just a coincidence. It could be a message, Mike, just letting you know that they know you're here, but if so, they won't do more than hang around." I don't know if that satisfied anyone, but our minds were eased when the car turned onto another road.

The Camino Real, where we'd always stayed in the past, hadn't changed. As we arrived, a car pulled in beside us and a man stepped out carrying a large automatic weapon. He stood with it at the ready as his passenger went into the hotel. "Welcome to San Salvador," I laughed.

Bill Dale and Bert Whittier, the writer of the piece, now entitled *La Lucha* ("The Struggle"), welcomed us. Gene had arranged for us to shoot (perhaps not the best word under the circumstances) on a small cooperative called Tres Ceibas, just outside the city. We'd start first thing in the morning, which gave us time to go across to the *supermercado* and get some clean underwear, toothbrushes, and other necessities.

Not wanting to create trouble for the project, we didn't set up any meetings. We'd make a few stops whenever there was time, but it was safer not to stir things up. My great regret now is that we didn't go up to the UCA and see the Jesuits—those incredibly brave priests we had always relied on in the past—who would be brutally murdered by the Salvadoran military just a few months later.

The day at Tres Ceibas was a perfect example of life in El Salvador. The people were typically warm and generous, thoughtful, industrious, and anxious to help. The leader of the community, a quiet, powerfully built man, gave no sign of concern at our presence, despite the fact that, as Gene told us, he'd already been tortured because of suspected guerrilla sympathies. There was no interference as we did our work, but a stir arose with the news that our host's brother had been picked up by the military. We offered to pack up and leave, but he insisted we stay. We asked Gene to make sure, but the man was confident the incident was completely unrelated to our presence; it was the usual harassment. So, nerves raw, we kept at it. Erin got a bit too much sun, and a young woman put her in a hammock and sat fanning her until she cooled off. When we finished, I gave my Swiss Army Knife to our *compañero*. It might not stand up to the kind of jobs he'd subject it to, but I wanted to show my appreciation in some way. From the first days in camps so many years ago, I've always found Salvadorans to be amazingly sweet, eager to be helpful, and grateful for any positive attention.

When Bill and Bert went off to do some stuff that didn't involve me, I took Tom and the kids around. We visited a wretched shanty-town on the edge of the city beside a dump. The conditions boggled the mind. Families lived in dirt-floored cardboard shacks propped up with odd pieces of wood scrounged from wherever they could find it. Filthy children played in the dump, rooting for things they—or perhaps the family—could eat, sell, or use. Despite it all, a sweetness emanated from the toothless smiles of women older than their years framed in the doorways of their junkyard homes, their children waving shyly from behind them. Up the hill, a school, maintained by money from the church, was led by the young Padre Jimmy, a *Norte Americano* hero intent on letting these kids know they weren't invisible. Love, attention, and respect. It's amazing how simple—and powerful—it can be.

Another stop was Bethania, the camp just outside the city. As always, the sights and sounds of the children broke our hearts. Tom noted that the one toy the kids had to play with—and they did so with joy—was a rubber ball. He couldn't get over the fact that this ball they were joyously running with and kicking and tossing about was flat.

The journey finally over, I again encountered the re-entry phenomenon, but this time it was shared. We all knew what we had seen. Sharing it made the burden lighter.

After having some time to reflect, Mike decided to try college at San Diego State, even though he still didn't know what he was interested in studying. And, just as my son was leaving home, I got a job that would be shot out of the country. Being given a first-class ticket to a foreign land and offered a chance to live there for weeks on someone else's dime has always been part of the fantasy of being an actor for me. Except for the lousy timing with Mike's departure for school, this new job was a dream. It gave me the opportunity to live in London and work with Bob Foxworth again, our first time since *Questor.* Since Mike would not be far from home, I could check in when I got back, so he forgave me for not being there to see him off.

Shelley was able to come over for a couple of weeks in the middle of the shoot, making it even more fun. The picture, *The Price of the Bride,* wasn't particularly notable except for an incident during shooting that always makes me smile. TV movies are all about the money, which means getting the job done on time. The budget is always very tight, and keeping to the schedule is key. If you run into problems, it can be a nightmare, so you can generally tell if things aren't going well by the increasingly harried look on the faces of those watching the clock. The director for this production, Tom Clegg, was a nice guy, a very good technician, and extremely focused on the schedule. Bob and I, along with a terrific British actor named Peter Egan, were clearly able to do the work, so Tommy didn't spend much time with "interpretation." We'd come into a new situation, talk it over briefly, block out the scene, and take a seat as the crew set everything up. Then we'd come back in and shoot it. Tommy would then swipe his hands together as if to say, *That's it, we've got it,* and move on.

On one particularly harried day, Tommy needed to accomplish a critical scene with limited shooting space. There was no room to maneuver the camera. As he told us the problem, he kept glancing over his shoulder at the hovering assistant director who was looking at his watch. Could Bob possibly do it from here? "Sure." "You can?" "Sure." "Wonderful, wonderful, but then, Mike, that would mean you'll have to . . ." "No problem, Tommy." "Really?" "No problem at all. And I can use this line to move around to here." "Really? Oh, that's bloody good; then I won't have to move the camera! Bob, you're okay with that?" "Sure." "Mike?" "Yup." "Then we've got it." Swiping his hands in his *That's it* gesture, he started out of the room. "Whoa, Tommy!" Bob and I yelled, just as he got to the door. "We do still have to shoot it." We all roared with laughter as he said, "Oh, yes. Right! Right you are!" and headed back into the room.

During the shoot, I was invited to meet with a local group opposed to U.S. involvement in Central America. It was a nice home in the Mayfair section of Central London, and a pretty good crowd was on hand. As angry as I was about Reagan's policies, I was totally unprepared for the anti-American vitriol spewed by some in the group. I particularly remember the playwright Harold Pinter giving voice to some of the most cynical assertions I'd yet heard about the history of U.S. expansionism, the insanity of its anti-Communist hysteria, and the brutality of its outreach. It was an interesting lesson. Though I shared their opposition to the policy, I was deeply offended by the absence of any awareness of the hard work being done by citizens and leaders in our country to set things right. There seemed to be a need to lump us all into one thoughtless, heartless, exploitive, self-indulgent mass. I didn't like it. For me, America is an ideal, an experiment, and for all the extraordinary things we've accomplished as a nation—and there are many—we haven't yet lived up to that ideal. But that doesn't make us the monsters that Pinter and the others were painting us to be. It's a mistake to ascribe the stupidity and arrogance of those in power at a given time to the entire country and condemn all as a result. America may or may not be the last best hope of the world, but it is without question the most powerful nation on the globe today, and it has at its core the most humane and forward-looking principles known to mankind. We can't throw away the promise of America because some arrogant fear-mongers currently have their hands on the reins. Let's get their hands off the reins and let the values that have inspired people the world over lead us toward the heights we know we're capable of reaching. I tried to say that to Pinter and the others at the meeting. What came out, I'm not sure, but I left there knowing that we had a lot of work to do to regain our place as the beacon of hope for the world.

Once back in the States, Marvin and I got the go-ahead to make another movie, one of the first for Turner Network Television (TNT), Ted Turner's company. The idea grew out of my 1976 tromp through the New Hampshire snow with Jim Hightower, campaigning for Fred Harris. "It's the smell of money"—the comment justifying the awful odor from the pulp mill in otherwise beautiful Berlin, New Hampshire—struck me at the time, then was repeated word-for-word a few years later in a rancid-smelling town in Oregon. Our story presented the dilemma faced when a man discovers that the company providing the economic mainstay for his community is secretly poisoning the environment, spewing chemical waste into the local water. In our story, his child dies as a result. Once he uncovers the problem, he can't get the company to take responsibility to fix it and his neighbors and the authorities won't help because of the company's economic clout. We said that a decent person, faced with these circumstances, could become frustrated enough to deal with it himself.

It turned out to be a pretty damned good movie, if I do say so myself. Michael Pressman directed a lovely script written by Albert Ruben, and we put together a terrific cast, including Tess Harper and Helen Hunt, to tell Al's version of the story my friend David Reiss and I had sketched out. Of course, nothing is easy in this business. The original version of the story we pitched to Ted Turner had our leading man go to the offending plant, order everyone out, and blow the place up. Ted loved it. As we got going, however, Turner's minions got cold feet and decided that our hero shouldn't commit a violent act. We fought, insisting it was an appropriate response under the circumstances and that he was willing to stand his ground and take the consequences. But they had the wallet. Our negotiations ended in a compromise, with my character instead taking a sledgehammer to the offending machinery. Oh well . . .

We had a good time putting the picture together, only to run into more problems with Ted's new executives before it was aired. First, they didn't like the name: *The Smell of Money*. They tested titles and came up with *Incident at Dark River*. I hated it, but that's what it would be called. Next, they expressed concern about some of the language in the film. By today's standards, it was laughable: a few "Gods," "hells," and "damns." We said the language was appropriate and would not, in context, be offensive. Cable organizations don't have the same restrictions on language as do the broadcast networks, but the new executive, Scott Sassa (who went on to become the head of NBC TV in the '90s), had a sudden concern for his audience's sensibilities. After a long debate, we prevailed, or so we thought. All was agreed, and the picture was locked, meaning that nothing could be changed without a great deal of effort and expense. When I proudly watched the premier broadcast, however, the dialogue was interrupted a number of times by scratchy little sounds that blocked out certain words. Despite our agreement, Sassa'd had the "offending" words removed—without telling us about it or even having the decency, if it had to be done, to let us do it correctly. We were furious and let him have it, using a few of the words he had bleeped and several others for good measure. He later apologized, but the damage had been done.

Chapter 17
STALEMATE

etween jobs and trips, I stayed with the Giarratano campaign,
working the phones, doing radio and TV interviews, and flying to Richmond for meetings. Joe's lead attorneys at this
point were Dick Burr and Steve Hawkins from the NAACP Legal
Defense Fund (LDF). Dick, a soft-spoken Southerner, had been
fighting the death penalty for years and would go on to become one
of the preeminent death penalty defense attorneys in the country.
Steve Hawkins, a young African-American out of Harvard and the
NYU School of Law, later left the LDF to head the National
Coalition to Abolish the Death Penalty. They generously made me
part of the defense team so I could have access to prison visits, strategy sessions, and the meetings they were now having with Governor
Wilder's legal advisor, Walter "Mac" McFarlane. Mac was a thoughtful, careful man who appeared to be playing it fairly straight, but no
one knew for sure whether he was more focused on doing justice or
protecting the governor.

Then out of the blue, I received two intriguing—and seemingly
conflicting—invitations. The first came from Senator Christopher
Dodd on behalf of the National Democratic Institute for
International Affairs, asking me to be part of an election-monitoring
delegation to observe the upcoming vote in Czechoslovakia. The
second, from the PAX World Foundation, was to join former Senator
Charles Percy and my friend former Congressman John Anderson on
a "Mission for a Just Solution in the Middle East." I reviewed the
proposed schedules and saw that I could just finish the Middle East
trip in time to hop over to Prague. My brain was in a spin, but

Shelley said it was too good an opportunity to pass up, so I signed on for both.

In late May we gathered in Washington, D.C. for briefings by the State Department and consular officers from the countries we'd be visiting. State's assurances that the U.S. was acting as an honest broker in the region didn't square with what I'd seen two years before, but I held my tongue. Our group was larger than the earlier delegation and heavily weighted toward clergy of various denominations. Rabbi Bob Marx from Chicago was a chess player and brought a portable set, hoping to find a patsy. I said I'd give it a go, and we ended up having our very own traveling international chess tournament. Mike Beard, founder of the National Coalition to End Gun Violence, was part of the group and had recommended me. I had done some work with Mike over the years and admired him. Another member, a young lawyer from Baltimore named Rick Schaeffer, was a family friend of Alan Alda's. We had a lot to talk about and became good friends.

This trip followed a different route, touching down first in Damascus, then Cairo, on to Amman, and finally into Israel and the Occupied Territories. Unfortunately, little had changed. While the very tentative talks between the U.S. and the PLO continued to offer a slim ray of hope, they were not viewed positively by the Shamir government and had done little to calm tensions in the region.

Damascus seemed brighter and less forbidding than I remembered. After getting the lay of the land from Ambassador Djerejian and suffering through another, blessedly short, session with the snide Foreign Minister Farouk al Sharaa, our primary meeting was with President Hafez al Assad himself. Known for "Hama rules" and a fierce grip on authority, Assad was surprisingly affable in our meeting. He could afford to be. Charming a party of Americans would be good for his image. He allowed any questions and answered all, giving the impression of one seeking to find a way to resolve the region's problems peacefully. These guys don't get to be where they are by accident.

A bus trip to a hospital on the edge of the Golan Heights was yet another lesson. Israeli military outposts visible across the hills made clear the strategic significance of the position, overlooking as it did the kibbutz and farms in the Galilee below. Inside the now deserted hospital, we were shown signs of destruction supposedly caused by Israeli troops who had overrun the Heights and then the hospital, shooting up the place in the process. Holes in the walls from machine-gun fire infuriated some in our group, but something about the scene troubled me. Questioning the guide, I pointed out that the holes were in a quite regular pattern and continued into and down around the walls of a flight of stairs. "How could somebody shoot into these walls without being caught by ricochets from his own weapon?" The guide had no answer. Suspicious, I persisted and finally learned from someone with a less jaundiced view that the holes in the walls were from rivets that had once held huge decorative ceramic pieces in place. No Israeli machine-gun fire had raked the halls of that hospital. It's hard, when trying to sort these things through, to separate out the passion and keep your eyes on the ball.

A meeting with the Grand Mufti of Damascus was largely ceremonial, but interesting. Assad was a Baathist like Saddam Hussein and practiced a more secular version of Islam. The faith, though respected, didn't seem to have the sway there that it did in some other Arab countries.

In Cairo we met with Boutrous Boutrous Ghali, then Egypt's Minister of State for Foreign Affairs and later Secretary General of the UN. He may have been tired of entertaining well-meaning American delegations, or maybe it was an off day, but I found him arrogant and imperious. Maybe he was frustrated at his impotence in the face of what he probably saw as Israeli intransigence.

We met with the head of the Red Crescent Society, Dr. Fathi Arafat, Yasser's brother. The resemblance was striking; he couldn't have hidden it if he wanted to. An energetic and jolly man, Dr. Arafat proudly showed us around his large, modern, well-stocked medical complex. The Red Crescent Society is an international aid organization, part of the International Federation of Red Cross and Red Crescent Societies.

With more time in Cairo, some of us walked through the city, marveling at the history unfolding before us. We visited one of the great mosques and took an evening ride on the Nile. Seeing so many Egyptian men walking along hand in hand, one of our group took this customary practice as a sign of homosexuality (an example of how we view others through the prism of our own cultural experience). The next day we traveled to Giza to see the Sphinx and the Pyramids. Both are dazzling sights, mysterious and compelling. Entering the tomb in the center of the Great Pyramid suddenly brought up my old claustrophobic panic, and I had to let the group go without me. It took some time to work up the courage to make a dash through the small tunnel, look around inside, and race back out, but I was proud to have accomplished it.

While our trip to Jordan didn't include a visit to the astonishing Petra, it did offer two opportunities I hadn't had before. We got to sit in on a session of the Jordanian parliament that offered a vivid demonstration of the contending forces King Hussein faced. The debate was lively and loud, and a particular assault by one Palestinian was riddled with harsh anti-Israel rhetoric. While I'd read much about King Hussein and been so impressed with his brother, the volatility of this debate helped me appreciate the thin ice the two had to regularly traverse. This time we had an audience with the king himself, who knocked me out. As gentle, genuine, and articulate as his brother Crown Prince Hassan, the king, not tall but nonetheless physically imposing, emanated a sense of power and authority that was quite attractive. One could only imagine the pressure that a huge and restive population of Palestinian refugees in his own country, a belligerent—or at least unyielding—Israel to his west, and more radical Arab states to his north and east could bring to bear, yet he was courageously outspoken about his relationships with all of them. Clearheaded, hopeful, and determined that a solution could be found, if there was an honest broker in this whole dynamic, this was the guy.

Before leaving for Israel, Rick, Bob Marx, and a few of us got taxis to take us to a place I knew from my last visit: the best Chinese restaurant in Amman. No one would believe such a place existed, and something about the oddity of the search tickled us all. I couldn't remember the restaurant's name, but the cab driver got us there, its actual existence causing even more yelps of glee. It was a wonderful dinner.

We arrived in Israel the day after an attack by a splinter group—the Palestine Liberation Front—on the beach at Tel Aviv. Fruitless and self-defeating, it resulted only in the death of the four Palestinians, further inflamed the fears of the Israelis, caused the cut-off of talks between the U.S. and the PLO, and cemented the image of Palestinians as ruthless terrorists in the eyes of most of the world. For us, it underscored the degree to which the fate of the region was in the hands of the most radical elements on both sides. With even the most tentative contacts broken off every time an act of violence occurred, the whip was in the hands of the worst people, who could obstruct any serious effort toward peace. Israel's requirement of a set period in which no violent acts occurred as a precondition for such talks made matters even worse. It was a self-defeating position that empowered hard-liners on both sides of the divide.

Evidence of the human cost of this stalemate was everywhere. Once in our hotel, we learned of a fast for peace by over forty leading Palestinians that was taking place in East Jerusalem. Several of us immediately went to show support for this nonviolent action and were welcomed under a canopy erected as protection from the sun. The group, dressed in black, had been there for twelve days. It included Jonathan Khutab, the attorney from Law in the Service of Man whom I had met on my last trip; Faisal Husseini, an often-imprisoned, longtime activist and official of the PLO; and a woman whose face I recognized but whose name I couldn't remember. I said hello, confessing that I knew we had met but couldn't remember where. She smiled, saying she didn't believe we'd met but that I might have seen her on television. She was Hanan Ashrawi, the extraordinarily articulate woman I had first seen on Ted Koppel's powerful Israeli-Palestinian Television Town Meeting and had seen inter- viewed many times since. I was embarrassed, not only for the goof, but by the turning of the tables. There have been so many times that people have come up to me and said some version of the same thing—"I know we've met but I can't remember where"—and I've had to find a way to respond in the same manner while trying not to sound self-important.

Here it was in a nutshell. Decent, intelligent, dedicated, peaceful Palestinian patriots staging a nonviolent demonstration in what was once their capital city, asking to be given the respect and attention they deserved as human beings and leaders of their community. They didn't support the insane attack on Tel Aviv. They didn't want to drive Israel into the sea; they wanted only to be given the right to live in peace, to be free of the occupation, to determine for themselves the form of their government, to establish a self-sustaining country, and to join the community of nations. I was embarrassed that we could do so little as they thanked us for caring enough to come and pay our respects.

Our meetings with officials were a repeat of those two years ear- lier. Defense Minister Moshe Ahrens, in particular, defended his bel- licosity by referring to "little Israel," suggesting that a puny state in the midst of a sea of haters could cede nothing. This ignored the mil- itary officers of the Council for Peace and Security, who said "little Israel" could easily take care of itself. Shimon Peres, the Labor Party leader, was disappointing as well, taking a very hard line. Clearly this wasn't a time for politicians to discuss peace, dialogue, or a two-state solution.

My second visit to Yad Vashem, the Holocaust museum, again provided brutal testimony to the obstacles faced by those with hope for overcoming the trauma of the past. All were deeply touched by the visit, an experience I wish everyone could have. Rick, my young lawyer friend, was utterly overcome by it.

Our trips into Gaza and the West Bank were devastating. In

Rafah Camp, we saw the wreckage of many demolished homes. In Jabaliya Camp, a couple of us went into a small cement-block home for thick, bitter coffee. As we sat on the stone surface in the open entry, I saw the top of the cap of someone approaching, the rest hidden behind the wall. But we had just come in that way and the wall was barely three feet high. Soon a man crept in and my confusion was replaced by shock. Apparently very old—we were later told he was 104—he was crawling on hands and knees. Nodding and smiling, he pulled himself up to us and reclined on one side to join us for coffee. Our host made introductions, explaining that the new guest was unable to walk after having been beaten by IDF troops. Our conversation continued, but I could barely pull my eyes from the smiling, wizened face of this ancient creature, now accustomed to crawling from place to place.

In Gaza City, UNRWA officials told our group of having treated the wounds of 173 children who had been beaten by the IDF in the past three months. Later, in the Arab-run hospital, we were again shown X-rays of patients with "crowd control" rubber or plastic bullets lodged in their bodies—in the abdomen, against the spine, in the skull. I spoke to the son of a bandaged woman who had been beaten until her face was misshapen and her skull fractured while trying to protect him from an Israeli soldier.

In Beit Sahour, residents explained that they had staged a tax revolt, crying, ironically, "No taxation without representation." They were placed under siege and had their goods seized. In Ramallah, schools remained closed. In Bethlehem, where a church had been erected over the site of the manger, artifacts of which decorate the homes of believers the world over at Christmas, Arab houses had been raided and ransacked. In East Jerusalem, a group of Muslim and Christian religious leaders joined in song, calling for dialogue between the Israelis and the PLO.

At a gathering in Jerusalem, I saw Anne Nixon, the young Save the Children worker who had taken our delegation through Gaza two years earlier. She told me about the research she was doing on the plight of children in the Occupied Territories and the problems that had arisen around a report she was just completing. She'd begun writing "The Status of Palestinian Children During the Uprising in the Occupied Territories" as part of her job with Save the Children/U.S. But as the resulting picture became more and more damning of IDF tactics, she was told to stop. With a lot of time and effort already invested in it and believing the report offered an important view of the conditions impacting Palestinian children, she appealed the order. Her superiors at Save the Children/U.S., however, were adamant: Her work must stop; Save the Children/U.S. would have nothing to do with it. Angry at what she thought a cowardly act on the part of an organization dedicated to the welfare of the world's children, she turned to Swedish Save the Children (Radda Barnen). They were familiar with her research and commissioned her to complete the work. Now, the Swedish group was getting no cooperation from Save the Children/U.S. and was having difficulty getting attention to the report in the States.

I asked for a copy of the Executive Summary to look over right away and the four-volume report as soon as possible. It exposed a hideous mess. According to a later *Washington Post* story, "*Israeli soldiers trying to quell the West Bank–Gaza uprising have inflicted on children more than 150 deaths, thousands of beatings and gunfire wounds, and tens of thousands of other injuries*" during the previous two years.

As our next meeting was with Shmuel Goren, Chief Coordinator of Civil Administration in the Occupied Territories, I raised the issue. A crushingly arrogant bastard, Goren smugly dismissed the report as biased, overblown, and full of lies. He added that it had been repudiated by none other than the head of Save the Children/U.S., who had not only "disassociated" his organization from it but had "denounced it as inaccurate." Suspicious and frustrated but having no way to know what Save the Children/U.S. might have said, or why, I had no choice but to leave it for the time being. Later in the meeting, I asked about a matter that had been reported to us by an Israeli human rights group. He said the only people who made reference to the case

I'd cited were "enemies of the State." This guy was truly a putz.

As we prepared to leave, we heard the dispiriting news that the U.S. had vetoed a UN Security Council resolution on sending observers to the Occupied Territories. With a lot to think about, we headed west.

In Frankfurt, Germany, I jumped ship, making a connection to Prague to meet the election-monitoring group. This was a new part of the world for me, and anticipation was high. Upon landing I was taken to a Soviet-style hotel that was newer than most of the buildings I saw coming from the airport, and quite stale and utilitarian. As I walked in, the delegation had already gathered around a large table, and the members were in the process of introducing themselves. Their combined pedigrees were very intimidating. These were historians, foreign affairs specialists, academics, politicians, journalists, businesswomen and men—and there was me. When it came my turn to offer credentials, all I could think of to say was my name. They looked at me expectantly, but, unable to think of anything that would have meaning in this company, I sat mute. I'm afraid it must have appeared that I was suggesting my name was enough, but, in fact, I was so intimidated I couldn't think of anything to offer that would justify my being included. Finally, Senator Chris Dodd leaped to my rescue, explaining that I had just come from two weeks in the Middle East with a peace delegation.

Later, a few of us went to dinner at a local restaurant and I got a sense of some of the participants. A nonpartisan event, it boasted a bipartisan delegation. Just to my left, a man quickly exposed himself as the legendary, boorish, ugly American. He was a Republican, apparently quite rich and a major donor to his party. Besides giving the waitress a bunch of unnecessary guff, he quickly began sounding off on a number of issues. I particularly recall a shot he took at Lyndon Johnson, who, according to a book he had read, exaggerated his own importance by telling stories to an obviously impressionable "young girl who sat on the foot of his bed." He had no sooner finished the sentence when a woman across to my right leaned over and said,

"I beg your pardon. I was that young girl at the foot of his bed." She was Doris Kearns Goodwin, the Pulitzer Prize–winning biographer, and she immediately set him straight. I quickly learned to adore her. Another woman at the table with whom he argued until she too shut him up was a professor of International Affairs named Madeleine Albright, later Bill Clinton's Secretary of State. This guy couldn't win for losing.

In Prague, we met with leaders of the new government—formed after the fall of the Soviet-sponsored Communist regime in December 1989—and those who aspired to leadership. There was great pride evident in the smile, the look, the step of so many we met; soon-to-be-elected President Vaclav Havel seemed to be the model. A soft-spoken man of great humility and extraordinary dignity, Havel impressed us all. In addition to the widespread sense of promise and excitement, we learned of the enormous difficulty involved in working out the unique needs and desires of the distinct peoples involved—the Czechs and the Slovaks. Those considerations presaged the later split into two separate countries, Slovakia and the Czech Republic, resulting from the dissolution of the federation three years later in 1993.

Our delegation divided, one group to be poll watchers in Prague and the other headed to Bratislava. Though I'd have preferred to stay in Prague with its ancient, graceful buildings and cobbled streets, my name was picked for Bratislava. Driving south it quickly became clear that the Communists had ravaged the countryside with little if any concern for the environment. There were signs everywhere of carelessness: abuse of the wooded areas, deserted mines, factories left to molder once they had served the purpose of the State. This new country had a lot of work ahead.

Bratislava was far less attractive than Prague, its construction more in the stolid, utilitarian Soviet style. Someone suggested the city may have been far more greatly damaged in World War II than had Prague, which could explain the difference between them. Whatever the cause, Bratislava suffered by comparison. The people, however, were every bit as enthusiastic as the Czechs about the day approaching. For the most part, we were welcomed—the lone exception being the surviving functionaries of the collapsed Communist regime now acting as election officials. This caused some concern, and we were encouraged to watch closely in certain voting precincts to ensure that proper procedures were followed.

On the day of the election we arose early and went in teams to our assigned polling places. Our first, on the second floor of a school, took my breath away. People had obviously been assembling since the early hours, and the line of expectant voters extended down the hall, down the stairs, out into the street, and a full block away. The young, the old, the lame, and even the severely disabled waited quietly, patiently, the very picture of dignity, for the chance to perform their civic duty. Tears stung my eyes as I considered this tribute to democracy, and my stomach tightened as I thought of its lackluster counterpart at home.

The day was a triumph in every way. Even in those places where we'd been warned to be especially wary, the process went off in an orderly manner. Some of the old-line functionaries we had been cautioned about certainly didn't look happy, but they did their jobs. When there were problems, monitors took the questions to government-appointed agents who resolved them. I saw no serious missteps in the entire process. We turned in our reports and, our job done, headed back to Prague for debriefing and a celebration. And it was a doozy! Thousands of people gathered in Liberty Square to hear Paul Simon sing of a "Bridge Over Troubled Waters," and the people of Slovakia and the Czech lands celebrated into the wee hours, exulting in their new freedom.

The next day, in a post-election symposium on democracy, members of our delegation were invited to give their impressions. Most of our members were properly respectful, congratulating the citizens of Czechoslovakia on their extraordinary transition. A few went a bit overboard, fairly smacking their lips at this victory over the Evil Empire and even implying a sense of authorship, an attitude I found galling. Senator John McCain declared that one of the primary reasons for this victory over oppression was "the United States' steadfast support for human rights." So when my chance came, I noted that, after having spent the prior two weeks in the Middle East and seeing a decided lack of U.S. leadership, there was clearly a great deal yet to be done in our world. I hoped this extraordinary development could inspire others to act in as courageous a manner. But it was a bit presumptuous, I added, to gloat about the United States' steadfast support for human rights here when it was failing so miserably in lands not so very far away.

The return home was a jumble of compressed nerves, time, and emotions. It was great to see everyone and again try to explain all I had seen and done, but I had to deal with the hangover of the Save the Children debate. I called James Bausch, head of Save the Children/U.S. and explained my concern, asked him to endorse Anne's report, and offered to join him in a press conference as he did so. With a less-than-friendly reaction, he ended the call quickly. Frustrated, I wrote him about the burying of the report, an act I found inexcusable in light of the mandate of his organization. I was angered at Shmuel Goren's use of his name to discredit Anne's work. If Goren had spoken truthfully, I wanted to know what Bausch's problems were with the report, which had not only been encouraged and supported by Radda Barnen but had since been endorsed by Save the Children/U.K. If Goren had not spoken truthfully, I wanted Bausch to set him straight. I sent copies of the report to Congressman Lee Hamilton and others in the hope that someone would pressure the Israelis to meet their responsibilities regarding the behavior of members of the IDF in the Occupied Territories, especially toward children.

Sadly, my efforts ended mostly in frustration (with the minimal satisfaction of learning that I caused Bausch to "go into a cold sweat, hyperventilate, and feel humiliated"). The *Washington Post* ran its editorial and a few in Washington expressed muted concern. But the impact of Anne's report in the States, despite wide circulation and general endorsement among our allies, was negligible. After a series of increasingly heated letters with Bausch, it was clear that he was unwilling to associate his organization with a report critical of the IDF in any way. He wrote a meek letter to Goren effectively washing the organization's hands of any part in what he called the "Swedish–Anne Nixon report on Palestinian Children."

"We did not and do not intend to state any opinion about this report, as doing so is clearly not the business of our organization," Bausch whined. I was furious. At the height of my anger I contacted some people on Bausch's board and laid out the situation. Some shared my anger at his cowardice. A couple said that Bausch, like many others, was fearful of criticizing Israel out of concern that right-wing Jewish groups in the States would mount a campaign against Save the Children that would impact its income stream and thus its ability to do its work. This was borne out in the first line of a Bausch letter to Goren, thanking him for his "fast and generous action to correct the mistaken impression that may have been conveyed by the *Jerusalem Post* that Save the Children/U.S. might be hostile to Israel." It made me sick.

Chapter 18
"IN POLITICS . . ."

Back in the "real" world, my very patient partner Marvin heard from Lifetime Television about a script we had submitted earlier. It was a complex thriller about a writer who becomes the target of increasingly frightening events that parallel plots he has written, all just as he's becoming involved with a young admirer. Lifetime was then establishing itself as a women's network, and the executives liked the story but wanted us to flip the genders, making the writer a woman and the admirer a younger man. Flip the genders? Interesting idea, so we set to work with the writer.

At the same time, the Giarratano case was coming to a head. More interview requests came in and the pressure mounted. Meetings with Mac McFarlane, Governor Wilder's legal advisor, had me hopping to Richmond and back when I could, seeing Joe when possible. The more I did, the more I liked him. Rick Schaeffer, from the last Middle East delegation, lived in Baltimore and was interested in the case. He came over to meet Marie, Joe, and the others and ended up getting deeply involved.

At one point, we heard that Governor Wilder had a political guru and a decision of this magnitude would never be made without his approval. We dug up his name and number and I left a message—ultimately a series of messages—asking for a meeting. Hearing nothing, we assumed we were being blown off, so focused our attention on Mac and the public campaign. As the case became better known, we were targeted by angry segments of the press and local pro-execution forces, including the Attorney General's office. Things got pretty sticky, but eased up when we started getting support from outside the circle of "usual suspects." With conservative newspaper columnist James J. Kilpatrick expressing doubts about Joe's guilt, we got a bit more legitimacy in some eyes.

And I actually got a call from the guru, who agreed to meet, but only in secret. Late one night, Rick and I went to an unimpressive motel in Richmond and up to the designated door. A short, thin, dark-haired, bespectacled man let us into an unlit room, and we talked for some time without the lights ever being turned on. It was bizarre, even more so because a human life was hanging in the balance. The conversation was stilted as we sat in the dark, Rick and I in chairs against the window, the man on the bed. He talked generalities and we kept bringing it back to the case. We emphasized the political upside for Governor Wilder: a cut above the average politician; a courageous man who'd take an unpopular step in the interests of justice.

Rick had worked out a plan that was quite ingenious. The governor would grant a conditional pardon, lifting the conviction and sentence of death in exchange for Joe's agreement to stand trial again. Before the pardon, Joe would waive his protection against double jeopardy, agreeing to be retried with the guarantee that all evidence would be presented in court. The result of the trial, including the possibility of another death sentence, would be accepted without equivocation. It was a win-win proposition for Wilder, but risky as hell for Joe, particularly given the campaign against him by Attorney General Mary Sue Terry. She would scream, shout, lie, cheat, and steal before admitting a mistake. But Joe seemed content with this deal. I suspect that he had lived for so long believing he was guilty that he wanted to go through the process legitimately so there could be no question about the result.

After laying out the proposition carefully, we waited for a response. There was none. Thinking he might be afraid we were taping the conversation, Rick took a cue from *All the President's Men* and said if the guy agreed and would take it to Wilder with his endorsement, all he had to do was stand up for a moment and then sit down again.

As he sat there and looked at us, my heart sank. After an eternity that was probably only a minute or so, he said, "In politics, the death penalty only cuts one way. You kill." Then he got up and left.

I was stunned. We sat there trying to find some ray of hope. Marie, who had been through many of these campaigns, would be heartbroken, but she would put it away somewhere, take a drag off her cigarette, reach deep into her reservoir of faith, and say in her soft, slightly raspy Southern drawl, "We'll just have to try harder." Dick and Steve, who had no faith that a politician would do the right thing simply because it was the right thing to do, would just keep on trying to figure out a way to get past the twenty-one-day rule.

It was Joe I was worried about. Over the past couple of years, I had come to care deeply about him. His keen mind and good heart were always at work, mostly trying to figure out ways to help others. One of those he helped was Earl Washington, a mentally retarded man on death row whom Joe was convinced was innocent. And he turned out to be just that. Helped by an attorney Joe had urged to take on the case in 1985, Earl's sentence was commuted to life in 1992, and he was freed years later.

But in that motel room, I was sick. Suddenly the size, power, and imperious nature of the machine we were facing seemed overwhelming. Truth didn't matter. Justice didn't matter. Politics mattered. That is, politics defined not as doing good, but doing whatever's necessary to stay in power. I had allowed myself to believe that there was something called right and wrong. I had thought that if I could just get to the person on the other side and tell the truth, he'd have no choice. He'd have to set things right. What a fool I was! What a naïve dope. This was the Big Leagues. I was just an actor. What the hell was I doing playing with a man's life?

So back we trudged. When we met with the team, they said thanks for trying. It was worth the effort, they said, but no one was surprised. Marie said, "Well, we'll just have to try harder." So that's what we did.

* * *

At home everyone was doing well. The script for Lifetime was coming along and would be ready in a few weeks. My world was operating on so many different levels it was hard to keep track.

Then Marie called. Joe had been given a date. They would kill
him on February 21, 1991. We went crazy, getting everyone we could
think of to write Governor Wilder, working the press, meeting with
Mac McFarlane. In mid-February, Joe was transferred from
Mecklenberg to the death house in Richmond, and a few days before
the execution Dick, Steve, Marie, and I went to see him. Once down
in the bowels of the old building, the guards let him out of his death-
watch cell, and we sat around a worn table about ten feet from the
door behind which sat the electric chair. It was cold. Everything
about the place was cold. And spare. As always, Joe took an active
part in discussing the strategy. Mac had all the material. He understood our offer and had assured us that Governor Wilder understood
it as well. Mac had some concern about whether the governor actually had the authority to order a new trial, but we reassured him.
Once Joe had waived his double jeopardy rights, all the governor had
to do was commute the sentence, thereby voiding it, and leave the
indictment in place. That meant the state would have to try him a
second time. Now it all rested with the governor. Would he have the
courage to commute a convicted double murderer whom the
Attorney General insisted was as guilty as sin? I kept thinking, *In politics the death penalty only cuts one way* . . . and praying that Joe
wouldn't ask me to be a witness at the execution. I don't know that I
could have turned him down, but the idea made me want to puke.

As we gathered our stuff, Dick asked Joe to tell me about the
table. "Oh, this?" Joe asked, pointing down at the table around which
we had been sitting. Dick nodded, and Joe said, "This is the cooling
table." After being electrocuted, his body would be too hot to touch.
Guards with asbestos gloves would quickly lift him out of the chair
and lay him on this very table until he was cool enough to be moved.

I hugged him. He thanked me for caring and said he loved me. I
could hardly speak. The next morning I flew home. I tried to behave

normally but felt like a bag of sticks. On February 20, sixteen hours before Joe was to die, Marie called. Mac had come through. Governor Wilder had commuted Joe's sentence to life with the possibility of parole because of "possible innocence." Her voice was thick. She knew little. She'd call when she knew more. I was shaking so hard that Shelley had to put down the phone. And then she held me as I sobbed.

After collecting ourselves, we talked. Elated that Joe's life had been spared, we were still frustrated because Wilder had given only half a loaf. In the deal we had proposed, the Attorney General would be forced to retry him or drop the charges. With the confession debunked, the case wouldn't hold up and Joe would be free. In simply commuting the sentence from death to life in prison, Wilder left the decision regarding a retrial up to Attorney General Mary Sue Terry, a woman dead-set on becoming Virginia's next governor. Because any waves created by a reversal in Giarratano's case could be used against her, there would be no retrial.

So, Joe was saved from frying but thrown into the fire of those who believed he had beaten the system. In his first post–death row prison, Powhatan Correctional Center, a rumor "somehow" spread that Joe was a snitch. It was false, of course, but virtually another death sentence in prison. He was targeted, threatened, harassed, and beaten while complaints sent through prescribed channels were ignored. We kept pressure on, and he tried to stay in his cell. But a corrections system is a virtual fiefdom, and if someone inside is in harm's way, there's little those out in the world can do. Except Marie. She got word to the governor that it would not look good if his only death row commutation ended up murdered in prison under the watchful eye of his Department of Corrections. Joe was moved from Powhatan and assigned to Augusta Correctional Center in the far reaches of the state close to the West Virginia border where, for a while, he was safe.

My relationship with the Cult Awareness Network grew and I joined their board of advisors. It's called a "pretty board" among charitable groups—experts and well-known people establish their bona fides and raise their profiles. I was glad to be asked because I admired those on the board, but also because CAN had helped me better understand the damage done by these cults' use of seductive tactics on the lonely, the weak, and the unwary. No one had bitten on the satanic cult movie idea—fascinating, but too creepy for most—but getting to know Cynthia, the Executive Director, and learning what CAN did for people made me want to help. I wrote a fundraising letter and agreed to appear at a benefit in Los Angeles. Then the fun started.

I got a call from Heber Jentsch, one of the mucky-mucks of what they call the Church of Scientology, telling me I was being duped. CAN, he said, was a terrible bunch, claiming to save people who didn't need saving and didn't want help. CAN was full of liars, connivers, and manipulators, and I should steer clear of them. After we disagreed for a while, he invited me to lunch so he could clarify things and introduce me to someone the nefarious CAN had kidnapped.

We met at a restaurant not far from my office, and Heber was gracious and charming, if oily. He produced a scrapbook of clippings and crowed about what his organization had done for the Hollywood community, insisting all the terrible things others said were lies. When I asked about the CAN kidnapping, he introduced a young man in his early twenties who said that after he joined the group and separated from his family, his parents had tried various ruses to get him back.

"Right," I responded. "So?"

On their last attempt, they had insisted he come to their house. Once he got there, they brought out two former Scientologists who wanted to talk to him about the organization.

"I see," I said. "And where does CAN come in?" His parents had called CAN, who had recommended these people. "Okay, so what happened?"

"My parents wanted me to talk to them," he said. But he wouldn't talk to them and wanted to leave.

"And?" I asked.

"And I left."

"Uh-huh. Did they try to stop you?"

"They told me I was making a mistake."

"Right. I mean, did they . . . grab you, hold you, physically try to stop you?"

"No."

"And you left?"

"That's right."

I turned to Heber, who seemed a bit flushed—whether from anger or embarrassment, I couldn't tell. "I'm sorry," I said, "I don't get it. How is this a kidnapping, and how is CAN responsible for it?"

There was more fluster and bluster, ending with my thanking him for the lunch. It was clear from the scrapbook that they did a lot of service to the Hollywood community, but so what? Mussolini made the trains run on time. I thought it was tragic that the kid had been separated from his family, but that was something Heber would have to live with. And the kid. And his family. As for the kidnapping, I said he should be embarrassed. This outrageous libel was exactly the kind of supercharged paranoid nonsense that made people see Scientology for what it was.

A couple of weeks later, I drove up to the house in Beverly Hills for the CAN fundraiser and people with video cameras were everywhere. Some stood on the street to take shots of me parking and going into the event. Once out of the car, two more, one with a camera, the other simply wild-eyed, raced up and began yelling at me, demanding to know why I was persecuting them. Pretty bizarre stuff. I went in, despite their promises of my impending doom, and met some very grateful, very normal-appearing people. *Man*, I thought, *these folks have a lot of guts to take on that crazy bunch.*

Stepping out of that Byzantine dimension and back into what we like to think of as normal, Marvin and I readied the now-altered Lifetime script for production. They insisted we shoot it in Vancouver, British Columbia, which was just beginning to be used as a cheaper alternative to shooting in the States. We wanted to do it at home, but were given no choice by those who were writing the checks. We hired a director, cast the major roles, and moved north to set up shop.

The movie, a good if unremarkable potboiler, provided one truly noteworthy moment. Having cast the major roles at home and arranged transportation and housing for our actors, we had to find additional Canadian actors to fill out the cast. This takes attention; although we speak the same language, Canadians pronounce certain words differently, making an otherwise unobtrusive supporting role suddenly obtrusive. But we did well, finding talented, thoughtful actors who spoke "American." The crew came together nicely, and the civility and gentility of Canadians in general made for a happy shoot. We had a panicky moment when our male lead backed out for another movie role. This put us in a spin until we replaced him, but that was quickly, if reluctantly, done. We scouted and secured locations, took care of thousands of details, rehearsed and got ready to shoot.

At 2 a.m. on the day we were to begin, the phone in my hotel room startled me awake. The manager for one of our leading players was on the line, saying the actress couldn't do the job and had to go home. "Go home?" I sputtered, suddenly wide awake. "Go home? She can't do that. We start shooting at 8 o'clock. She's in the first shot! What do you mean *go home?*" She was sorry, but there had been an emergency; her client was distraught and had to leave. I couldn't believe my ears. This was nuts. Leave? "Are you crazy? She can't leave. We have a hundred people ready to go to work in just a few hours."

All apologies, the manager insisted that her client was simply incapable of working and that I'd have to understand that.

"Well, no," I said, "I don't understand that." Then she said she had already called the head of the company that was putting up the money and let him know. "You did what?"

She kindly repeated it and added, "He'll be calling you."

As if by magic, my other line began ringing.

"What the hell is going on up there?" he shouted over the line.

"That's what I'm trying to figure out," I responded.

"You've got a picture to shoot!" he yelled. "You start tomorrow!"

"Thanks for the reminder!" I yelled back. "Is there another reason for this call?"

Things were not going well. I got the idiot off the line and then dealt with the fool. Or was it the other way around? I said that I understood, that I appreciated her call, and that I'd go up right now to her client's room and see if I couldn't just figure out a way to resolve this.

So up I went and knocked on the door. She let me in. She was a wreck. She was crying. She paced. I paced. We paced. There had been a call from home. There were the kids, her husband. There was trouble: Maybe a child was sick; maybe the roof had fallen in; maybe she was having an anxiety attack. I couldn't tell for sure. It was a very iffy situation. We walked and we talked, and we talked and we walked. We went for miles in her suite, probably carving a path in the rug. I tried to reassure her. Whatever the problem was, we'd do everything we could to help. We'd fix the roof; we'd bring her family up here if that would make her feel better. But she had to understand that we couldn't simply shut down the production and send everyone home. We had a picture to make. She had a job to do. We had a hundred folks out there beginning to set up the shoot.

Maybe it was the fact that someone was paying attention. Maybe it was the walking and the talking. Maybe it was the wonderfully therapeutic manner with which I disguised my terror. Maybe it was all a bad dream. But little by little she calmed down and began to think it through. Little by little there was less panic in her voice, and soon . . . we were okay. She knew she had a job to do. She knew the situation at home (whatever it was) would ultimately be okay, especially if her family was able to come up. Everything was oooookay, right? Right. Okay. Let's try to get some sleep.

And that—except for a slight hiccup the next day when she walked into the edge of a door and cut open her forehead—was that.

Once we got on track, the picture came off without a hitch. Just another day of making movies.

In June my daughter Erin, my Golden Girl, graduated from high school. Brilliant, gorgeous, wonderfully coordinated and enormously talented, she'd been extremely shy and reluctant to step out on her own for years, a result, I fear, of anxiety produced by the divorce. Finally gaining confidence, however, she responded to the challenge of high school studies, social activities, and sports, became an all-around champ and was presented the Headmasters Award in recognition of her multidisciplinary achievements as four proud, teary-eyed parents stood and cheered. That she followed this by going to Vassar College, 3,000 miles away, was almost more than we could believe.

President Bush the elder did his best to ruin my summer by earmarking an extra $21 million dollars for military aid to El Salvador, a hideously insensitive act in view of the army's murder of the Jesuits a year and a half earlier. Incensed, I wrote an op-ed (*USA Today*, July 24, 1994, see www.mikefarrell.org/publications/salvador.html) excoriating the mindlessness of the decision. Not only sickening and infuriating, it flew in the face of advice from his emissary in El Salvador. Years later a secret "eyes only" memo from Ambassador William Walker to Bernard Aronson, a State Department apologist for this criminal policy, was unearthed by the National Security Archive. Written months before President Bush decided to send the additional $21 million to the murderers, it was entitled, "Reaching the End of the Rope." Stamped *SECRET*, it read:

> Despite advancements in other areas, on the Jesuit case the ESAF [El Salvador Armed Forces] remains committed to a hermetic conspiracy to protect its own at whatever cost. USG [U.S. government] pleas, threats, turning on and off the military assistance spigot, and appeals to institutional honor have all had the same results—zilch. We have made enough demarches and agreements—our position is

clear to the ESAF. I reluctantly conclude MGB [Defense Minister] Ponce is a fatally flawed leader. Absent immediate turn-around, and despite the downsides, I recommend that the GOES [Government of El Salvador] be informed that we will not move on their pending requests.

It made my blood boil. Clearly the siren song of anti-Communism was irresistible to the Bush Administration, trumping justice, decency, and any vestige of honor that might have been thought to remain.

As Erin prepared for Vassar, Mike decided to take some time away from school. He said he was wasting his time and my money. I wasn't thrilled, but we agreed that he would take the time he needed to fig-ure out where he wanted to go in life, and he'd seriously consider returning to school later. Mike had been fascinated with martial arts since he was quite young, and it had turned into an impressive disci-pline. This in turn led to an interest in Eastern philosophy that I found hopeful. We'd see.

Erin, on the other hand, had wrestled her current demons to the floor and was ready to make the plunge. Taking her to Vassar was one of those parental delights, at once heartwarming and heartrending. The campus was gorgeous, everything one dreams about in a college, assuming one dreams about college. The idea that my child would spend four years here being exposed to the best education possible was both thrilling and intimidating. I was thrilled to be able to make it possible, thrilled that she had qualified to come here, and dogged by the vestige of a feeling that missing college had left me somewhat unprepared for life. Envy? Maybe. It was certainly admiration for Erin's ability to put her fears behind her and tackle this challenge. And tackle it she did.

Leaving our baby girl to the horrors and delights of college life, Shelley and I headed down to Virginia to visit Joe. After facing some initial testing at Augusta, he had done well. The warden liked him and supported Joe's idea for bringing peace to a typically troubled institution. With the support of Marie and *Washington Post* columnist Colman McCarthy, a longtime supporter, Joe and a cellmate founded Peace Studies, ATV, an inmate-run alternatives-to-violence program. I was a founding board member.

Augusta is way the hell out in the western reaches of Virginia, not far from the West Virginia border, as we found out by missing the turnoff and getting well into the new state before realizing our error. Finally at the prison, I experienced the usual dull ache that comes with seeing a place where human beings are warehoused. Even if occasionally under the leadership of enlightened administrations, prisons in America were well described by the incarcerated author Jack Abbott as "animal factories." Pulling across the inevitable flat parking lot toward the razor-wire-covered fence we could see the solid gray buildings, their slit windows peering out suspiciously.

Late because of our inadvertent trip into West Virginia, we were afraid we might not get to see Joe. Once through the initial gate, we found our way down a chain-link tunnel to reception and were soon in the office of Warden Lonnie Saunders. A pleasant, soft-spoken African-American, Saunders received us graciously and seemed sympathetic about our getting lost. He dropped something about not getting too many television celebrities out this way before allowing with a smile that he'd let us see Joe even though visiting hours were over. He called Major Braxton, a strapping black man with military build, bearing, and uniform to match, who made no secret about being a fan and treated us like old friends. We were registered and searched, then led into a locked area where we relinquished our driver's licenses before moving out into the yard. Braxton took us into an office to wait while he went to get Joe. Later we found out that he had given us his own office for the meeting.

It was great to see Joe and wonderful to have him meet Shelley after all they had heard about each other. He looked good and sounded even better. He had high hopes for the Peace Studies program and had begun to outline classes in the philosophies of Gandhi and Martin Luther King, Jr. Joe was enthusiastic about beginning literacy programs and essay contests, and was even hoping to start computer training. I was amazed at his enthusiastic description of what could be done for the inmates here. Watching him explain the benefits of the program to Shelley, I couldn't help thinking that if a lot of people in this state had had their way, they'd have killed him months ago.

That autumn, CAN held a conference on destructive cults in Los Angeles. Dr. Louis Jolyon West and Dr. Margaret Singer, widely respected psychiatrists, addressed the issue. It was extraordinary. People picketed, others tried to sneak in using fake press credentials. Anyone coming or going was harangued by super-aggressive types, most of whom were identifiable as Scientologists either by what they said or what was on their signs. I'd already seen a bit of this behavior and had been warned about it, but the degree of vitriol unleashed against us was truly shocking. Psychiatry is roundly despised by Scientology and its founder L. Ron Hubbard, a science fiction writer and true loon. Ironically, Scientologists denounced CAN as a group that controlled people's minds.

Not long after that, I got a call on a private line from a man who apologized for intruding and said he was the press agent for my friend Harry Morgan (M*A*S*H's Colonel Potter). He was sorry to have to tell me that Harry had suddenly passed away. Taken completely by surprise, I was devastated. I love Harry, had seen him not long before, and planned to see him again soon. And now this. I couldn't believe it and didn't know what to do. In tears, I told Shelley, who was stunned. I had an odd feeling because I'd never known Harry to have a press agent, but I was so shocked I couldn't put my thoughts together. Could it be a hoax? Who would do such a thing? Finally I called Barbara, Harry's wife. She said hello, sounding fine and giving no indication anything was wrong. I asked if Harry was okay. She asked if I wanted to talk to him. I almost wept again. I had a wonderful talk with Harry, who laughed it all off with the old line, "Reports of my demise are exceedingly premature."

The more I thought about it, though, the angrier I got. That evening I got another call, this time from two men claiming to be from a radio station, wanting my reaction to Harry Morgan's death. I cursed the sons of bitches, and when they laughed, I blurted out, "What church are you from?" They quickly hung up. For the next few months, calls came in the middle of the night, every night, pulling one crappy stunt after another. I kept the phone beside me after the first few wee-hours calls, and I'd pick up the receiver and say, in a pleasant, informational tone, "Hubbard was crazy." The first couple of times, I heard an audible stumble on the other end. And then the calls stopped.

I can laugh about it now, of course. As an "enemy" of Scientology, assuming it was them, I was "fair game." They once had a division called the Guardian's Office doing their dirty work, though it was supposedly disbanded in the 1970s after criminal indictments were issued for breaking into government offices. Today, the Guardian's Office has been replaced by an Office of Special Affairs that some believe still carries out the harassment and "dead agenting" (spreading malicious gossip to discredit an enemy). It would be hard to believe, if there weren't so many tragic examples. Ask those who've tried to get to the bottom of Scientologist Lisa McPherson's mysterious death. They seem to have finally lost interest in me (unless writing this sets them off again), but it's disgusting to think of the lives that have been wrecked and families torn apart by clowns like these.

Scientology is also aggressively litigious. Their hatred and fear of CAN was so intense that a series of expensive lawsuits drove it out of business a few years later. (One of Hubbard's favorite techniques was to use lawsuits to harass, discourage, bankrupt, or destroy his enemies.) The infuriating irony is that once CAN went into bankruptcy, its name and corporate assets became available and were bought up by . . . you guessed it. Now the wounded parents who call the Cult Awareness Network looking for assistance are "helped" by cult apologists.

Chapter 19
STATE KILLING

Nineteen ninety-two was a busy year. In January, a UN-brokered peace agreement was signed (by Nidia Diaz, among others) in El Salvador. The accords were "aimed not only to bring about a cessation of conflict, but also to . . . promote democratization and reconciliation among Salvadorans." A year later the UN Truth Commission report said 75,000 Salvadoran lives had been lost in the twelve-year war. (Maria Julia Hernandez of Tutela Legal says there were probably twice that.) The "vast majority" of human rights violations were committed by the military, the government-allied paramilitaries, and the "death squads." The U.S.-funded, -trained, and -maintained army was guilty of massacres at El Mozote and the Rio Sumpul (as reported by Ray Bonner, Chris Hedges, and others), the murder of the Jesuits, and complicity in the assassination of Archbishop Romero and the four American churchwomen. Roberto D'Aubuisson was specifically denounced for his involvement in the murder of Archbishop Romero, but U.S. complicity in this horror went largely unremarked.

Days after the Truth Commission issued its report, the National Assembly of El Salvador, controlled by members of the right-wing ARENA party, enacted an amnesty law to protect perpetrators of crimes committed during the conflict from prosecution. Impunity continues. (One of the perpetrators of Archbishop Romero's murder was found guilty of crimes against humanity in a Fresno, California federal district courtroom, however. On September 3, 2004, Judge Oliver Wanger found the defendant, Alvaro Saravia, who had been living in Modesto for thirteen years, responsible for arranging the murder of Archbishop Oscar Romero. Stating that "the damages are of a magnitude that is hardly describable," the judge awarded $10 million to the plaintiff, a relative of Romero's whose identity remains secret for reasons of his/her safety.)

In March, I got a call from Dick Burr, who had represented Joe. He and Steve Hawkins were about to lose a client in Oklahoma and needed desperately to get the state's new governor, David Walters, to listen to some facts they thought might persuade him to delay the execution. Their client was to die in two days, and Walters had ignored them. Would I come to a press conference asking the governor for a meeting? Once again, I thought, *In politics, the death penalty only cuts one way.* Sure I would.

The next day I was in Oklahoma City with Dick and Steve, preparing to meet the press. Robyn Parks, scheduled to die the following day, was, as is typical for death row inmates, an indigent young black man who had lousy, court-appointed representation at his trial. As his execution date approached, Henry Bellmon, the outgoing governor, had wanted to grant clemency, but the Pardon and Parole Board, which in Oklahoma must agree for clemency to take effect, had refused. The new governor, David Walters, was letting things move forward without comment. Dick and Steve had turned up evidence suggesting that the shooting could not have happened as was claimed by the prosecution. If Walters would hear them out, there was a chance to save the young man's life.

The press conference was a hurried affair; some in attendance were quite hostile to the idea that a famous actor from California would fly in and expect the authorities to jump. I tried to avoid the fight they were picking and said that I had worked with Dick, Steve, and the NAACP Legal Defense Fund for years, that I knew them to be diligent in the pursuit of justice, and that justice, it seemed to me, was as important to the people of Oklahoma as it was to Americans everywhere. Robyn Parks might be guilty as charged, I said, but if the evidence these lawyers had found was as significant as they claimed, it seemed only fair that Governor Walters hear them out. He was the only one who could intervene at this point. All we were asking for was a meeting.

Their cheap shots aside, we got the meeting. We went to the governor's home, passed through a security check of unfriendly state police, and waited while he met with someone else. When that meeting broke up, Walters showed some men to the door before coming to meet us. Steve noted that they were from the Attorney General's office. Not a good sign. Walters, a Democrat, was a well-educated, fairly progressive man, but the pressure was heavy on him tonight. Beyond thanking him for taking the time to meet us and offering some words of praise for Dick, Steve, and the LDF, I kept my mouth shut as the two of them laid out the case for the governer's intervention. The meeting didn't last long, and Walters was studiously non-committal. He thanked us for coming, assured us he would give these arguments serious consideration, and said goodnight. There was a heavy sense of foreboding in the car as we drove away.

Dick went off to file a last appeal while Steve headed to McAlester Prison, a couple of hours away. He asked if I'd come, saying Robyn would like to meet me. So we piled into the back of an old van and headed into the night. We rode in the back with Clif Everhart, a former Oklahoma cop who was the investigator on the case. Clif was full of stories about how lousy the Oklahoma system was and kept us entertained—if stories about corrupt cops, paid-off judges and a racist system can be entertaining—most of the way to McAlester. Arriving at the small town, we made our way through the dark streets and were passed through the prison's gate without quibble. Up a rough lane, the prison walls stood to our right, a looming fortress. To our left was a grassy, tree-filled, parklike area that soon revealed a large house with lights in the windows. It was the warden's residence, and we were expected. Steve and I were welcomed by the warden, who thanked us for coming. The fact that we were here in the middle of the night seemed to bother him not at all. As he repeatedly thanked me for being there, I got the impression that what bothered him, if anything, was that a man would probably die in a matter of hours under his authority.

After a phone call approving our entry, we were back in the van and headed out around the big walls and down to the H Unit. Steve had tried to prepare me for the structure, which houses death row and the segregation cells. On the prison grounds but outside the huge walls of the old fortress, H Unit was often described as being underground. While that's not technically true—the entrance and main floor are at or just below ground level—it does sit in a kind of hollow with earthworks built up on its sides to prevent access to natural light. There are no windows. Inmates can never see the outside, let alone the sun, and even the air is pumped in by machine. It appeared, as we got out of the van, as if you could walk up to the top and over and down the other side, like taking a hike on a hill. But instead of ants, gophers, or moles, inside this hill were captives. Entering H Unit was like going into a tomb or an underground shelter. Once past the guard at the entrance and through a turnstile device, we walked down a long, sterile, almost futuristic tunnel into the unit itself. In the visiting area, there was a wall, regularly pierced by windows, slightly reminiscent of the teller stations in a bank, except for the stools on our side. I stood back while Steve went up and presented his credentials to the guard on duty, who passed word back to bring up Robyn Parks.

It was quiet except for the occasional distant slam of a barred door or clang of a lock. Periodically a uniformed officer walked by. Then a black man appeared in the window, and Steve quickly went over to him, explaining what had happened. We still didn't have any answers, but he deserved to hear what we knew. I began to feel very conspicuous, not only because the guards kept giving me looks, but because Robyn kept looking over at me as Steve spoke to him. I assumed I'd be expected to talk to him, but had no idea what to say. The circumstances were so otherworldly that I was dumbstruck. I kept thinking I shouldn't be there at all. Maybe he only wanted to talk to his lawyer or somebody he knew. He should probably spend this time with his family. What the hell was I doing there, anyway?

Before I could work myself into a state of apoplexy, Steve said, "Robyn would like to talk to you." As I walked the few yards over to him, he smiled, and when I reached the window, he put his hand up on the glass or Plexiglas or whatever the hell it was. It was a greeting, a way to almost shake hands. I put my hand up against the glass opposite his. It's not the same as touching, obviously, but it's an attempt to connect.

I don't really remember the conversation except that I was utterly inept and he was kind. He thanked me for coming to Oklahoma, thanked me for helping him. He said he knew Steve and Dick were doing everything they could and he appreciated it all. He said that he was sorry we had to meet this way and he hoped, if things worked out, we could perhaps meet again. Here was a guy facing death in a matter of hours, and he was trying to make me feel better. I don't know that I'd have had the courage.

Somehow we got through it. Steve then had some more words with Robyn who, after a last wave and a mouthed *thank you* to me, went away with a guard. It felt so odd and so wrong to walk away, knowing that in a few hours they'd strap him down and kill him. And that's what they did.

A week after Robyn was killed, I got a letter from Clif, who had stayed with him until they took him to be executed. "Even at that late hour," Clif said, "Robyn was upbeat and more concerned about others than his own future . . . Robyn said, 'I have nothing to worry about. I did nothing wrong and God knows it.'" Clif also relayed Robyn's final statement in which he thanked a number of people for trying to help him. The fact that he included me made my throat close.

"I know that one day my innocence will be proven. I hope that on that day the state of Oklahoma and the entire world will stop and take a very close look at what they are doing. I pray that no more innocent people will have to die for no reason."

The specter of state killing came closer to home with the scheduled execution of Robert Alton Harris in San Quentin's gas chamber. The first execution in our state in over twenty years, it was creating a storm of controversy. The news media ballyhooed the image promoted by the prosecution of a smirking, heartless killer who brutally exterminated two boys and then casually ate the hamburgers his two victims had just purchased for lunch.

Amnesty International asked me to help with a videotaped packet of information on the case that would be presented to Governor Pete Wilson. The video, which I hosted and narrated, was something of a first in clemency appeals. It offered medical testimony by a doctor and information about Harris's life that had not been brought out at trial. As it showed, Harris was a victim of fetal alcohol syndrome and resultant brain damage. The tragedy of his life began before birth, with an alcoholic mother. Then an abusive father, finding the boy slow and dull, singled him out for beatings, the description of which beggared the imagination. None of this, the video made clear, was meant to excuse his actions. Hopefully, though, it provided context that would allow the governor to see that there was no social benefit in killing a severely damaged man that would not be equally realized by commuting the sentence to life in prison without the possibility of parole. After giving the tape to Governor Wilson and getting no response, we released it to the media at a press conference at which the doctor who discovered fetal alcohol syndrome explained it and identified Harris as a victim. I simply said that we have to consider one's life experience in these matters. "We've all heard of someone being 'beaten within an inch of his life.' Robert Alton Harris was repeatedly beaten within an inch of his life, and now the state of California wants to take the last inch."

Governor Wilson refused to intervene, and the execution protocol went forward. Hundreds gathered in Los Angeles and at the East Gate of San Quentin to protest the execution while the Ninth Circuit Court of Appeals and the U.S. Supreme Court battled over Harris's death. The Ninth ordered the execution stopped, and the Supreme Court overturned their stay. The Ninth stopped it again on different grounds, and the Supremes again trumped them. The two courts parried for hours in this gruesome duel, with Mr. Harris being taken into the gas chamber and brought back out again, before the Supreme Court finally ordered that the Ninth interfere no more. I don't know enough about the law to be sure if that had ever happened before, but the legal community was outraged.

Robert Alton Harris died in the gas chamber early on Tuesday, April 21, 1992, his death captured on videotape at the order of Judge Marilyn Patel. The tape created a tug-of-war when the warden seized it immediately after the killing and refused to turn it over until Judge Patel threatened to lock him up. A later hearing convinced the judge that execution by lethal gas constituted cruel and unusual punishment, and the gas chamber was subsequently outlawed in California.

During that frustrating time, I got to know people who were part of Death Penalty Focus, a San Francisco–based organization working to abolish capital punishment, and was asked to join their board of directors. Seeing that this was going to be an ongoing struggle that needed more than an ad hoc approach, I agreed.

Chapter 20
SILENCE . . .

In the spring, I got a call from Paul McCleary, head of the Christian Children's Fund (CCF). Working with Emory University, McCleary was taking a small group to Jordan to inspect self-help, development, and medical programs with a special focus on children. He'd heard of my interest in the area and wanted me to join them. Concerned about the implications of an avowedly Christian group going to a largely Muslim region, I said I'd think about it. I checked McCleary out with friends, who described him in the most positive terms, saying that he was always respectful, congenial, sensitive, and welcoming of all faiths and beliefs. I got back to him and asked if there was a chance to go into Israel and the Occupied Territories. He didn't have any plans to do so, but had no problem with my going across if I chose, so I agreed.

Paul is a big man, if small in stature. He's warm, charming, incredibly smart, deeply religious without being oppressively so, and extraordinarily passionate about the children of the world. He's a Methodist minister who had once headed Save the Children, my sparring partner of a couple years earlier, though his tenure had preceded Mr. Bauch. Before that, he headed Church World Service and other organizations. Clearly, what's important to him is service—and children. Our companions on the trip included Dr. Dean Wilcox, a public health specialist out of Emory University's medical school in Atlanta, and Dr. R. Jack Sadler, a Virginian on the board of the Christian Children's Fund. Both were quiet, thoughtful men, and I enjoyed their company.

We flew directly into Amman and headed straight to one of the community groups that CCF was helping to support. This was my first trip to the region without an overt human rights agenda, and it was interesting to see what was being done for the children. Her Majesty Queen Noor was personally involved with the first program we saw. Although not there on the day we visited, we were assured that she spent a good deal of time with the children. She is apparently greatly loved.

Beyond the opportunity to appreciate some of the work being done for children, in both Jordanian and assimilated Palestinian families and those still in the refugee camps, the trip allowed an opportunity to see the successes of King Hussein's enlightened leadership. Jordan, or at least the parts of it we saw, remained the most modern and cosmopolitan of the Arab nations I had visited. Though they haven't eliminated poverty or fully overcome some of the less beneficial aspects of ancient tribal culture, the king's education and his appreciation of technological advancement and modern social improvements were evident in the pride of the Jordanian people. Women, for example, were actively involved in all aspects of business, as well as other parts of society. While not universally so, the progress in that direction was obvious.

Visiting the centers, Dean was touched by the response to his question about so much focus on child development when there were many other pressing problems in the country. "Dr. Wilcox, nothing is more important than preserving our culture," he was told. War, if it came, would inevitably involve Jordan and cost the lives of many. The children who survived must be able to rise to positions of leadership and ensure that Jordanian culture is maintained. Again the possibility—perhaps inevitability—of war was not only on these people's minds; it was a critical part of their plans for the future.

Dean was particularly interested in a water reclamation site near the Dead Sea. With the Centers for Disease Control (CDC) in western Africa, he had helped develop a treatment for acute diarrhea and the resultant dehydration in infants, a primary cause of child death in the underdeveloped world. Countless children's lives had been saved using a "home-made" liquid solution that included protein and nutrients derived from tilapia, a fish common to the area that could be bred in ponds. Here by the Dead Sea, he was thrilled to see a Bedouin "relocation" community where the very process he helped develop was a part of their sustenance, training, and education program.

Then I was thrilled to again have the opportunity to take in the extraordinary beauty of the ancient city of Petra. Aside from Paul, none of the others had been there, and it was almost as much fun to see the looks on their faces when we came out of the narrow canyon into the valley of tombs as it was to see this splendid place again myself. We walked farther that day than we did last time, exploring more of the ancient site, and ended up taking a much longer route over the hills and back to the hotel. I don't know how old Paul was at the time, but he was very impressive. In his enthusiasm, he led us to one discovery after another, leaving younger men panting in his wake. And on one of our evenings in the city, I took the group to the best Chinese restaurant in Amman.

When Paul mentioned my plan to travel across the Jordan River, Jack Sadler said he'd like to go along, so the two of us got a bus from Amman. Jack had never been in this part of the world and was a bit nervous, but his enthusiasm for seeing the Holy Land overcame his anxiety. With no delegation and no guide, we were just two American tourists on the bus. As we approached the Israeli checkpoint at the border, there was a perceptible rise of tension among the passengers. The Arabs traveling through were quiet and businesslike, as were the IDF guards, but there was a palpable sense that things could change in a heartbeat. The searches were thorough, lengthy, and, in some cases, apparently quite grueling. But everyone was careful to do what was necessary to get by, and we crossed through without incident. Because Jack and I carried little and had American passports, we had a much easier time of it than many of the others.

Passing through Jericho, Jack was thrilled to see where Joshua had "fit the battle." As we moved across the West Bank toward Jerusalem, he was stunned, as I'd been the first time, at the size, scope, and dominance of the settlements we passed. The word "settlements" doesn't prepare one for the reality. Even larger in size and number than my last visit, they were truly an outrage. Once in East Jerusalem, we found our way to the Old City, which was much more active than the last time, a result of the hope arising from the Madrid talks. Walking the Via Dolorosa is always an eerie experience, but as the Intifada was muted at this time, the market was alive with people, its shops and stalls buzzing. The ironic sight of small Palestinian children running through the narrow lanes with toy machine guns clutched at my stomach. With access to the Temple Mount open, we left the war behind and took in the beauty of the Dome of the Rock and Al Aqsa Mosque, considered one of the three holiest shrines in the Muslim world.

Jack wanted to see a woman whose school for children was supported by the CCF. After a search, we found the place and were lucky enough to catch her, a straightforward, no-nonsense Englishwoman who was wonderful with the kids but merciless about the occupation and the price paid by her wards. The school was in a small court and didn't have much to offer, but her enthusiasm and energy made up for a lot and the kids seemed well cared for. After a too-short visit, we headed back to catch the bus for Jordan, once again making our way through thousands of years of history on the trip back to Amman.

Later that spring Richard Walden, founder of Operation U.S.A., invited me to meet Mrs. Sadako Ogata, the UN High Commissioner for Refugees. Mrs. Ogata had heard of my travels and wanted to know if I'd consider a trip for the UN. I said I'd be happy to help if I could and left the meeting wondering if anything would result.

Soon after, Shelley's mother Elsa Rose passed away, the cruel thief Alzheimer's having taken its toll. Unable to help her mother beyond comforting her and seeing that she was cared for, Shelley had begun volunteering for the Los Angeles Alzheimer's Association shortly after Elsa was diagnosed and has never stopped. She travels the country speaking and making appearances, testifies before congressional committees, uses her celebrity to bring attention and money to aid research, and has been tireless in working to end this awful curse. A member of the national board of directors of the Association, she is one of their most valuable assets.

In July, Amnesty International called again, this time working with the NAACP Legal Defense Fund on an upcoming execution in Utah. Steve Hawkins was representing the condemned man, an African-American named William Andrews. Along with another, Andrews had taken part in the robbery of a business that involved overpowering and tying up a number of customers. He claimed to have been outside when his accomplice murdered some of the hostages in a particularly cruel manner: forcing them to drink Drano before shooting them. The murders had naturally outraged the community, and because murder during the commission of a felony makes everyone involved "death eligible," both were sentenced to die. The verdict against Andrews came despite his insistence that he had not taken part in the killings and hadn't even known they were happening. The two were tried separately, the other man first. When Andrews's case went to the jury, someone left a drawing in their room: a stick figure in a noose, with the admonition: *Hang the Nigger!*

The state of Utah is under the thrall of the Church of Jesus Christ of the Latter Day Saints, also known as the Mormons, whose history includes open discrimination against black people who were disdained as the descendants of Ham. Despite the fact that these racist teachings have since been repudiated and stricken from Mormon instruction, some felt that continuing bias in the community, evidenced by the ugly note, affected Andrews's sentence. Steve and the people at Amnesty asked me to facilitate meetings they were having trouble setting up—one with the church leadership and another between Governor Norman Bangerter and William Andrews's mother.

I met Steve and Amnesty's Ashanti Chimurenga in Salt Lake

City. Our first meeting, with elders of the church, was short and unavailing. While the note and its implication were troubling, they felt the changes in church doctrine on racism had been appropriately communicated to the membership. Unwilling to interfere with the operation of the law, there was nothing they could do.

Next, I met Steve and Mrs. Andrews outside the governor's mansion. She was gracious and thanked me for coming, but was quite reserved. Considering the situation, I wasn't surprised.

We didn't have to wait long for Governor Bangerter, but you could cut the tension with a knife. In his office, the governor joined us around a wooden table rather than remaining behind his desk, a gesture I appreciated. But that was all we got. Steve made his case, touching on all the salient points, without getting a response. Sensing that we weren't getting through, Mrs. Andrews began talking about her son, about the horror of the crime and her own confused feelings. She knew that he'd done wrong, but he hadn't killed anyone; taking his life would be neither right nor fair. My heart ached to see this good woman plead—not beg, but plead—for her son's life. She fought back tears and maintained her composure, but the strain was obvious. How does one survive this?

When Mrs. Andrews ran out of words and the governor said nothing hopeful, the meeting reached one of those points that I sensed would end with him looking at his watch and thanking us for coming. Knowing what that would mean for William Andrews, I couldn't stay silent. I reminded the governor of the tragic aftermath of the recent verdict in the Los Angeles trial of the policemen responsible for the Rodney King beating and said those who care about our society should consider it a national wake-up call. All of us, but particularly the leaders, needed to reassess some of the assumptions we live by but rarely examine. Without mentioning the Mormon Church's history, I pointed out that latent racist tendencies are an inevitable carryover from the days of slavery, segregation, and Jim Crow, and that we owe it to ourselves to recognize this, to do everything in our power to acknowledge it, and, more important, to change it. Missing my point entirely, Bangerter expressed his concern that racial unrest might result from Mr. Andrews's execution. Didn't, I wondered, his concerns subtly underscore my very point? But how to express that without going over the same territory again?

The governor looked at his watch and begged our pardon. Together we rose, doing the incredibly painful dance of pretending we didn't know he had already decided to kill Mrs. Andrews's son. We shook hands, thanked him for his time, and left. Once outside, somehow clinging to her dignity, Mrs. Andrews quietly expressed appreciation for my help and went off with Steve. And I went home, "free, white, and twenty-one," and needing to scream. Bangerter did nothing, and William Andrews is no more.

Marvin and I were moving through the painful process of trying to develop a wonderful book into a motion picture. The book, *In Silence* by Ruth Sidransky, is the story of her life as the hearing child of deaf parents in 1930s–1940s New York. Ruth's mother, a beautiful, shy woman, and her father, a vibrant, brilliantly vivacious character, lived in a world of silence that required their daughter to be interpreter, translator, negotiator, and often parent for her parents. We had been deeply moved by the book, had come to know Ruth, and were thrilled when Marvin's friend Bruce Rubin, the highly regarded screenwriter of *Ghost* and *Jacob's Ladder*, introduced us at Paramount Pictures and helped us secure a deal to develop it. After months of discussions, meetings and greetings, promises and reassessments, we were cast adrift by one of those too-regular seismic events in Hollywood: regime change at the studio. Amazingly, given the new-broom-sweeps-clean policy that usually accompanies such developments, we survived and were assigned a new executive. This led to more meetings, a slightly lower budget projection, discussions of less-pricey writers, and finally the go-ahead to scout New York locations. That was a very good sign because Paramount was putting up some money and, we hoped, getting a little bit pregnant. Before we could leave, however, somebody pulled the plug on the trip, executive shuffle struck again, and we were back at square one.

Given the crazy-making nature of trying to do something creative in the face of money-crunchers and terminally job-insecure development executives, it was always a relief to get away from the lunacy of Hollywood and deal with something real—like the death penalty. Learning that Bonnie Raitt's fall tour included Richmond, I asked if she'd set aside some tickets so Marie could raise funds for the Virginia Coalition on Jails and Prisons. Bonnie agreed, and I flew in. We had a ball. Bonnie was wonderful, as always, and the show was a smash. We did a lot of press, getting in a few good licks about Joe, the death penalty in general, and the work of the Coalition. Marie was thrilled though a bit off balance, since Willie Leroy Jones was scheduled to die very soon. But she rallied and left Willie for a while to come to the show, almost breaking down as Bonnie took time between numbers to talk about her work.

We beat our brains out to get *In Silence* moving again. The studio had been so passive that I was relieved, if taken aback, to be contacted by Mrs. Sadako Ogata. She had been serious about my taking a trip for the UNHCR and had in mind a doozy—to two areas of concern. The first was Somalia, where a collapse of civil government and a struggle between two warlords complicated a drought-related famine and left people starving in frightening numbers. Those with enough strength had staggered across the border, creating a mammoth refugee emergency just inside Kenya. Those left in Somalia were dying. Her second concern was Bosnia, where what had been dismissed as an age-old ethnic conflict was laying waste to the country, and generating what looked like a genocidal campaign against Bosnian Muslims. In neither case had the world shown significant concern. The UNHCR was doing its best with both emergencies, but absent greater international support, these situations, already catastrophic, would only worsen. Mrs. Ogata hoped that after seeing it for themselves, a group of people who could command media attention would help awaken the

U.S., and perhaps the rest of the world. She knew there was some danger, but thought it critically important.

The result was . . . well, how many experiences can alter one's life dramatically? I guess I'm still finding out. The entire trip was a journey into fear that forced me to deal with some personal demons, the power of which I had barely glimpsed. I made lifelong friendships, witnessed suffering that rivaled anything I had yet seen or heard about, and, once again, was inspired by the selfless devotion of talented, dedicated people who would neither tolerate nor ignore human suffering.

In Somalia our little troupe braved dangerous flights, mine fields, gun-toting children, the danger of attack by hostile forces, and a level of death and human misery that defies comprehension. The harshness of this reality was ameliorated, though, by the courage of those who rose above the strife to help their neighbors, and by those from outside who rushed in to assist. The International Medical Corps operated a M*A*S*H-like surgery in the midst of turmoil that defined heroism. And even with the daily horror of bodies left beside the road like trash, the disease-ridden camps and clinics, and the carnage from the fighting, the eye-popping beauty of the Somali people was a miracle impossible to ignore. My own nearly crippling attacks of claustrophobia during this trip led not only to personal discoveries, but to acts of kindness and generosity on the part of my colleagues— one in particular—that will never leave me. And somehow there were moments of great joy and even hilarity.

In Bosnia we were smaller in number but exposed to no less. From survivors of the Serb concentration camps we learned of torture, rape, and slaughter. We picked our way through war in a convoy of unarmed UN supply trucks, every nerve ending at attention. We sneaked under guard through "sniper alley" into Sarajevo, then made our way carefully in this once-beautiful city to hear and convey messages, dodge sniper bullets, and witness daily acts of astonishing courage. And we are richer for it. (See "Somalia/Bosnia Journal" at www.mikefarrell.org/Journals.html.)

* * *

Every return from these forays into other worlds made me more deeply appreciative of what I had been given in life and more intent on doing what I could to respond to injustice. Sometimes there would be nothing I could do, but when I could, I tried. At a minimum I could use the public forum available to me to let others know what I had seen.

In February of '93, former Congressman Dave Nagle called. Iowa, one of then thirteen states in the country without a death penalty, was under pressure to reinstate it. An open session in the Iowa State Senate would debate the question, and if I'd come, I could address the body. It was a scary notion but Dave thought it would help.

After a quick flight to Des Moines, it was straight to the Capitol for a press conference and no second thoughts. Iowa had long been firmly in the ranks of non-killing states, but a typically loud and angry element, sure there was no satisfaction until blood was spilled, had pushed the issue until it might pass. The press conference was fortunately absent the fire-breathers, so we got through it—into the Senate chamber and right to the podium. A clever parliamentarian, Dave ceded his allotted minutes so I could give a quick historical perspective and then focus on the political nature of the modern American death penalty, ending with a few specific cases as illustrations. My full presentation can be found online ("Iowa State Legislature Speech," www.mikefarrell.org/speeches.html), but here's a brief excerpt:

- Barry Lee Fairchild is soon to be executed in Arkansas for the rape/murder of a white nurse. New evidence shows that he was the fourteenth black man to have been brought into the sheriff's office. Each was told they had proof he had done it. Each was beaten in an attempt to extract a confession. The other thirteen refused to submit. Barry gave in. The difference is that he is mentally retarded.
- In January of this year, Charles Stamper was carried to the electric chair in Virginia after being lifted by three guards out of his wheelchair.

- On November 20, 1992, Cornelius Singleton was electrocuted after signing, with his X, a confession he couldn't read. He had an IQ of approximately 61.
- In January of 1992, Rickey Rector, who had been effectively lobotomized by a self-inflicted gunshot wound at the time of his crime and had virtually no comprehension of his situation, was led to his execution. He left the dessert from his last meal waiting in the cell for his return.
- In Florida in 1990, Jesse Tafero's head was set afire during his execution. Tafero's codefendant was later freed when the prosecution's case was disproved.
- This month, the Supreme Court of the United States, in the *Herrera* case, held that innocence was not sufficient justification to stop an execution—a decision Justice Blackmun, in dissent, said was "perilously close to simple murder."

I spent a restless night, flew home, and didn't know the result until Dave called the next day to say that we had won. Iowa remains a non-killing state today.

In the spring I lost my sister. Sally wasn't sick for long, which is a blessing, and the doctor assured us she didn't suffer. But the hammer of mortality comes down with a deafening thud, leaving one helpless before it. After a brief and unsuccessful young marriage, Sal had married again, this time to a jerk. I think the insecurity caused by her bad eye cast a shadow over her life, particularly her view of herself, which never allowed her to claim the person she was. Terrifically bright, unfailingly sweet and ever thoughtful, she allowed herself to be subsumed by her husband's trail of failure. The family accepted him for her sake, but he was a bigot and, I later came to believe, an abuser. They made their home in Oregon. There were visits, but the relationship was strained; familial but not intimate. To her great credit, Sal raised three beautiful kids and fought to protect them from the damage of her failed marriage. She struggled to find ways to express the beauty of her nature. She finally left the moron, a profoundly positive and healing step, only to have her ability to enjoy a new life of freedom and self-discovery abruptly ended by cancer. Kathy, Jim, and I followed our mom behind the casket down the aisle for the funeral mass, astonished at Agnes's strength, unbelieving of the suddenness of it all, hopeful that there was comfort in the ritual, and prayerful that there was finally release for Sal. Beyond my sorrow about what might have been—should have been—there continues a deep and echoing sense of loss at her death.

Chapter 21
CATHEDRALS

L ater that year I was invited by Pat Keohane, warden of the federal penitentiary in Terre Haute, Indiana, to preside at graduation exercises for inmates who had done sufficient work to earn degrees. Though he disagreed with my position on the death penalty (his institution housed the federal death row), Keohane knew of my interest in prison reform and thought the inmates would appreciate my being there. I said I'd come if the trip included a tour of the place.

The prison was more modern and cleaner than I expected. On a large plot of land outside Terre Haute, it housed two separate facilities: a secondary prison for minimum- and medium-security inmates, and the primary one for maximum security. Keohane is a big, bull-necked, powerful-looking man with a surprisingly gentle, amiable manner, and I liked him at once. After I met the staff, who quizzed me a bit about my interest in prisons and my position on the death penalty, their initial reserve seemed to ease a bit, and there were even words of approval, if not agreement.

The graduation was set for the afternoon, so I went over to the minimum/medium-security side, where two or three hundred men greeted me warmly. I hadn't prepared anything, so just explained why I was there and offered to shoot the bull.

There were plenty of questions about M*A*S*H, quite a few about Hot Lips, of course. Some wanted to know about Hollywood and how much money people made, I made, they could make. We had a pretty good time. Talk of the prison system and the death penalty segued into complaints about their situation, which many felt—no surprise—to be unfair, and the drug laws, which they saw as nonsensical. About two-thirds of them were there for drug-related crimes. When I asked how many were involved in additional crimes, violent or otherwise, most of the hands dropped. There's got to be a better way to deal with a public health problem like drug abuse than putting people in institutions where they learn how to be real criminals.

For the graduation we passed through the inevitable gates, security areas, and self-locking barred doors into a large hall where thirty or forty men sat on benches before a podium. Staff and some visitors helped fill the room. I had heard about the group being honored, many of whom were receiving their GEDs. Others were getting college degrees, and two were to receive advanced degrees—all of which was encouraged by the administration. Ironically, some of these men who had studied so hard to better themselves would never see the outside of these walls.

As the exercise began, some of the educational staff spoke, showing pride in their students. Keohane thanked the men for their hard work and offered hope that this would be a ticket to a better life. Then he introduced me. I talked about The House and what I was taught there, about the capacity to transform one's life, and about the ability to make a contribution in whatever circumstance we find ourselves. Finally I talked about the importance—actually the necessity—of love, attention, and respect in all of our lives. Keohane asked if I'd help pass out the certificates of achievement, so I got the chance to shake each man's hand. I was touched by their gratitude.

After it was over, the warden took me on the tour. I was impressed that we went everywhere unescorted, passing through large groups of inmates in the recreation and mess areas. If someone had a bone to pick, we would have made very convenient hostages. Going through the crowds, I noted the number of men who greeted him familiarly in what seemed a genuinely respectful manner. As we moved along, the glances slid from him to me, with eyes widening and smiles breaking out. Hands stretched out to shake mine, and men said, "Hey, man, what're you doing here?" "Hey, how you doin'?" "Where's Hot Lips?" "How's Hawkeye?" "Thanks for coming here."

We went into the segregation area where hard-core and troublesome inmates were housed. Some of the doors were solid with small Plexiglas windows. The most we could do was look in, sometimes to get a wave in response, often to be ignored. In one area a wing extended off the hall with a row of cells visible on one side. It reminded me of the death row at Tennessee State Prison so many years earlier. From down at the end, we could hear screaming curses from what was a very angry if not completely crazy man. Keohane looked a question at me, I nodded, and we walked down the row of cells, the volume increasing as we neared the end. A good-looking, muscular black man, probably in his thirties, stood there clinging to the bars and raining curses down on the world, the institution, and, when he saw us, the warden, at the top of his lungs.

Keohane addressed him by name. While the volume decreased, the rant continued. His complaint was apparently well known to the warden. As his agitation lessened, the two were soon conversing, the prisoner maintaining a very loud but more rational tone. After a moment, the warden nodded his head to me and said, "Recognize him?"

The man shifted his eyes quickly toward me, away, and then looked again, quizzically. "FBI?" he asked the warden.

"Nope," Keohane replied. "You ever watch M*A*S*H?"

The head snapped back to me, his eyes widening, his mouth moving into a smile. "No shit!" Suddenly a different person, he stuck his hand out through the bars and said, "Hey, man, how the fuck'r you doing?"

I shook his hand and said, "I'm doing fine, man. How the fuck are you?" We all laughed. He was a very bright guy, and when our time was over I felt odd leaving him there. He thanked me for coming and said he hoped I'd come back. I said I'd like to, though I haven't. Pat Keohane left for another institution a few months later.

Walking out of the maximum-security side, the warden invited me to meet his family. I discovered the reason—or at least part of it—for his gentle manner when I met his wife and son in their modest but lovely house on the grounds. His son has Down's syndrome. From the Special Olympics, I've come to know those with Down's syndrome as some of the most loving and uncomplicatedly sweet human beings in existence. Those who deal with them, whether parents or caregivers, cannot avoid being affected by their pure hearts. I'd be very surprised if Pat Keohane's sensitivity, his awareness, and his humane manner toward those in his charge didn't have a lot to do with his son.

Dick Burr called me a few weeks later. He was trying to save the life of Gary Graham, another young black man scheduled to die in Texas for a hotly contested murder. Graham's conviction was based on the testimony of a single eyewitness. Two other witnesses who had seen the perpetrator just as clearly—perhaps more so—said that Graham was not the man. Their statements never made it into court, however, and Burr was trying very hard to stop the execution in order to get all the facts admitted. I wasn't able to make it in time for the press conference Dick had set up, but I called Danny Glover, who flew down. In the ensuing weeks, Danny and I did a lot of press on the case. I appeared on a couple of television shows debating members of a bloodthirsty Texas group that wanted more and quicker executions, pulling out all the emotional stops in their advocacy. It was chilling. Dick did get a stay of execution, thankfully, and the struggle continued.

Hardy Jones, a documentary filmmaker specializing in environmental issues, had been working for some time on the loss of underwater coral reefs and the danger signal this was for the environment. In the summer of 1993, a project came together that had my kids and I diving in the South Pacific to point out the harm being done and how to correct it. Taking Shelley and the kids made it a particularly glorious experience. Erin, Mike and I became certified scuba divers with a few weeks instruction (Shelley said she'd stay in the boat, thank you), and off we went to Tahiti. Diving off Bora Bora, we saw damage to the fragile coral ecosystem by silt from poor agricultural practices and, more directly, by stupid tourists who drop anchors on it or cut off pieces to take home. We then flew 500 miles north to the Rangiroa Atoll, where the extravagant colors and living sculptures of coral reefs are so miraculously, deliciously thrilling they make you want to pray. The wonder of their delicacy, the genius of their construction, is breathtaking—which can be a problem when you're dozens of feet underwater. Thanks to the too-often-ill-used magic of television, we were able to bring *Cathedrals in the Sea* to a worldwide audience courtesy of the Audubon Society.

An atoll is a circular reef, a ring with a lagoon in the middle, usually with one or two openings through which water feeds in and out with the tide. This phenomenon created one of the most thrilling experiences I've ever had. One afternoon we took the boat out onto the ocean side and, after giving a hammerhead shark time to go away, went into the water and down about 120 feet, deeper than the kids and I had ever gone. Following our guide to the opening of the breach in the reef, we waited for his signal to move into the current. Holding there, we were treated to an astonishing sight: a school of sharks, above us and a bit farther into the reef. Our guide had told us what to expect, but I was completely blown away. They were gray reef sharks, at least 500 of them. And beyond them, the guide pointed out excitedly, was a school of barracuda. I found myself hoping that his excitement was *excitement* excitement and not anxiety or perhaps terror.

Soon some of the sharks came our way. I kept reminding myself that we'd been told they were not a danger unless we did something silly. I wasn't sure, though, what constituted silly to a shark. Erin and Mike had settled into a little bowl to watch the extraordinary show. Seeing a shark heading toward them, I quickly swam down and put myself between my kids and the intruder. It was an instinctive parental act, but as I did it I almost laughed (also not a good thing to do underwater), thinking that if this guy really wanted them, going through me would not be that big a problem. Thankfully, he or she just took a look and went on by. Before long the thrill of having good-sized sharks coasting by to look us over became almost commonplace.

Our guide waited for the tide to kick in, after which he signaled us out into the current away from the wall of rock. It was like nothing I've ever known. We flew! We just put our hands out like Superman as the tide propelled us along at what seemed an incredible rate. The rock wall slipped by beside us, fish rode along on the current with us, and the school of sharks, feeding on the delicacies brought their way by the tide, remained in place above as we passed beneath. In too short a time the ride was over, leaving us in the gorgeous lagoon, again surrounded by nature's delicate beauty.

Then I had another, slightly different adventure. Having been down to such a depth, we had to come up at a regulated pace in order to avoid nitrogen bubbles in the blood: "the bends." We gathered together and I checked the meter showing how much oxygen was left in each of the kids' tanks. They were fine. When our guide came over to see if we were okay on oxygen, I gave him the thumbs-up. As he turned away, I noticed I was having difficulty breathing and realized I hadn't checked my own gauge. Looking down, I found my meter in the red. Suddenly there was nothing coming through. Nothing. This was not good. I looked up and saw the guide swimming away toward the cameraman. Turning, I saw Mike going after him. Trying not to panic, I turned further and spotted Erin. Thank God she was looking right at me. I gave her the hands-across-the-throat sign meaning "no air," and she, sweet child, understood immediately. Swimming to me, she took two breaths and passed her breathing tube over. I took two and handed it back. It worked just as it was supposed to. We continued this routine as we rose slowly toward the surface, making sure we didn't ascend any faster than the bubbles from our common mouthpiece. When we finally broke out on the surface, I thanked my lovely daughter for her great presence of mind and for saving my life. The guide splashed to the surface a moment later, panicked at having lost sight of us, but I said there was no problem, thanks, I had Erin to take care of me.

* * *

Making progress with *In Silence* at Paramount, Marvin and I brought in Corey Blechman, who had done the first two drafts of *Dominic and Eugene*. He was soon off working on the script, while I considered an offer that would take me away for a few weeks. David W. Rintels, who had written and produced *Choices of the Heart*, about the four church-women in El Salvador, had since become a good friend. Along with many highly regarded films, David had written a wonderful one-man play about Clarence Darrow that Henry Fonda had performed to much acclaim. David planned to restage the play with George C. Scott, but that had apparently changed because he called and asked me to do it for a six-week run across the country. I was equal parts thrilled and panicked at the thought. Darrow is one of the great heroes of the movement to abolish the death penalty. Even without having seen the play, I knew it would be a great fit from that per-spective. And what I knew of him beyond that was certainly enticing. But I still had to deal with the panic. I had done plays, of course, including the Kennedy one-man show. But that had been on tape, not before a live audience, and wasn't really a fair comparison. The offer, however, was real, and I had to respond. Then I learned that David would direct the show. How could I pass it up?

It was a great experience and I'm thankful for it, but doing a one-man show is damned hard work. Beyond the research, rehearsal, and learning techniques to keep from losing your voice, being on stage maintaining a character—The Character—for a couple of hours all by yourself is a hell of a task. I read everything I could get my hands on about Darrow and really enjoyed getting to know him. An extraor-dinarily intelligent man, he was profoundly committed to social justice, highly sensitive to the suffering of others, terribly sexist, egomaniacal, generous, carefree, careless, powerful, and deeply principled. And what a mind! The toughest thing about doing the show was the absence of other actors to check with, talk to, complain about, care for, worry with, and lean on. Sometimes you want to say, *God, it's really working tonight, don't you think?* Or, *What happened to that laugh?*

I'm sure there was supposed to be a laugh there. Or, Is somebody groaning out there or is that snoring I hear? I ended up talking to the mirror a lot.

Into 1994, Joe Giarratano continued to do well. His Peace Studies program developed a great record at Augusta. Marie kept me up to date. I was able to recycle some computers and word processors for Joe's classes. Colman McCarthy arranged for students from D.C. to talk to Joe and some who had gone through the program. These criminals and wastrels were surprisingly open to lessons about dignity, their innate value, and the power of nonviolence. As the training continued, no one who took part had a disciplinary write-up. The media gave the program's success, and Joe, a great deal of attention. It was what you hope for in these situations, yet Joe was still behind bars.

Patch Adams called looking for advice. As a result of his book about greed in the health care industry, some big-name producers and agents were trying to get the rights to do a movie about his life. I just love Patch, who is truly one of a kind, and we'd stayed in touch since the Russia trip. A revolutionary in clown's clothing, he's a doctor who wants only to serve humanity. He's incensed that people in this country go without medical care while doctors, pharmaceutical companies, and hospitals get rich. As a result of the book, he'd been flown out to Hollywood, chauffeured, wined, dined, and generally given the treatment. He hated it.

"Mike," he roared, "I don't know these people, and I don't trust them. And they certainly don't know me!"

The Hollywood folks were taking the wrong approach with Patch, but I gave him the best advice I could: There might be a lot of money in it for the free hospital he wanted to build.

"But I know you, and I trust you. Why don't you do the movie?"

I explained that we didn't have the kind of access the others were offering and couldn't provide the same potential for success. But he kept insisting, and we decided to give it a try.

Marvin and I took the idea to Barry Kemp, the creator of Shelley's show, *Coach*. Barry had proven to be every bit the decent guy Shelley pegged him for at the outset. *Coach* was shot at Universal, and Barry's deal there included making features, so we went to see him. I told Barry how Patch and I had met in the Soviet Union. We described his energy and optimism, his "I wake up every morning and decide it's going to be a joyous day" intentionality. Marvin, who can be pretty cynical, talked about how charmed he was by Patch's innocent enthusiasm. We pitched a Patch movie as a kind of *Good Morning, Vietnam* in the medical world. Barry loved the idea, and we struck a deal. It was the beginning of a long, twisting, pothole-filled road and this, as it turned out, may have been the best part of the experience.

Chapter 22
SACRED AND PROFANE

J oe Ingle was right. The machinery had not only cranked up; it was devouring us, eating away at the soul of the nation, though most Americans didn't yet know it. But there were people who did. It was an uphill fight, but the company was good.

Leonard Weinglass came to see me. Len had endeared himself to many—and become Public Enemy #1 to many more—with his defense of the Chicago Seven after the debacle of the 1968 Democratic Convention. He now represented Mumia Abu-Jamal, a black activist condemned for the murder of Philadelphia police officer Daniel Faulkner a dozen years earlier. Abu-Jamal, long a politically active, very articulate critic of police racism in the City of Brotherly Love, and a man with no criminal record, became a *cause célèbre* during the trial and more so once convicted. While not unusual as a black man on death row for killing a white, he was rare in being able to write, broadcast, and argue his case to great effect. Adopted by many in the left as a prime example of the racism in the system, his case took on unusual political significance. While the facts around the shooting were cloudy—and witness testimonies before, during, and after the trial contradictory—there were also many problems with the case, including the behavior of the judge. Evidence of coerced testimony was rampant, and the history of the Philadelphia Police Department reeked of racism and corruption. One of the more troubling aspects was the prosecutor's assertion that the wounded Abu-Jamal had shouted out a confession while in the company of police at the hospital, a claim directly contradicted by the written report of the officer with him at the time. Not mentioned by police until two months after the incident, the recall of the confession was extremely timely, given the Department's need for a defense against Abu-Jamal's suit for physical abuse. It was hard to believe that two veteran officers forgot such a key piece of evidence until it was needed for the state's case.

Many believed that Abu-Jamal was an innocent victim of a racist police conspiracy and loudly demanded his immediate release: the chant *Free Mumia* becoming a regular part of social justice demonstrations. The Pennsylvania Fraternal Order of Police (FOP) had taken up the cudgel, using Officer Faulkner's widow Maureen as the up-front figure in their campaign to kill Abu-Jamal. Len thought he had a good chance of getting a new trial based on the record, but it would take money. He asked me to co-chair the Committee to Save Mumia Abu-Jamal with Ossie Davis, a man I greatly admired, to raise funds for the defense. This was a can of worms, but I liked Ossie, had faith in Len, and believed the death penalty an abomination. I agreed, with the caveat that it be clearly understood that I thought Mumia Abu-Jamal deserved a fair trial, not that I was convinced of his innocence. None of that mattered, of course. I was immediately slandered on television and in the press as a know-nothing, out-of-work actor looking for attention, while the pro-Mumia side was pissed at me for not declaring him innocent. We raised some dough, however, and Len went to work.

Because Barry Kemp's contract was with Universal, we had to piggyback our deal onto his. Once that was settled, he negotiated the deal for the Patch movie with the studio. Because these things move at a glacial pace, I accompanied two Human Rights Watch researchers investigating conditions on the U.S.-Mexico border. HRW had issued reports the two preceding years, finding Border Patrol agents responsible for beatings, sexual abuse, rape, and murder. The agents often escaped prosecution due to false reports, cover-up by fellow officers, and a tendency to close ranks against victims, witnesses making charges, and investigative agencies. The Border Patrol is part of the

Immigration and Naturalization Service (INS), and its commissioner in 1992, Gene McNary, refused to meet with HRW and dismissed its report out of hand. The relationship improved with the appointment of a new commissioner, but the behavior of the agents remained pretty much the same.

Allyson Collins and Lee Tucker, a researcher/investigator and a lawyer, met me near San Diego, where we interviewed the head of the Border Patrol's western region and some of his agents. We rode out on patrol, examining the areas most used by people coming across, then went into Tijuana, Mexico, to see things from that perspective.

The Border Patrol has a tough job and the political pressures are huge. They're battered from all sides: by racists and nativists, anti-immigration forces, and open-border advocates, as well as those concerned about refugee rights, drug smuggling, documentation, worker's rights, and the effects of this service-level work force on both countries' economies. Politicians are notorious cowards on the issue, aware that the regional economy depends on a continuing flow of workers, but unwilling to face the issue squarely for fear of offending voters on one side or the other. HRW's concern is straightforward: People who are apprehended coming across the border illegally still have rights and should be treated fairly and appropriately. Unfortunately, as sometimes happens with those in authority, some Border Patrol agents have adopted an "it's war" attitude. Harassment, brutality, rape, and even murder can result.

On the U.S. side, we encountered a friendly openness that quickly degenerated when we cited specific instances of criminal behavior on the part of agents. The political pressure we understood, but there was no excuse for violence and abuse against people who were, after all, primarily looking for work. In Tijuana we met people who had been cruelly beaten by BP officers. One man, arrested with a group that included his pregnant sister-in-law, had objected when an officer beat the woman because she had been unable to kneel at his order. The officer, whom the survivors claimed was drunk, shot him. Charges were filed and the incident investigated, but the witnesses were held in custody, where they say they were harassed and intimidated. Faced with official disbelief, the woman's husband offered to take a lie detector test, but it was never administered. When the gunshot victim died, the family was sent home. Complaints from the Mexican Consulate met the response that the agent's actions were in accordance with INS regulations. Other reports of shootings, beatings, and sexual abuse got the same treatment. Those to whom we spoke in Mexico had little respect for the BP agents and no faith that anything would be done for those who suffered at their hands without meaningful leadership from Washington.

We then flew to Tucson, Arizona, and drove to Nogales, a town that straddles the U.S.-Mexican border. Nogales got far less attention than San Diego, and things were worse. The facility where detainees were held, a hot, dirty place, lacked even the required posters informing them of their rights. On the Mexican side, we met a young woman who had come through the fence with a friend in order to shop. Picked up by a BP officer, she was taken to a deserted area and raped. Despite intimidation from investigators, she pressed charges. The agent was indicted, but the County Attorney dropped the charges in return for a "no contest" plea to a lesser offense. The agent got a year in jail. Other women told stories just as lousy or worse, but few had any hope of holding the men accountable. Authorities on the Mexican side were frustrated at being unable to protect their people or even work satisfactorily with their counterparts across the border.

Back in Tucson we met with Justice Department prosecutors and attorneys for non-governmental organizations fighting for the rights of detainees and citizens of Latin American descent who were harassed and even imprisoned on the suspicion that they were illegal. It all felt sadly familiar, as these were some of the same people who had offered sanctuary to refugees from the terror in El Salvador and Guatemala. Refugee issues are a major problem, rife with racist policies, beliefs, and practices, and won't go away without courageous leadership on the national level. (For the HRW report, go to www.hrw.org and see "Crossing the Line—Human Rights Abuses along the U.S. Border with Mexico Persist Amid a Climate of Impunity.")

Time brings change and growth, and sometimes more than you expect. My daughter Erin, the kid who had been afraid to leave the house alone, spent her junior year at Queen's College in London. Mike was out in the world trying to make sense of things. And at home we had a scare. My mom was getting on in years, and we wanted her to come live with us, so Shelley found a new home complete with a guest house for Agnes. As always with a new place, work needed to be done. While inspecting some reconstruction with Tom Callaway, our friend and designer, Shelley slipped and fell between the exposed beams of an upstairs bathroom. Tom caught her before going all the way through, but she suffered broken ribs and terrible bruising. The examination showed two things that needed further testing: one was related to her heart and the other indicated potential liver problems. The heart question was easily resolved, but the elevated liver enzymes set us on an odyssey that continued for years.

In late August, Nebraskans against the Death Penalty asked for help in stopping the first execution in their state in thirty-five years. Harold "Wili" Otey, another black man sentenced to die for the rape and murder of a white woman, had been represented by an attorney with little experience. Otey had maintained his innocence for the seventeen years he'd been on Nebraska's death row, and during that time he'd become a different man from the illiterate racetrack worker who'd been convicted, even in the eyes of the authorities. He'd written three books of poetry and earned so much trust that he was given extraordinary freedom of movement within the prison. But his time had run out. The governor offered to consider clemency if he'd express remorse for the crime, but Otey said he couldn't pretend sorrow for a crime he didn't commit.

I went to Lincoln for a press conference calling for clemency, sat in with people trying to work out a last-minute deal, and took part in a demonstration on the Capitol steps.

Given the chance to meet Wili, I was shown into a small room in the prison. After a short time he came in by himself. No guards. These meetings are always difficult because you don't know what to expect, but Wili was calm, quiet, a very dignified man. He said thanks for coming all this way just for him. I didn't know quite what to say, but he was very peaceful and took pains to show that my being there mattered.

Wili Otey died in Nebraska's electric chair. His lawyer said he made no final statement, only mouthing the words *I love you* to her before the guards pulled the leather mask over his face. Outside, drunken members of a cheering crowd shouted, "Fry the nigger!"

A month later I got a call from Dale Baich, Ohio's Assistant State Public Defender. Following the example of Robert Harris's case, Baich made a videotape for Governor George Voinovich, asking him to stop the execution of Anthony Apanovitch. He had discovered evidence of Apanovitch's innocence that had been kept from his lawyers at trial, and he wanted me to host the video. I don't know if the tape made any difference, but Baich got the case back into court, and Apanovitch remains on death row today, awaiting the results.

That fall, as Marvin and I were looking for a writer for *Patch* at Universal and still stuck in neutral with *In Silence* at Paramount, I got a call from the "little giant": Paul McCleary of the Christian Children's Fund. He was going to Cuba, hoping to find ways to ease problems created by the collapse of the Soviet Bloc and the continuing U.S. embargo. Shortages of medicine, medical equipment, school supplies, and other essentials were devastating the Cuban people— particularly the children. Paul thought there must be a way around the limitations laid on by our ideologues to get help to those who needed it, and he wanted me with him.

I'd never been to Cuba and had mixed feelings from conflicting reports, so I agreed. The charismatic Fidel had charmed many

Americans who saw the benefits of his *revolución* even as the human rights community reported strong-arm tactics, repression of dissent, and concern about religious freedom. Neither a Solidarity groupie nor an ally of those to whom he was the devil incarnate, I took a kind of "Swiss" position. I was concerned about human rights and suspicious of the closed political system, but strongly opposed to U.S. belligerence, believing an end to the embargo and better relations would do more to open Cuban society than our idiotic attempts at assassination and economic strangulation could ever bring about.

Paul assembled a well-rounded delegation: a congressional aide, a writer, a doctor, and three people from philanthropic foundations, one of whom was my old friend Janet Shenk from Arca. I brought another to the party by calling my then-agent, a great guy named Jack X. Fields, to say I'd be out of touch for a bit; when he heard where I was going, he wanted to come, too. Jack arranged cases of medicine to take in and was a funny, charming, generous, and always self-effacing companion.

The trip was equal parts hilarious, infuriating, and educational. I was surprised by the fervor of the Cold War mindset that hit us even before we left the country. Our welcome in Cuba, on the other hand, was for the most part as gracious as one would expect for a party openly disagreeing with U.S. policies. We were treated to the expected dog-and-pony shows demonstrating the wonders the regime had wrought in spite of the harassment, intimidation, and economic interference from Uncle Sam. A number of these achievements were pretty impressive, I will say. Literacy, below fifty percent during Batista's time, had nearly doubled, with the average Cuban completing the tenth grade (while the rest of Latin America still averaged a fifth-grade level). Over ninety percent of Cuban homes had electricity—again, almost double what it was before Castro. Government-supported programs were ambitious and impressive, showing exciting progress in biotechnology and medical research, but shortages were painfully obvious, particularly in hospitals and schools.

People made do with less, largely thanks to the U.S. embargo.

Havana, storied and historic, was a delight on many levels, but the shortages were clearly evident. Most of the cars were older U.S. models, and fuel was scarce. Buses and some cabs mixed with motorbikes, bicycles, and a lot of pedestrians.

The richness of Cuban culture was everywhere, but a flight to the interior and a trip into the mountains to see the work of the rural medical practitioners were the highlights of the trip for me. In one small town we were received like visiting royalty as we presented the medicines Jack had provided. Then, on a tour of their pitifully supplied hospital, Jack spotted an ambulance up on blocks. Learning that it had been out of commission for months because it lacked tires, he got out his Canadian credit card (spending U.S. dollars is prohibited by U.S. law) and arranged for new ones.

Prisons weren't on our agenda, but I did talk to Ricardo Alarcón, President of the Cuban National Assembly, about human rights. Wary, he said the term *human rights* is subject to selective interpretation and that Cuba gets special scrutiny due to pressure from the U.S. But, he said, some of the criticisms were just, and steps were being taken to correct things. Yet the reports that indict Cuba for abuses, he said, ignore provocation from the north, including armed men from Florida, like those who had been dropped off a boat the previous month. Human rights, then, couldn't be easily discussed when attacks were continuing. He had a point. Whether American intelligence or anti-Castro groups out of Florida operating with a wink and a nod from the U.S., such attacks made it harder to fairly criticize Cuba.

Some of our toughest visits were to the special facilities for kids with medical problems. Seaside resorts for the wealthy during the pre-Castro days, they now served as treatment centers for diabetic and asthmatic kids. And I'll never forget the unit for Children of Chernobyl. Dr. Steven Ayres was a Christian Children's Fund board member and a public health specialist who had recently traveled to Byelorussia, where he worked with victims of the fallout from Chernobyl. He was impressed with the work being done in Cuba—they had treated over 12,000 kids with radiation sickness. The rest of us were just heartbroken. Hairless, anemic, weak, in some cases cancer-stricken with not long to live, they were playful and excited at our visit. This is where Jack knocked me out. Long a believer that photographs steal a part of your essence, he always avoided having his picture taken. But when a couple of the kids asked him to pose with them, he said yes without hesitation. That will always hold a special place in my heart. (For a full account, see "Cuba, Today," at www.mikefarrell.org/Journals.html.)

Shortly after we returned from Cuba, a DNA test moved Governor Wilder of Virginia to stop the execution of Earl Washington, whose case Joe Giarratano had championed for years. On the last day of his term, Wilder acted. Once again, however, he commuted Washington's sentence to life in prison instead of releasing him. Even though the DNA test clearly showed that the murder had not been committed by Earl, Wilder would let him spend the rest of his life in prison. Politics can be disgusting.

With Farrell/Minoff still in a holding pattern with *Patch* and *In Silence* as 1994 wound to a close, I tried not to think too much about what was coming. I'd gotten a call from Mrs. Ogata's office just after the slaughter in Rwanda, an orgy of blood that sent shivers down the spine. As in Bosnia, the world had chosen to turn away as somewhere between 500,000 and 1 million human beings, mostly of the minority Tutsi tribe, were massacred in less than three months. Authorities dismissed the atrocity as an "ancient tribal conflict" about which "good people can do nothing." To his everlasting shame, Bill Clinton dithered, squirming to avoid the word "genocide," the use of which would legally require action. This cowardice prevailed until the frenzy had largely passed and the expatriate Tutsi army, the Rwandese Patriotic Front (RPF), had established some control. The killing almost over, relief agencies were overwhelmed by the flood of refugees, their task complicated even more by the fact that those pouring out of Rwanda after the slaughter included many of the killers.

The first call from Mrs. Ogata raised the question of a trip to Rwanda, but it was postponed because a cholera epidemic had worsened the refugee situation. Things had now settled a bit and the trip was back on.

If Somalia and Bosnia had been a journey into fear, this was an adventure in terror. The idea of mad, rioting crowds hacking their victims to pieces with machetes conjures up all my deepest fears. And this wasn't just mindless carnage; it was planned and orchestrated. Brute power lashing out murderously is the stuff of my most ferocious childhood terrors and probably the origin of my need to understand and control. What I knew of Rwanda from reports in the press and Human Rights Watch told me it was the worst of my dreams and then some.

The trip was tough, but although frightening at times, it was never terrifying. As usual, my childhood nightmares had been magnified by the perspective of powerlessness. Becoming aware of one's strengths in such situations is an effective antidote.

Bloody murder suffused Rwanda, and the country's future was trapped in it. We visited the main prison in Kigali, packed so densely the people had to sleep in shifts. Making our way through the human sea inside was a challenge on every level. Men and women were separated more by agreement than architecture. Nuns and priests were charged with complicity, even participation, in the murders. People of all ages, many claiming innocence, sought our attention, while others cast baleful glances or pretended to ignore us. Given the heat and overcrowding, the conditions were disgusting, but those in charge did what they could. It was a fetid pit of human anguish.

Southeast of Kigali the government had left one of the massacre sites, the church at Ntarama, as they had found it, so that others could witness the carnage for themselves. I will never forget the skeleton of a man in the churchyard among the remains, still partly wrapped in the garments he wore when murdered—his arms and legs frozen in the posture of one running, a gruesome tableau of motion. Not far away, the skeletons of a number of children were gathered and I saw that this man had been killed while striving to protect his child. I still think of him, blessing his courage. Inside the church . . . well, I tried to describe a sanctuary carpeted with body parts at the beginning of "The Killing Ground" (see www.mikefarrell.org/Journals/Rwandaindex.html). It will never leave me.

We followed the refugees to Goma, Zaire (now the Democratic Republic of Congo), and into the camps maintained by the UNHCR. Those providing aid faced the same dilemma: how to justify food, shelter, and comfort for mass murderers who were still making nightly forays back across the border to continue the job. Seasoned relief workers, used to spending day and night in refugee camps, left these before dark. It's hard to walk through areas housing thousands of people in harsh conditions, but the presence of those who would kill us if they could added a new element.

The trip marked me, I think. We're all informed by every experience, and one can't come close to that kind of savagery without being somehow changed. I don't remember a conscious decision; no resolution suddenly formed itself in my mind. But I know I've never quite left it behind.

One night, not long after my return, Shelley and I were having dinner with Joe and Judy and some friends. There was a quiet moment, and I apparently drifted. I was brought back by Joe's voice: "Where did you go?"

I had been holding a glass of red wine, staring into it, and just kind of went away. I smiled, shrugged and apologized, but Joe reassured me that there was no need for that. He said it looked to him like a sacramental moment. Maybe it was.

Killing serves no human purpose. Killing in America's prisons is a cleaner-appearing, more "acceptable" version of the butchery in Rwanda's churches. As one dies at the hands of another, the killer dies in part as well. In this civilized, sophisticated, God-fearing, law-abiding country, those who stand by in silence, whether they understand it or not, are part of the killing.

Chapter 23
DEVIL'S CHAIR

Nineteen ninety-five was a bloody year. The Iowa Legislature again debated reinstating the death penalty. Again, we beat it back. A campaign to stop the first Montana execution in fifty-two years failed when Governor Mark Racicot killed Duncan McKenzie, who had been on death row for over twenty years. Illinois Governor Jim Edgar turned a deaf ear to pleas we had solicited from Senators Carol Moseley-Braun, Paul Simon, and the entire Congressional Black Caucus to stop the execution of Girvies Davis. Davis, an illiterate black man, was convicted largely on the basis of a hand-written confession he had supposedly given police. And then he was dead.

Mumia Abu-Jamal's case exploded as the new governor of Pennsylvania, a politically ambitious Tom Ridge (later the manipulator of the colored lights of Homeland Security), signed a death warrant despite ongoing appeals. Bellows arose from both sides and I was pulled into the fray, doing radio and television interviews, debating Abu-Jamal's former prosecutor on *Larry King Live* and the head of the Pennsylvania Fraternal Order of Police on CNN, responding to editorial attacks (see "Is It Wrong?" at www.mikefarrell.org/publications/isitwrong.html) and hate mail. Len Weinglass came through, frustrating Governor Ridge's ploy, and the struggle in the courts continued.

Steve Hawkins and I met in Little Rock for a press conference and clemency plea on behalf of Barry Fairchild, a mentally retarded African-American on Arkansas' death row. But Governor Jim Guy Tucker was unavailable. And Fairchild was soon dead.

* * *

A huge part of what saved me from even considering despair was the graduation of my glorious daughter from Vassar College. She had triumphed over her personal demons, had done exceptionally well academically and spent time abroad, as well as playing point guard on Vassar's varsity basketball team from her sophomore year on. The graduation exercise was lovely, as you'd expect from Vassar, and was proudly attended by her brother Mike and, as Erin introduced us to a friend, "all four of my parents." After a drive across the country on her way home from school, she blew all of our minds by announcing that, since she had so enjoyed herself at school in London, she was going to go back, get a job, and live in the city for a while.

A call from Vermont law professor Michael Mello prompted a campaign to stop the execution of Joseph Spaziano in Florida. Spaziano's was a truly extraordinary story that should be a motion picture. After more than twenty years on death row and at least five execution dates, we finally forced the state to reluctantly back off its intention to kill an innocent man. Though they still refuse to admit a mistake, as with Giarratano, justice may yet prevail.

Meanwhile, at Augusta, Giarratano's Peace Studies program became its own worst enemy. Prisoner-run programs succeeding where the Department of Corrections (DOC) failed didn't sit well with Virginia's new governor, George Allen, or Ron Angelone, his new DOC head. Angelone, a veteran of the vicious Texas system, immediately set out to establish his supremacy, and Joe Giarratano, a high-profile convict who had beaten the system and refused to play dead, topped off his hit list. Peace Studies/ATV was shut down, Giarratano was busted for taking a hit of some contraband wine, and things went from bad to worse. Augusta was shaken up, the Assistant Warden for Programs was transferred, and Joe was moved to Buckingham Correctional Center, where he was again labeled a snitch. He tried to handle himself carefully, but the rumor had the desired effect and Joe was stabbed. He survived, frustrating many, I'm sure.

* * *

Despite all their talk, Universal downgraded *Patch*, and we were told to make do with a less-than-A-list writer. Undaunted, we found a funny young guy named Steve Oedekerk to do the script. We brought Patch out, giving Steve the chance to experience this 6'6" elf with shoulder-length hair, handlebar mustache, outlandish clown clothing, and a smile that embraces everyone within view. Before it was in vogue for waiters to say, *If you need anything, my name is _____*, Patch never failed to ask the name of a waiter or service person and thank him or her personally when leaving. With Steve's eyes now a bit wider, we gave him our vision of the picture, answered his questions, and sent him merrily on his way.

In keeping with the general tone of the year, the wonderful *In Silence* began to look less and less likely. Marvin and I talked yet another development executive into letting us rewrite the script, but Paramount said, *Close, but no cigar*, and we were on our own.

We found a well-connected agent who liked the script and wanted to talk. I had always thought of Robin Williams as Bennie, the magical, ebullient man who was Ruth's deaf father. For my money there's no better physical actor than Robin. With the right director, he could be brilliant as a man who had no hearing and no words, yet was eloquent.

Well, wonderful things sometimes do happen in this business—or almost happen. The agent passed the script on to Robin, who apparently liked it, and asked if we'd be willing to fly to San Francisco for a meeting. Are you kidding? We met Robin's wife Marsha for lunch and a freewheeling discussion. She had a lot to say about what Robin did, so we loved hearing that she thought it was perfect for him. After lunch she drove us to their house where we met Robin, if briefly. We'd met before and I always found him very sweet and quite shy, though one wouldn't get that impression watching him on stage. He came into the room wearing bicycling gear; he'd either just come in from a ride or was heading out for one. He spoke very softly and was quite deferential, saying nice things about the script and mentioning a particular scene that he found very powerful. Then he left.

The whole encounter was a bit odd, but I remembered Marvin's advice years ago about *Dominick and Eugene:* If things are going well, don't argue. We talked to Marsha for a while longer, and everything seemed great. Needless to say, we were thrilled. On leaving, it seemed the deal was as good as done. Robin Williams was going to star in our picture. Bennie and Mary and Ruth would come to life. There would be tears and cheers and awards, and everyone would live happily ever after.

Not so fast, Johnson! Marvin and I were bouncing around back at the office, grinning and trying to figure out what to do next, when Marsha called and said something had come up. Robin's schedule had changed, and the whole thing was off. "Off?" Off. "Maybe . . . when he finishes whatever has come up . . . ?" No. She was sorry, but it wasn't going to work. Goodbye cheers and awards; hello tears. Jesus, did she let the air out of our balloon.

1996 started out with a bang. Literally. Before it was heard, I joined a broad-based campaign that included Human Rights Watch, Amnesty, the ACLU, dozens of legal experts, celebrities, and concerned psychiatric professionals. Our goal was to pressure Illinois Governor Jim Edgar to commute the death sentence of Guinevere Garcia, who had given up her appeals and "volunteered" to be executed. An addict and incest victim with a history of physical and sexual abuse, she had simply given up hope. Edgar acceded, and the commutation came just hours before her scheduled execution. When she got the word, this bitter young woman whom they had insisted wanted to die, affirmed her desire to live by gracefully thanking those who had championed her cause.

The bang came later that month, when John Albert Taylor, another "volunteer," died by firing squad in Utah. I hosted an online "death watch" with a connection to Taylor's attorney, who hoped to change her client's mind. A "volunteer" is a death row inmate who forgoes all legal appeals and says get on with it. It's a form of state-assisted suicide; they fold from the stress of living under the sword of

Damocles. Taylor thought the horror of his being killed by a firing squad (an option in Utah) would awaken America to the brutality of the system. I've heard it too many times; those who feel their life counts for nothing want to believe their death can count for something.

The *Patch* script Steve Oedekerk turned in was only a fraction of what we'd hoped for. It was fairly funny, but slick and superficial, never getting to the richness of the character. It wasn't just that Patch was funny, after all; it was the creative and courageous way he used humor. The army brat, the child of a distant father, the gangly loner and science nerd who had no friends and lost the one adult who believed in him to suicide, the young man who teetered on the brink of self-destruction, committing himself to a mental institution as a last hope, had finally, through the force of a singular will, turned his life into a wacky ode to joy. This antiauthoritarian, antic, impulsive, iconoclastic, bizarrely funny man was a human whoopee cushion who delighted in knocking down the walls of pretension and offering laughter, love, and truth in their place. Steve got some of the jokes, but he missed the Patch that would give the story meaning. Fortunately, as the draft went up the rungs at Universal, everyone agreed. So back Steve went, armed with our notes and encouraging words, to do a second draft. And we crossed our fingers.

California executed two men that year, William Bonin and Keith Daniel Williams. Each time, I stood with hundreds of others at the East Gate of San Quentin opposing it. I was now president of the board of directors of Death Penalty Focus, but the camera teams and reporters focused on me because of M*A*S*H, wanting to know how I could champion the life of a brutal, sadistic killer. I wasn't supporting the killer, I said, or the killings; I abhorred them, just as I did the arbitrary, ritualistic taking of life by the state. I believe we injure ourselves and cheapen our system in the process; we teach our young exactly the wrong lesson. The media enjoys playing back the horror stories of the crimes rather than examining what it does to us to kill.

With a sexual predator and serial killer like Bonin, the deck was pretty well stacked. But it was as important to stand against the killing of the hated Bonin as it was to express shame a few months later at the execution of the mentally damaged Danny Williams.

At home, Shelley began to experience some odd symptoms. They made no sense to us or to the doctors who were trying to understand the abnormal liver counts. She felt okay, but was losing weight and had periods of sudden exhaustion. Then she'd snap out of it and be fine. She said her tongue sometimes felt thick and heavy and she'd have trouble pronouncing words. I didn't want to alarm her, so didn't let on how worried I was. And I'm sure she was doing the same to protect me. She was working on *Coach* and still enjoying it, but she worried that the speech problem might make people think she was drinking or using drugs. We tried our doctor, an alternative healer, a neurologist, and a speech pathologist, but all were stumped.

We decided to have a meeting with Barry and the cast: Bill Fagerbakke, Jerry Van Dyke, and Craig T. Nelson. It's good we did, because they'd been worrying, at one point even considering an intervention. They adored Shelley and, once they understood, couldn't have been more supportive.

A liver specialist finally gave us the news, good and bad. The fatigue, weight loss, facial puffiness, and difficulty with words were from extreme hypothyroidism. With appropriate medication, she was her old self in no time. The bad news was that she had serious liver disease and would need further tests. Now, though we didn't know what the future held, at least we knew what we were dealing with. Through it all, this lovely woman, this bright spot in my life, soldiered on with her incredibly positive spirit.

A script on which Marvin and I had been working got a green light from an unusually bright and sensitive executive at USA Television (he was, of course, later fired), and we were lucky to get Jim Frawley to direct such powerful actors as Jill Clayburgh and Missy Crider. *Sins of the Mind,* as USA insisted we call it, was a powerful story of a bright young woman who, as a result of undiagnosed brain damage from an accident, loses all social inhibition and begins acting out in increasingly intolerable ways: lying, cheating, stealing, and becoming sexually predatory. Based on a true story, the film dramatizes her moral collapse, the near destruction of her family, and her eventual salvation by a pioneering psychiatrist working with therapies for sexual deviates. It's a terrific film, a powerful moral tale showing that there's always a reason for human behavior.

The entire process—from pitching the idea to USA through writing, approving, casting, shooting, editing, and turning over the finished film—didn't take more than six or eight months. Comparing that to the leaden slog we were subjected to on *In Silence* and *Patch* made us wonder about the business we were in.

Meanwhile, back in Virginia, Ron Angelone, head of the DOC, had Giarratano shipped from Buckingham back to Augusta without notice. Then, in the middle of the night, he had Joe flown in the governor's private jet to Utah. Transfer to an out-of-state prison isn't unusual, but a midnight ride in the governor's plane showed that Joe was getting special attention.

The press, intrigued by what appeared to be retaliatory treatment, pestered Angelone for an explanation. Joe, he claimed, was not only a killer but a ringleader and troublemaker. For his own protection, Joe would never see Virginia again.

Uinta 1, the pit of Utah's state prison system, is a primitive place. Inmates with no awareness of their rights struggled to survive. Profiled as a threat, Joe was kept in solitary confinement on meager rations. Maintaining his own counsel and lying low, he was eventually allowed minimal contact with other inmates. We located him, then friends at the Salt Lake ACLU checked in, and Joe's situation improved. With access to other prisoners, Joe began cataloguing illegal conditions. He was particularly offended, he told me, by the use of the "Devil's Chair," a restraint device so torturous that strict guidelines limited its use, guidelines assiduously ignored in Utah.

When we finally got the new version of the *Patch* script, we were again disappointed. Steve still hadn't broken the surface of the characters, so we began thinking of other writers. Luckily, Steve was then hired to write and direct another project, which left no time for us. Good for him and good for us. We didn't want to hurt his feelings, but we needed a writer who could take *Patch* to the next level.

With the heads of the Utah system unconcerned about the dangers of the Devil's Chair, Joe wrote the U.S. Justice Department. However, before Justice got seriously involved, Michael Valent, a mentally ill inmate, died after being strapped in the chair for sixteen hours. Furious, Joe filed a lawsuit and got a judgment against Utah's DOC for unlawful use of the instrument. An administrator sacked in the resultant housecleaning was Lane McCotter, next to be heard from when he was hired by the Bush Administration to run Abu Ghraib Prison in Iraq.

Utah had had enough of Giarratano, so in March 1997 a deal was worked that landed him next in Joliet Prison, southwest of Chicago.

Chapter 24
NOT SO FAST, JOHNSON!

T he *Patch* story became a saga in itself. Though it stretched over a couple of years, I'll try to string it together here to keep you from getting dizzy—but if it works, I'll be surprised. Universal brought in new executives, Marc Platt and Kevin Misher, from Tri-Star. They liked the project, but fear-of-saying-yes-itis bogged it down. Everyone knew the script wasn't what it should be, but months passed without a whimper. *Patch* was dying and we couldn't seem to revive it. Finally, Misher suggested finding a director who could move the project off the dime. We agreed, as long as it was understood that Steve's script wasn't the movie we wanted to make. "No problem."

So we went from talking about writers to talking about directors. We met two of them who agreed with our take on the film. But they were not, we learned, strong enough to get the picture moving. Why meet them, one might ask? They might work if another element could be added, Misher said. Like a star.

Then Steve called. His star was on the rise, but he hadn't forgotten *Patch*. He'd given the script to his friend Tom Shadyac, a hot young director currently finishing *Liar, Liar* with Jim Carrey. Shadyac, on the strength of two big-grossing movies, *Ace Ventura, Pet Detective* and *The Nutty Professor*, plus the buzz on *Liar*, would certainly be able to get the project made. But we didn't want *Patch* to become a silly, superficial comedy. Yes, lots of people like the movies Shadyac makes, but that's not what we wanted for *Patch*.

Stuck, we called Patch. He loved our idea of doing a smart movie—funny but meaningful—but he also understood the value a big hit could mean in terms of money to build his free hospital. Ultimately, he said he'd trust us to do the right thing. God. Well, at least we should talk to Shadyac—so we called. No response.

After a while things seemed to start moving at Universal, but no one said a word to us. All we knew was what leaked back. Shadyac, we heard, had expressed interest in working with Robin Williams. Apparently someone then talked to Williams and a meeting was arranged. Next we heard that an agreement had been struck for Robin Williams to star in *Patch Adams* and Tom Shadyac to direct. All of this was interesting, of course, but a bit odd to be getting it through back channels since we were supposed to produce the movie. So we called again. This time a meeting was set up.

Tom Shadyac is a smart, young, very verbal guy with a congenial and disarming air. He was quick to offer that we'd be taking something of a risk with him. His track record, he admitted, might not inspire confidence in people who wanted to do a picture containing the deeper elements of Patch's story. But he understood Patch, knew a good deal about medicine, shared Patch's views in many respects, and thought this was an important career step: a movie with something to say. Regarding the meetings we'd only heard about, he apologized, but said these things were sometimes best handled privately, on the basis of personal relationships. He was good. Our remaining concern was Steve. They were close, and Tom seemed intent on giving him another shot at deepening the script. We thought he didn't have the ability to deliver what we needed, but we knew we had to tread carefully. Tom assured us that he'd work closely with Steve and if it didn't work, we'd all move on. The meeting ended with a sense of cautious optimism.

Only later did we find out that nothing would happen for a while because Steve was finishing a film and Tom, once he wrapped *Liar, Liar*, was getting married and headed on a honeymoon. So we waited.

Next, Steve called to warn us that Brian Grazer, a big-time producer, was "putting on a full-court press" at Universal to glom onto *Patch*. Grazer, who had produced *Liar, Liar* with Shadyac, saw *Patch* as a potential hit and planned to take over. Tired of being jerked around, we set up a meeting with Casey Silver, Universal's head of production. Casey, a studio-politics pro, was "happy to see us" and had Kevin Misher there for backup. After he made nice for a bit, we said we'd heard some talk. *Well . . . yes.* Casey had been wondering if, for his own comfort, he might need to bring in someone he had worked with before. Knowing what we knew, it was an interesting exercise to watch this bullshit tumble forth. No names were mentioned. Casey insisted he meant no offense to the team already assembled. But since he hadn't worked with any of us and didn't know Robin at all—and since a great deal of money would be at risk if all the deals went through—he wanted to know how we'd feel if he decided to bring in another producer.

A lousy idea, we said, not to mention an insulting one. We'd been in the business a long time. We'd dealt with every conceivable production problem and could handle any that arose. We had a personal relationship with Patch, knew Robin, knew what the project should be, and didn't need another producer. And did we say insulting? *Well . . .* Casey hadn't expected us to come on quite so strong. He'd have to reserve the right to bring in someone if necessary, he hemmed, but he'd give our words serious consideration. And he'd talk with Shadyac.

We had another meeting with Tom, who waffled. It's hard to say no to Grazer, he told us. The man's powerful. When the studio pushed him on *Liar, Liar,* Grazer got them to lay off. We puffed him up a bit, reassured him that we were experienced producers and that Barry Kemp had lots of clout with the studio. It was tough, but he finally agreed to tell Casey that Grazer wasn't necessary.

Jeeeesus! Welcome to the big time.

Patch now moved from the whisper to the speak-out-loud stage, at least for some. A studio press release put *Patch Adams* on Universal's 1998 schedule; in a *New York Times* interview about the opening of *Liar, Liar,* Tom said his next project was *Patch Adams*; and Barry mentioned it in a *Los Angeles Times* interview. So, when Army Archerd of

Daily Variety asked what was up after our Jill Clayburgh picture, I told him about our relationship with Patch and the picture that seemed to be resulting from it. The next day, when Army's column said *"Robin Williams can thank Mike Farrell for his upcoming project,"* Kevin Misher called, saying we should do no more publicity without clearing it. Surprised, Marvin asked why. Kevin said he wanted "no feathers ruffled" by having names left out of publicity. What? Whose name had been left out? "There was no mention of Marsha Williams as producer," he said.

"Well, there's a good reason for that," Marvin replied, "no one ever mentioned Marsha being a producer." Misher insisted we had been told, and Marvin responded, "We've actually not been told much of anything by you guys and, by the way, we aren't too happy about it." Kevin then said the meeting with Casey Silver was about Marsha being a producer. "Horseshit! That meeting was about Brian Grazer, and we said no. Part of Casey's excuse was that he didn't know Robin, remember? Had never worked with him. So don't give us that crap!"

Kevin huffed and puffed, then said, like it or not, Marsha Williams was now a producer and we should clear any press releases having to do with *Patch* so his office could be sure no one would get upset.

"Should we take this call to mean that Marsha was upset by the article?" No answer. Was Marsha's nose out of joint or was Kevin covering his ass?

Now, painfully aware of having been hung out to dry by Marsha— or Marsha and Robin—once before, we put in a call to welcome her and tell her that her participation was new information and no insult was intended by leaving her name out of the *Variety* mention. Happily, she was warm, friendly, and looking forward to a good working relationship.

Bringing Patch up to date was fun, but we had to keep his enthusiasm in check. We had to remind him that not everyone should be assumed to share his altruistic vision. While for Patch the project meant that his dream of a free hospital in rural West Virginia could become a reality, for the others it might only be about making money for themselves.

Finally, all deals resolved, we sat down in a conference room. Marc Platt made nice noises and passed the baton to Tom, who outlined the schedule: Steve would be available in July and they'd work together on the script; preproduction would start September 15; we would begin shooting on January 15, 1998. Marsha added, "And the picture will open on December 12, 1998." Concerned that this didn't leave much room for another writer, I asked why we had an opening date for a picture that didn't yet have a completed script. Because, they answered, Robin has a picture to be released in mid-September of 1998 and they had to guarantee a ninety-day window for promotion. Star power.

Finally, a discussion of the script allowed Marvin, Barry, and me to be very specific about the problems we had. Notes were taken, agreement expressed, and we were on our way.

As Steve and Tom worked on the script that summer, Patch was taking part in a clown camp in the Bay Area and we all agreed to meet. An excited Patch called to say Marsha had invited him to stay with them for a couple of days, so Marvin called Kevin Misher to find out about our travel arrangements. Told that only the "creative team" would be included, Marvin said we were part of the "creative team" and Patch expected us to be there. Kevin said to make our own arrangements; we'd be reimbursed. Uh-oh.

Like unwanted in-laws, we flew to San Francisco, got a hotel and a cab to the restaurant, where we found Marsha, who was exhausted, just having flown in from setting up Robin's next picture in Hungary. Then up came a limo with Tom and—surprise!—Steve. Get the picture? If not for Patch, we'd have just gone into the kitchen and started washing dishes.

God bless Patch, his enthusiasm set the tone and the dinner was actually pleasant. Steve said he'd be working closely with Tom on the script. Robin worked late and didn't make it, so Marsha, Tom, Steve, and Patch went off in Marsha's car and Marvin and I hitchhiked back to the hotel.

In the morning we all met at a university where Patch was speaking to a group of medical students. His presentation went wonderfully, but Tom, Steve, and Marsha left before it was over to see Robin, who had to work that afternoon. After his speech, Patch spent the better part of another hour autographing copies of his book, talking, making jokes, and dispensing hugs and humor to an adoring crowd of students who couldn't get enough of him. It was pure Patch. Too bad the trio missed it.

After reassuring a disappointed Patch that they meant no offense by their early departure, we headed back to the airport knowing that if we'd ever been there, we certainly weren't in Kansas anymore.

When Tom and Steve's script arrived, it was like we were speaking different languages. Gags, funny lines, and situations appeared, but there was no depth of character, none of the reality that everyone had agreed was necessary. Steve had reached his limit a long time ago, but what concerned us now was Tom. This is the guy who saw the project as a career step away from superficial comedies. Step to *what?* became the question.

Time was short, so we had yet another big meeting. This time the studio execs included VP Stacy Snider, perhaps to make a point. All of them, thank God, echoed our concerns about the script. Steve was there this time and gave a lesson in what a little success in this business can do: The nice young man we had originally met and liked had somehow morphed into an arrogant prick. His sarcasm was shocking, both because it was unlike anything we'd ever heard from him and because the executives just sat there and took it. Some apparently very thick skins had been donned for the meeting. Universal must keep them in a closet somewhere. New notes met nods and words of agreement from Tom—silence from Steve—and off the two went.

Back when I was a process server, I knocked on a lot of doors while those inside pretended they weren't home. Same feeling here. The execs all smiled benignly, and Marvin, Barry, and I barely managed to get out without screaming.

The new script arrived. No surprise: a huge disappointment. Some minor changes, but nothing significant. With the picture already in preproduction, it was panic time. We went to see Kevin Misher, who was noncommittal, saying the other executives hadn't yet read it (an unwritten law forbids junior executives from having an opinion before their superiors).

"For the record," I said, "we need a new writer."

After a beat, he replied, "Off the record, I agree. But if push comes to shove, I'll deny I said it. That's a real political problem here." Well, finally, some (not exactly) straight talk. "Political problem" clearly meant that Tom was committed to Steve and we could forget all the other bullshit. While the gloves weren't exactly off, we got the message.

Hoping against hope, we called Marsha. Just in from Hungary again, she agreed, saying, "I wouldn't show this script to Robin." We talked new writers. The jokes were there, but we needed an Alvin Sargent. Marsha suggested Richard LaGravenese and Eric Roth, both of whom she knew. This was nice territory; we were on the same track. Then she added that Tom was very much committed to Steve and that we didn't want to lose the director. Were we on the same track? She was to have a meeting with Tom and would talk about her concerns and get a sense of his openness to another writer. Perhaps, we suggested, we should be at the meeting. But no, she felt he'd be more open to her alone. She'd let us know. But if we wanted to send her our notes . . . Send her our notes?

A week passed with no word, so we made another call to Marsha. No meeting yet, but she was flying with Tom to North Carolina to look at locations and they'd talk on the trip. A location scout about which we knew nothing! This was excruciating. Clearly the phone lines were burning up and a power play was in the works.

As if to cement the fact, a call to Kevin Misher elicited the flat statement: "Tom is the director." Not exactly news, this clearly meant something more.

"And the writer?" Marvin asked.

"Steve is the writer. Steve has always been the writer," came Kevin's reply. The power play, it appeared, had worked. The studio blinked. Kevin said there would be one more meeting about the script and that was it.

Ready to bite through wire, we sat down and wrote an eight-page dissection of the script, laying out problems noted from the beginning—and agreed to by all—that had gone unaddressed. Barry said the script promised a disastrously superficial film and that a meeting was essential.

Kevin Misher responded, "Tom doesn't want another large meeting with the whole group where the script will be put through a torturous session like the last one." Instead he'd be calling us individually. Divide and conquer.

Barry got word that Tom had been put through a tough session with the Universal execs, but had brushed it off as typical anxiety before green-lighting a picture. In other words, they tried to lay down the law, he told them to go fuck themselves, and they chose to do just that.

Barry then heard from Tom's office about setting up a call for notes. Not on the phone, Barry said. He wanted a meeting and wanted us there, too.

When we showed up, Tom seemed surprised. The meeting was short and ugly. He deflected most notes and shrugged off others. Nothing we said mattered; he was the boss. He said the script had been shown to six people, in and out of the business, and they all loved it. (My God, *six!*) He said the picture's new line producer would give us a call and noted that a production designer, an assistant, and a casting director were now on staff. It was a galling demonstration of raw power. The lone pleasure I got was to hand him our eight pages of blistering notes.

We distributed copies of our eight pages to Casey Silver, Kevin

Misher, Marc Platt, and Stacy Snider with a request for whatever notes they had on the last draft. We also faxed the memo to Marsha with a request for her notes. Need I say we never received a response from anyone?

Some days later, Steve Oedekerk called to say our notes were insulting and inaccurate. I said they weren't intended to be insulting, but rather to strongly convey our serious concern that work was needed to make the script what we had initially agreed it should be. His pride injured, Steve launched into a long, defensive tirade. He had personally shown the script to twenty-seven people (twenty-one more than Tom!) in and out of the business, who had laughed and cried and loved it. They included, he said, all the executives at Universal and Robin Williams. Based on their reaction, it was clear that our notes were inaccurate.

Insulted and tired of being dicked around, Marvin wanted a meeting with Casey Silver. Instead, Kevin Misher called, saying he'd read our notes. When told of Steve's call, he was incredulous, dismissed it as nonsense, and said the battle wasn't over. Huh? Positions were shifting so fast I was getting dizzy. Misher said Steve and Tom would take one more pass, then Steve would move on, allowing us to bring in another writer who could work on it for a week and bring it up to snuff.

They'd played the game this long and wanted someone to fix it in a week? Shit. But at least we were talking about a new writer.

Barry finally got through to Marc Platt, who said his notes agreed with ours. While maintaining his "appreciation" for Steve as a writer, he agreed that someone else was needed to finish the script. We were clearly on a hell of a roller coaster ride, but for a moment, at least, it began to feel as though we were actually being heard.

That evening Tom called. He'd read the notes and said, "We're making different movies."

"I'm afraid you're right," I replied, "but we're still talking about our movie, the one everybody agreed to a long time ago."

Tom claimed he wasn't going for another *Liar, Liar*, but a picture with substance.

I said, "One-dimensional characters and unbelievable situations don't get you there."

He argued that *Good Morning, Vietnam,* often mentioned as a prototype for *Patch,* used a one-dimensional villain as a foil for Robin's character and it worked beautifully.

"Nobody said *Good Morning, Vietnam* was a perfect picture," I responded. "It was an example, not a model. Because some of the characters were one-dimensional doesn't mean you copy them; it means you do it better."

After we calmed down a bit, Tom stepped cautiously into discussing another writer. I told him the need was urgent and, when he asked for names, said, "Alvin Sargent, Richard LaGravenese, Eric Roth, Gary Ross." Tom reluctantly agreed that LaGravenese might be okay: He had worked with Robin and Marsha.

This being go-for-broke time, I told him that we resented being cut out of the process. The project came from us; we were hands-on producers and expected our agreement to be honored.

Tom: "Brian Grazer doesn't go on location scouts or sit in on casting sessions."

Me: "We don't sit in our office smoking cigars and making deals for other movies. This picture was ours before you came into it, and we care about it."

Tom: "You're talking about a community project."

Me: "Look, we don't want to direct the picture. We know there are areas that are out of bounds, but there are places we can be helpful." This project was personal, I said, and we had a responsibility to Patch.

Tom said he'd ask for help once decisions were boiled down to a couple of choices, but we would not be included in the entire process. As to the script, he'd bring Barry in to meet with Steve before the next draft.

Days later, Barry came out of that meeting guardedly optimistic. He thought they'd heard him somewhat, and Steve had another project to go to. That would, Barry hoped, give us time to bring in a new writer.

Marvin and I met with Casey Silver. We were pissed. We no longer expected much, but this was humiliating. He had allowed Tom to put the studio in breach of our contract. Casey pleaded for understanding, saying he was dealing with an 800-pound gorilla, or in this case, three of them.

"Two and a half," I said. Marsha's clout was all about Robin.

Casey said Tom was "an arrogant twelve-year-old who'd had a string of successes and was drunk on his own power." Then he immediately echoed Misher, saying, "But if you quote me on this, I'll deny saying it." We, of course, "had the moral high ground" (not a generally recognized location in this industry). He was sorry that this had happened on his watch and he had to take responsibility for it. But, he was "in the business of making pictures that make money," and he "had to make these deals." Poor guy. "Other than watching things more closely in the future," he said, he didn't know what he could do.

"Well," I said, "it looks like we're bringing in another writer. That's a good thing. You need to understand that this isn't a case where a quick-fix, one-week patch-up job will do it."

Casey said he'd stay on top of it, take a look at the next draft, and call a meeting where the problems could be discussed openly. Openly? That would be interesting.

Having heard nothing from the line producer Tom had hired, we set up a meeting. Fairly nice, if a bit smooth, he was clearly in a tough spot. Sets were being built in a warehouse rather than a soundstage in the Bay Area at a hit to the budget of "about $4 million," the price of doing a picture with Robin. That, together with Tom's openness to LaGravenese, sounded like Marsha was getting her way. This guy was very diplomatic, but he knew who was boss. He said he'd try to keep us in the loop. I wanted a copy of the budget. He gulped and said it was still "in the works."

"Fine. I want it."

The tentative budget made interesting reading. Robin, Marsha, their company, and Tom each made millions. That was bad enough. What really stuck was Steve Oedekerk, whose fee we had long ago negotiated; he was now both a writer and a coproducer, getting over a million dollars. All in, the budget came to almost $69 million dollars—ten times what it took us to make *Dominick and Eugene*. Our deal, negotiated at the outset, included Barry, Marvin, and me together for less than Steve was now getting alone. Clearly the "moral high ground" was an economic pothole.

The holidays and a vacation for Tom put us in a box. If the new version of Steve and Tom's script didn't come quickly, we'd literally be backed up against the start of shooting without time to bring in a writer to fix it. More hollering, nudging, arm-wrestling, and jockeying finally got us their latest version, which was exactly what we expected. Marc Platt then promised to get on his horse. His horse, however, threw him, as Richard LaGravenese, whom we had all been assured was available and interested, was now unavailable. Or uninterested.

A bright spot appeared when Platt then agreed to approach one of three other good writers: Paul Attenasio, Bo Goldman, or Phil Alden Robinson. Goldman was a friend of Barry's, and Phil (my compadre from Somalia and Bosnia) a friend of mine. So our hopes rose once again. We decided not to mention our relationships with either, assuming that would be the kiss of death. But I did call Phil, who had just had a much-loved project (that grew out of our time in Sarajevo) fall out at Universal.

"Well," he said ironically, "I'm available." I gave him the lay of the land, and he agreed it was tricky. But even without the offer, he said he'd read the script. He and Tom had met only once, but Tom had spoken admiringly of his work. Although I now knew that one shouldn't take Tom's words too seriously, this wasn't a bad sign. We got the script over to Phil right away and sent him Patch's book as well.

Before he got the book, Phil called. He'd gone through the script and certainly saw the problems: The main character learns nothing, the other characters were one-dimensional, scenes were written for the sole purpose of telling jokes, things were not set up, etc. In one quick reading, he'd gotten everything we'd been arguing for months. He said, "You get to page twelve, you know what the movie is. It's a series of jokes without a plot, any development, or any particularly interesting characters." The possibilities were there but weren't realized on the page. All this, of course, was music to our ears, in part because it validated what we'd been saying for so long, but mostly because it came from an intelligent, talented writer who saw the potential in the project and knew how to fix it. He still hadn't seen the book, so we asked him to just take a look at the forward. He called later and said, "This is great! Now I see this guy, I know who he is, and I know where this wants to go!" God, I loved him.

Then Kevin Misher called. We dummied up as he told us that Tom had given Steve the news that three other writers were being considered. Of them, he said, Tom was enthusiastic about Phil Robinson. I almost yelled, but didn't. We were calm, professional: "Well, we can't argue with that choice; he's certainly a fine writer." We thanked him, hung up, and exploded. I could hardly believe it. We'd have to handle it carefully, but we were finally getting our project back from this conniving bastard, and he wouldn't even understand how it happened!

Not so fast, Johnson! Phil was concerned about butting heads with the director. I understood but assured him he'd have everybody else's support. Then the studio started talking about doing the rewrite in a week or two. Phil told them he couldn't do what was needed in that amount of time; it was likely to be four or five weeks, maybe more. They balked, there was more talk, and it went quickly downhill. Finally, Phil called to apologize. He just couldn't do it in the time they wanted to give him.

Ach. Well, they brought in Paul Attenasio, evidently for a week or two, but Tom was in the driver's seat, and that, it seemed, was that. We were out of the picture, literally. I asked Marc Platt what the hell the point was in hiring Attenasio or any other writer if we couldn't talk to him. He said, "We're in Shadyac world now." He said Tom was passive-aggressive, and described a meeting in which he had made some mild observations about the script and Tom had threatened to walk off the picture.

Shooting began, and whatever good Attenasio did seemed to have been "fixed" by Tom and, of course, Steve, who magically reappeared. We got the notice of a "small read-through" followed by lunch and a "large read-through" for the people named. We were not among the people named.

Patch called about wanting to visit the set with his son. I told him it was probably best if I wasn't the one who asked. He called on his own and Tom said, "Send me a proposal." I truly wanted to strangle the bastard.

Marvin and I visited the *Patch* set twice and everyone was . . . nice. More importantly, Patch was able to come and bring his son. It was frustrating to watch the shoot. It was even more frustrating that I wasn't comfortable approaching Robin, whom I admire. Given the tension, I didn't want to cause him any more discomfort than was already evident on the set because of our presence. So I didn't.

Months later, Marvin and I flew to Phoenix, Arizona, for a sneak preview of *Patch*. We sat through a cartoonish version of what should have been a wonderful and meaningful picture. The audience laughed at the obvious jokes as Robin was clever and charming, if on the nose. But the core of reality we had fought for, the soul of the Patch we knew, was nowhere to be seen. We left quietly as the Universal executives happily collected the audience response cards telling them how funny it was.

Patch Adams was released in December, and we put on happy faces and went for the ride. I was pleased that a good editor had gotten his hands on the picture and made it far less painful. Some subtlety had been injected, performances were helped, and transitions made more sense. Though it didn't approach the picture it should have been and the critics saw through the artlessness of Tom's work, the final result, very much in the *Liar, Liar* mode, was less embarrassing than what we had first seen.

The film was a huge success financially, if not critically—but financially was what it was clearly all about. It literally saved

Universal's butt after a string of failures. So the passive-aggressive, arrogant twelve-year-old drunk on his own power became a genius, and all the game-playing, duplicity, ineptitude, wasted money, manipulation and ass-covering was forgotten.

And though no one begrudges anybody the right to make a buck, it's a bitter lesson that a picture grossing over $400 million did not put a penny of its profit into Patch Adams's dream of a free hospital.

Chapter 25
DIVINE PROVIDENCE

With time to spare during the *Patch* insanity, I took a motorcycle ride and made my first stop a visit with Joe. Set in the midst of a small industrial Illinois city south of Chicago, Joliet Prison is an ugly place that has dealt with many hard people over hard years. While its reputation would intimidate most newcomers, its appearance seals the bargain. Yet when I visited Joe, I discovered that he had worked out a relationship with the warden that was based on mutual respect. His primary observation was: "It's closer to home." The place was all right, he said, but he didn't plan to be there long.

Joe already understood prison politics at Joliet. The warden was a pro, and problems here, unlike Utah, were dealt with reasonably. Joe's biggest concern was Virginia. He needed to be there so the effort to get a new trial didn't founder.

I was still a naïve outsider, but the idea that this young man was so confident he could work the system to get home despite Angelone's truculence seemed a fantasy to me. I was more concerned about his health. He'd developed liver disease, probably as a result of early substance abuse coupled with years of prison food. He had sued to get the vegetarian diet that worked best for him, but the condition occasionally flared up and worried me. His fasts and hunger strikes probably didn't help.

In March of '97, Shelley finished her ninth and last season of *Coach*. Because she was feeling pretty good, we took off for a week in Hong Kong and another in Sydney, Australia. Then Shelley flew home, and

I realized one of my longtime dreams by spending a few weeks riding a motorcycle across that glorious country.

Once home, I was kicked around in the media for arguing in *USA Today* (see "re: McVeigh" at www.mikefarrell.org/publications/mcveigh.html) that executing Timothy McVeigh would serve no purpose but to make him a martyr in the eyes of other antigovernment fanatics. I was honored to be joined by Bud Welch, whose daughter Julie Marie was one of McVeigh's victims in the Oklahoma City bombing. After suffering the excruciating pain of losing his beloved daughter, Bud had gone from wanting to kill McVeigh with his bare hands to understanding that his death would neither bring back his daughter nor end the pain of her loss. Through this metamorphosis, Bud has become one of the most eloquent opponents of capital punishment in the country.

That summer, California was itching to kill Thomas Thompson, a death-row inmate who may have been as innocent as he consistently maintained. An already complex case was made more so by the prosecutor's misconduct—hiding evidence from Thompson's attorneys and changing his theory of the crime to convict both Thompson and his codefendant in separate trials. The codefendant, who was the victim's lover, had threatened to kill her. Thought by many to be the actual perpetrator, he got fifteen years while Thompson got death. We had unusual allies in seven veteran state prosecutors, who joined us in asking Governor Wilson to stop the execution.

Besides radio, TV, and newspaper interviews, I testified before the State Board of Pardons and Paroles, which was acting as a clemency board for the governor. They were a grim, unresponsive group that might as well have been sitting on cakes of ice. Their recommendation was secret, but no one was surprised when Wilson refused clemency. On execution day I chaired a press conference with experts who dissected the evidence, pointed out flaws that had caused a federal judge to overturn the case earlier, and criticized the governor's cowardice. Hours before Thompson was to be killed, the U.S. Supreme Court stopped the execution, causing the governor much-deserved embarrassment.

Shortly after that, I was appointed to the California Commission on Judicial Performance. A serious commitment, it meant joining a panel of lawyers, judges and others, investigating charges and disciplining any judges guilty of unethical or inappropriate conduct. The homework was prodigious, but I was honored to be asked, so put on a suit and played Commissioner Farrell for the next three years.

Bacre Waly N'Diaye, the UN Special Rapporteur for Extrajudicial, Summary and Arbitrary Executions, was touring the killing states, and I helped coordinate his visit to L.A., wrapping it up with a gathering at our home. A big man, bright and very articulate, N'Diaye was a lawyer from Senegal who was investigating death row conditions and letting our governors know about the international community's intention to abolish the death penalty. He told of meeting Governor George W. Bush of Texas, who was unaware of the obligations imposed by the International Covenant on Civil and Political Rights, a treaty to which the U.S. was signatory.

"Why should I care about this law?" Bush had asked.

"Because," Bacre responded, "your father signed it."

Following up, I drafted a petition to Governor Mel Carnahan of Missouri asking clemency for A.J. Bannister, who was soon to die. Even the arresting officer said there was no evidence to support the death penalty in this case. Paired with an appeal from the Organization of American States, our petition was signed by Gregory Peck, Jack Lemmon, Sean Penn, Edward Asner, and many other celebrities, as well as members of Congress and the clergy. But Carnahan ducked a delegation hoping to discuss the case with him personally, did a Pontius Pilate, and Bannister was killed.

That February I took on former Texas Attorney General Jim Mattox in an MSNBC debate about the execution of Karla Faye Tucker. Sentenced to die for a brutal murder fourteen years earlier, she'd had a personal transformation in prison, including a religious conversion that brought Pat Robertson, among others, to her defense. She married the chaplain, was esteemed within the prison for her work with other inmates, and even had the detective who originally helped secure her death sentence championing a commutation to life. But being Texas, it was more important to get their pound of flesh than accept that people can change. Karla Faye Tucker's plea is reported to have been mocked in a whiney voice by Governor George W. Bush.

In March, after experiencing an electric tingling zip in her right hip, Shelley suddenly couldn't walk without extreme pain. An MRI showed that the tip of her right femur had collapsed due to a loss of blood flow to the bone, a condition known as *avascular necrosis*. Her hip had to be replaced. I got the news first and had to tell her of this possibly life-changing development, something I wasn't sure how to do. When I broke it to her, though, she reached into that core of sweetness and wonder that daily affirms for me that she is the most decent human being I've ever known. She thought about it for a moment, and said it all in a word: "Gosh."

It's an awful, helpless feeling to have the one you love enter such a process, but we were of two minds about it. It's a damned shame she had to go through it, but how lucky we were that it could be done. Hip replacement has become commonplace in America today, and the advances in surgical techniques and the prosthetics themselves were amazing. It wasn't pleasant, but Shelley was a champ and recovered quickly, grateful to everyone and happy to be able to walk without pain.

That spring we stopped the scheduled execution of Horace Kelly, a deranged man on California's death row. In an editorial for the *Los Angeles Times* (see "Put an End to America's Death Machine" at www.mikefarrell.org/publications/deathmachine.html) and in debates with prosecutors and "victims advocates," I argued that it tortured the concept of justice to kill a man who, according to a prison psychiatrist, lived in a state of "bizarre delusions and hallucinations, incoherence, catatonic behavior, and inappropriate affect." Kelly, who believed he was a guard rather than a prisoner at San Quentin, had been living in his own excrement, surrounded by moldy food and soiled bedding. Despite a prosecution expert's claim that Kelly was sane enough to be killed because he was able to play tic-tac-toe, the execution was stayed. For now.

Then—surprise!—I was offered a job. As an actor, of all things. My agent sent a script and, if I was interested, an invitation to meet the producers. It was for a television series, which didn't thrill me, but I figured it wouldn't hurt to read it. And it was very good. The show was *Providence*, set in the city of the same name. But it was actually about divine providence in the lives of a family. Written by John Masius, it was an intelligent yet offbeat depiction of a real family with real problems, and it sucked me right in. I thought it was too smart to actually be picked up as a series, so I agreed to meet the producers. Before I could turn around, I was offered the role of Dr. Jim Hansen, a quiet, emotionally restrained veterinarian with a pushy, strident, unsatisfied wife, and two adult kids still at home: a very pregnant, about-to-be-married daughter and a confused son looking for the easy road to success. There was also a brilliant, successful plastic surgeon daughter. In the pilot, the daughter has left home but returns for the wedding, which is interrupted by the sudden death of the wife. Did I say it was offbeat?

My agent told them about the Commission: I'd have to be in San Francisco for meetings every few weeks. If they couldn't find room in the schedule, I wasn't sure it would work. So I was knocked out when the producer said: "Look, this is just a television show; we'll work it out."

Shooting the pilot was a ball. The cast was great; the director was terrific; the crew wonderful. Everyone had a good time. It didn't have a chance.

In May, the Mexican government asked for support in its suit against the United States based on the Vienna Convention on Consular Rights. Never heard of it? Unfortunately, neither have most police.

Along with most of the world, the U.S. signed the Convention in 1963, protecting the rights of citizens traveling outside their country. Article 36 says that if you're detained or arrested outside your country, you must be allowed to contact your consulate for legal assistance without delay. It's a good law that protects Americans who have legal trouble abroad, but it's also meant to protect those from other countries traveling here. While it's widely honored around the globe, in the U.S. most state and local authorities don't recognize the rights of foreigners when they're stopped or arrested. As a result, people have been charged, convicted, and sentenced—to death, in some cases—without being given the right to see their consul for help with language, laws, customs, etc. This is a violation of a person's rights under the treaty and a legal error that should reverse a conviction.

In one example, a Paraguayan national named Angel Breard was executed in Virginia despite a World Court ruling that the U.S. government should stop the process and investigate the abrogation of his rights under the Vienna Convention. It was an ugly international incident. Secretary of State Madeleine Albright actually called for the execution to be stopped, if only to ensure the safety of American citizens traveling abroad. She was ignored, however, and Breard was killed. The next week a Honduran was executed despite a plea from the president of Honduras to the governor of Arizona.

With more than thirty nationals on death row in the U.S., the Mexican government was asking Death Penalty Focus to support their appeal to the Inter-American Court. They argued that the right to consular contact without delay should be required, just like the Miranda warnings, when dealing with a foreign national. When we agreed, they asked if we would appear and testify. Thrilled at the chance, board member Steve Rohde, a constitutional lawyer, and I took off for Costa Rica.

It was exciting to be part of proceedings before the Inter-American Court. It was an impressive setting. The seven justices sat in full robes at the end of a large room in a colonial building that was, ironically, fashioned after the White House. The interior was complete with ceiling fans, and as the Costa Rican breeze blew through the open doors, I kept expecting Alec Guinness to slip in and join us. Among the familiar faces I saw that day was Juan Mendez; my old friend from America's Watch had since joined the staff of the Inter-American Court. (He's now the UN Secretary General's Special Advisor on the Prevention of Genocide.)

Once Mexico presented its case, delegations from El Salvador, Honduras, Guatemala, Costa Rica, the Dominican Republic, and Paraguay took their turns in support. Canada's observer didn't testify but was also in favor. The only opposition came from the U.S. Some very haughty suits from the State Department said that the Court had no jurisdiction, the Vienna Convention was not a human rights treaty, and Article 36 applied only to governments, not people. It was an embarrassingly arrogant demonstration and showed how we've earned the reputation that bedevils us internationally.

After the State Department folks walked out, it was our turn. Amnesty, Human Rights Watch, the Inter-American Commission on Human Rights, Death Penalty Focus, the Minnesota Advocates for Human Rights, a professor from the International Human Rights Law Institute of DePaul University, two other professors of law, three public defenders from Ohio, and a former justice of the Inter-American Court itself—all spoke in support of Mexico. The proceedings went on for over two days, and I was honored to address the Court (see "Address to the Inter-American Court on Human Rights" at www.mikefarrell.org/Journals/Costa.html). Without an ounce of objectivity, I can say that our combined testimony decimated the U.S. position.

It was wonderful to watch this exercise in international law, knowing that the founders of the U.S. had so inspired these folks that they had constructed a system of law modeled on our own. But it was sad to see that the system that had inspired them had grown so deaf.

From that triumph we came home to frustration. The U.S. Supreme Court had overturned the stay on Thomas Thompson's execution on a technicality. The federal district court had ruled that Thompson was erroneously convicted of capital murder and the Ninth Circuit Court of Appeals agreed, but then missed its own deadline. Due to that error, the U.S. Supreme Court had reinstated the death sentence. Furious, we stood vigil at San Quentin's East Gate on July 13, 1998, as Thompson was killed. His last statement said: "For seventeen years the AG has been pursuing the wrong man. In time he will come to know this. I don't want anyone to avenge my death. Instead I want you to stop killing people. God bless." Stephen Reinhardt, an eighteen-year veteran of the U.S. Court of Appeals for the Ninth Circuit, wrote in the *New York University Law Journal* that Thompson was *"the first person in the nation ever to be executed on the basis of a trial that an unrefuted decision of a United States Court of Appeals had held to be unconstitutional."*

And then *Providence* was suddenly picked up as a mid-season replacement, and I was a working actor once again. It was an odd feeling. I hadn't been particularly interested in doing another series, but I had such a good time making the pilot that this was a blessing. The producers had put together a terrific ensemble. Our leading lady, Melina Kanakaredes, is a young Greek-American as bright and talented as she is beautiful—and a dream to work with. The two kids (I still think of them as kids) who played Melina's sister and brother were a delight. Paula Cale, daughter Joanie, was gorgeous and wickedly funny. Adept at both comedy and drama, she brought to mind a young Lucille Ball. Seth Peterson, son Robbie, was equally gifted—always working, always stretching as an actor. Watching him in a play, Shelley had pegged him as a young Jack Lemmon. Concetta Tomei, who played my wife Linda, is a pro who always brings a special energy to the work. Concetta wasn't originally scheduled to be a regular in the series; her character died in the pilot. But television being what it is, the network insisted on resurrecting her after she got positive responses in viewer testing. John Masius, the show's creator, decided to bring her back every week in Melina's dreams, part of the wackiness that his eccentric view of life brought to the show.

Good actors, good directors, and a happy crew made for a pleasant place to work. Because the kids did the heavy lifting, my schedule was fairly flexible, allowing me to go to Commission meetings and the occasional something else.

In the fall of 1998, Marie called to say that Joe had done the impossible: He was back in Virginia. One last hunger strike and the Joliet warden had given him what he wanted in spite of Ron Angelone. I still don't understand how Joe managed it, but Angelone was obviously furious at being trumped and put him in Red Onion State Prison, Virginia's new supermax in the mountains of the state's southwest corner. Supermax facilities are built for the most dangerous inmates, who live under the most rigorous, cruel, limiting conditions. Joe getting put there was an example of the High Priest's vindictiveness. At Red Onion, Joe is in his cell twenty-four hours a day, with time out for a shower and what they ridiculously call "yard" (exercise in a narrow, concrete dog run lined with chain link and razor wire) a few days a week. Human contact is minimal, with even guards interacting through a small slot in the door.

These places are designed to limit the possibility of escape and to eliminate any chance for a violence-prone inmate to do harm. Extreme measures, when necessary, are supposed to be temporary. Like other supermaxes in America, Red Onion is a symbol of the "tough on crime" mentality that, officials have found, makes for good theater—and political hay. Tough talk and macho posturing are used to bring in votes from a population force-fed stories about monsters lurking, ready to spring out and do harm if not destroyed or locked away.

Supermax Syndrome is an arrow in the political quiver of the prison/industrial complex. Hundreds of millions of dollars and thousands of jobs are involved in creating and staffing these awful places. In rural communities like Pound, Virginia, McAlester, Oklahoma, and Pelican Bay, California, the supermaxes pour money into the prison construction industry, create jobs in areas of low employment, and draw votes for legislators. They also bring political and financial support from the increasingly powerful correctional officers' unions.

The rub is finding enough inmates to justify the supermax. Violent crime goes down when the economy improves, but somebody still has to fill the cells. Gangs are demonized enough to do it. And it's a great place to put a prisoner you hate.

Though contact with other inmates is limited, Joe helps with lawsuits and grievances even in Red Onion as we continue to struggle for a just resolution to his case. Years of solitary confinement have done little to dim his mental growth, but they've taken their toll physically. Deeply involved in philosophy and meditation, Joe's unwillingness to crack inspires awe among inmates—and even some of the staff. Ironically, as they pretend Joe is dangerous and hide him away, they're forced to confront his legacy. In 2001, Earl Washington, the mentally deprived innocent whose life Joe saved so many years ago, was released. In 2006, with the help of the Innocence Project and Marie Deans, a jury awarded Earl $2.25 million for wrongful imprisonment.

Shelley continued to show high liver counts, and her blood platelets were very low. Trying to solve this puzzle, we depended more and more on the team at the Liver Clinic at Cedars Sinai. Though she wasn't in critical condition, it was beginning to get scary.

In November 1998, Death Penalty Focus cosponsored the first Conference on Wrongful Convictions and the Death Penalty at Northwestern University's law school in Chicago. It was exciting to be among giants of the abolition movement like Steve Bright, Bryan Stevenson, and Tony Amsterdam. An historic event put together by the brilliant Professor Larry Marshall, the Conference presented to the world thirty of the then seventy-four men and women who had been charged, tried, convicted and sent to death row. Some of them had come within hours of execution, only to be finally exonerated and freed. In a moving ceremony, each took a turn onstage in the law school's auditorium before a crowd that included journalists and camera crews from around the world. It was simple, chilling, and effective, as each person came to the podium, introduced him or herself, and said, "My name is _____, and I spent X years on death row for a crime I did not commit. If the state of _____ had its way, I would be dead today."

The repetition of this simple litany was almost more than the viewers could bear. Each one then placed a flower in a huge vase, signed a declaration to Governor George Ryan, and took a seat. Some were dressed formally, some casually; a few were comfortable, the rest not. They were mostly men, mostly black, mostly poor. None had a significant education. They were America's forgotten made suddenly visible, and their collected presence spoke volumes. It was the most powerful event of its time on the subject of state killing, and it marked the beginning of the end of capital punishment.

Chapter 26
INSIDE

A t work one day on *Providence*, the doctor called to say he was putting Shelley in the hospital. He didn't make it sound urgent, and her sister Smokey was there to take her, so I finished work. When I arrived, she was being prepared for emergency surgery.

It was a long, terrifying night as Smokey and I waited. The surgeon finally came out to say Shelley would be okay, but it was close. She'd lost an enormous amount of blood from an esophageal bleed (a burst portal vein). He'd initially found so much blood in her throat that he couldn't see the problem, but because she was either going to bleed to death or drown, he'd rushed her into surgery. The burst vessel was a result of pressure from the liver problem we'd been watching, and he said there was a very real danger it could reoccur unless she had a liver transplant.

Shelley recovered quickly, but the future was cloudy. The thought of a transplant was almost incomprehensible. With my natural-food, alternative-medicine, there-must-be-a-less-invasive-way bias, I probably found it harder to accept than she did. But without fully buying into the idea, we agreed to put her on the list. Going into the program involved extensive tests, meetings, a good deal of reading, and a lot of soul searching. We held onto the hope that regular checkups and a watch on the blood platelets and liver enzymes, as well as periodic tests to ensure the bleeding didn't reoccur, would keep her well enough to avoid a transplant.

Despite our progress at inching the reality of capital punishment into the public consciousness, politicians continued to turn a deaf ear and the ritual continued. In the spring of '99, we fought to bring the facts of Manny Babbitt's case to Governor Gray Davis here in California. A slow boy still in the seventh grade at seventeen, Babbitt had dropped out and joined the Marines with some help from a hungry recruiter. He had gone to Vietnam, fought in the siege of Khe San, and come home a classic case of PTSD. Diagnosed as mentally ill but turned out on the street, he was eventually responsible for a woman's death in what looked like a combat flashback—he left the body toe-tagged, as he had been taught at Khe San.

We didn't ask that Babbitt be set free, but what was the point in killing a damaged man for something he didn't remember doing? He had been turned in by his brother Bill, a loving and law-abiding man who was assured that, because of Manny's sickness, the state wouldn't press for death. But they did. Now, the execution impending, the struggle for Babbitt's life intensified, with psychiatric experts and Marine veterans of Khe San trying to pierce Davis's mask of indifference. But the indifference wasn't a mask, and Babbitt died with no memory of the event for which justice was supposedly being exacted.

In April I was part of a Human Rights Watch inspection of McAlester, the Oklahoma state prison, with Jamie Fellner, an expert on prisons. Shelley was well enough to travel, so she came too. Part of HRW's research into supermax facilities, the trip offered a deeper look at the place I'd visited in the middle of the night years earlier when meeting Robyn Parks. (Jamie's report, "Out of Sight," can be read at www.hrw.org.)

These things are never easy. Corrections staff and administrators are often defensive, sometimes antagonistic. We were treated well by the folks at McAlester, though, maybe in part because of *M*A*S*H* and *Providence*.

The main prison is almost one hundred years old and reeks of the sort of history one really doesn't want to know too much about. The old building had a certain ghastly grandeur, but one couldn't escape the pain radiating from the walls. Outside, the McAlester yard boasted a renowned prisoner rodeo once a year; inside, the ghosts were everywhere. After a thorough tour, we were taken down to H-Unit, the newer, nearly underground supermax where I'd met Robyn Parks. Here, death row and segregation cells held troublemakers, snitches, those deemed incorrigible, and the condemned. It was as austere and mechanistic as I had remembered, more so once we passed into areas known only to staff and inmates. The airlocks were as claustrophobic as usual, but the death row cells truly gave me the creeps. Inmates were double-bunked in spaces smaller than the average bathroom, locked in twenty-three hours a day, elbow to elbow with someone who might well be psychotic, and with no way to call for help.

After the tour, Jamie and I were given separate rooms to do interviews. A guard intended to stay there with me, but I wanted the inmates to be able to speak freely. Though not happy to leave me alone, he finally brought in the first man and turned to go, the inmate's manacles remaining in place. I asked the guard to release the restraints on all the men once they were in the room. He did, though it really bugged him. I know what he was afraid of, but the men appreciated it and I had no trouble.

The interviews were heartrending (see "McAlester" at www.mikefarrell.org/publications/mcalester.html). There were sick men, ignorant men, defiant men, contrite men, those who denied guilt and others who owned it, all hungry for personal time and attention. All of them were wounded by life, by what they'd done, by the conditions here. I was drawn to some, repelled by others, and sickened by the experience. I hate these places. Cesspools of human waste, they reek of agony and error, fear and guilt, sorrow and rage and hopelessness. The fact that we've given up on fellow human beings, disdained the possibility of rehabilitation—or "habilitation," as Ernie at The House called it—is a colossal failure on our part.

Needing a breath of hope, Shelley and I flew from Oklahoma to Richmond, Virginia, where we presented an award to Marie Deans for

Virginians against the Death Penalty, then drove down to see Joe. A small mountain town in Virginia's southwestern corner, Pound has little to brag about and depends on the prison for jobs. Red Onion is a few miles up a lonely road, stuck into the side of a mountain, an impregnable fort surrounded by high fences and razor wire.

After a very long wait, I was taken through the locking system into a large empty room and directed to a seat before a Plexiglas window. Joe was delivered to the other side. He looked pretty good and was clearly glad to be back in Virginia, even here. The two guards stayed within earshot, so I tried to be careful. But Joe didn't seem bothered by them. He said that they treated him pretty well, for the most part, and that solitary confinement was something he'd become accustomed to over the years. If they thought this was going to wear him down, they had a lot to learn.

It was nonetheless hard to see him like this. Even on death row, we'd had contact visits. At Joliet we sat alone together in a visiting room with vending machines and space to move around. But this was Red Onion—supermax—and they didn't give an inch. As much as I hated it, I was still amazed at Joe. His ability to stand up to the system was astonishing. He was there because of Angelone's fury at being bested in this contest, and if this is the worst he could do, Joe was ready for it. From where I sat, the odds were against Joe, but the odds against his getting back to Virginia had been even higher, so Goliath had better watch his ass.

After *Providence* started shooting again, I got a call one evening from Dr. John Vierling, head of the Liver Team at Cedars, saying they had a liver that might be right for Shelley. I sat there dumbfounded as he told me that there was someone on the list ahead of her, but we should be prepared if that person wasn't available or the organ wasn't a match. Blindsided and confused by the call, I talked to Shel about it, and she didn't understand it any more than I did. Shaken, we waited, but heard no more.

* * *

A few weeks later, the good folks at *Providence* fixed my schedule so I could testify before the Illinois House of Representatives Task Force on the Death Penalty. The release from death row of thirteen innocent men had embarrassed them into commissioning this body to examine their death system. I figured this was more of a reaction to growing support for a moratorium on killing than a serious look at changing anything. But it was worth the trip.

Hearings had already been held in Springfield, the Illinois capital, before I headed to Chicago. Walking into the anteroom, I was greeted by Renny Cushing, then Executive Director of Murder Victims Families for Reconciliation, and some MVFR members, including Bud Welch, my friend whose daughter was killed in the Oklahoma bombing. Richard Dieter, Executive Director of the Death Penalty Information Center, saw me and said, "They want you now."

"They want me now for what?"

"To speak. They're waiting for you."

Oh shit. I'd hoped to get a sense of the room before being called on, but I followed Dick into a small auditorium with a couple of hundred seats facing a stage where the members of the Task Force sat. At the foot of the aisle, a small table had been set up for those offering testimony. It sat in the well just below the stage, looking up at the intimidating array of commissioners. It was easy to envision getting the old thumbs-down from the Chair, then having the floor give way below.

Dieter took a seat in the audience and pointed toward the table, whispering, "You've got ten minutes."

"Ten? I was told twenty!"

"We all were. They changed it."

The room was not full, probably fifty to seventy-five people sitting in clumps, only a few of whom looked familiar, but all of whom seemed to be staring intently at me. I went to the table with the statement I had scrupulously boiled down on the plane to just under twenty minutes, and pulled out the chair.

"Mr. Farrell," said the dark-haired man in the middle of the row of suits. "Thank you for making yourself available to us. You have ten minutes, at the end of which there may be questions."

"Thank you, sir," I replied, noting that the panel was all white, all but one male, and all business. "If I may, I was told I'd have—"

"I understand," he interrupted, "and I'm sorry, but I'll have to inform you when your time is up."

"I see. Then I'll have to try to edit as I go; so I hope you'll understand if I'm not entirely coherent."

Not a smile in the bunch. I began, excising paragraphs as I went, eyes falling on a thought, brain trying to quickly decide if it could stay or go. When time was called, a number of hands went up. One man took umbrage at my suggestion that killing by the state is at least as wrong as that done by an individual. We sparred briefly. I said state killing was cold, mechanical, and ritualistic, in part to spare the feelings of the "death squad" and in part to give it an aura of respectability. "Yet," I said, "research shows that those who take part in the killing process suffer nonetheless."

Did I feel no outrage at the act of the criminal?

"Of course," I responded, "I'm outraged by all criminal acts. They're wrong, sometimes horrible, and those who commit them deserve consequences. The consequences should be stringent, effective, appropriate, and consistent with our principles. If someone were to kill one of my loved ones, I'd probably want to tear the bastard apart with my bare hands. I hope I wouldn't, but I'd certainly feel that way. But we can't make public policy because of someone's emotional reaction to a personal tragedy. Putting the perpetrator in prison for the rest of his life without the possibility of release protects us all without making us stoop to his level."

"So," the legislator observed, "you're just against the death penalty. But I didn't hear anything about problems with its application."

"I think you did, sir," I responded. "The racism and the fact that it's only used against the poor are huge problems. Its use on the retarded, the mentally ill, and children is a scandal. And as you in Illinois are well aware, innocent people are repeatedly caught up in the process, condemning it entirely."

At that he leaned back with a smug look, as if to say, *I've got your number.*

A second legislator asked, "You mentioned the polls showing a majority favoring life without parole. What do you think of this recent Gallup Poll that says people were asked which they'd prefer and fifty-six percent said they'd prefer the death penalty while thirty-eight percent said they'd prefer life without parole? Where do you get your information?"

"I'm not familiar with that poll, sir, but Professor William Bowers at Northeastern University has done these studies across the country and his results show what I've indicated. Just last month a poll by the University of Virginia showed that even in a killing state, the majority prefers life without parole. Now, I don't bring them up to suggest we legislate by poll, but to point out that life without parole is popular and available. England's leaders abolished the death penalty when over seventy percent of their people supported it. Russia has just done the same thing in the face of seventy-plus percent support. And if your Gallup numbers are correct, fifty-six percent is a twenty percent drop in support from their earlier polls. That would make this a politically viable moment to do the right thing."

A third man complimented me on M*A*S*H and *Providence* and asked what had caused my opposition to the death penalty. Pleading a lack of time, I gave him a brief sketch and mentioned Joe Giarratano's case.

Then it was over. Looking for a seat in the audience, I was able to get a sense of the crowd. The right front section was the pro-death group. The MVFR folks, the religious and the abolitionists were further back, so I joined them.

A number of victims' family members testified, sometimes quite emotionally. It was interesting to see how they were orchestrated by the state's attorney's office. Venturing into the waiting room later, I found a young woman from the office cheering them on, insisting on "closure," saying the opposition was naïve, ignorant of reality.

Back inside we heard more from the group. As moving as their anguish was, I couldn't help but be struck by the recurring litany: the death of the perpetrator is necessary for victims' families to have closure. A woman in her twenties had a great deal of trouble getting through the story of the murder of her family when she was six years old. Asked what she was doing now, she said she was in college on a scholarship provided by a state-run victim's fund. The fact that she was still tortured so many years after the murderer had been executed certainly raised questions about closure.

Then the members of Murder Victims Families for Reconciliation came up. Having suffered the same fate, they claimed the death penalty had no value for them and no place in society, that there was no such thing as "closure." Instead, they'd found that healing and reconciliation only take place when one is ready to accept the reality of what has happened, deal with the grief, and get on with life. The pursuit of vengeance in the death of another not only demeans the memory of their lost loved one, it delays the healing process. Worse, they said, state authorities tend to sever relations with family members who don't pursue the death penalty, cutting them out of the loop and often depriving them of the services made available to those who cooperate.

The Chair underscored this bias by having all the MVFR members come to the microphone at once. He gave the entire group ten minutes to divide among themselves, despite the fact that he had just given the pro-death family members ten minutes each. It was blatant and shocking, but despite their muzzling, the MVFR folks were eloquent and effective. Bud Welch, who had testified in Springfield, stepped aside. Renny Cushing made a short statement and left most of the time for those from Illinois. One woman had not only suffered the loss of both parents but the additional horror of having her twin brother tried, convicted, and sentenced to death for the crime. Her brother, Gary Gauger, was one of the exonerated.

Two sisters said that after the murder of their entire family, they were virtually shunned by authorities because they didn't want death for the killer. Another argued that the killer of her loved one was too young to be sentenced to death. After their words, Renny asked for equal treatment for all murder victims' families, regardless of their position on the death penalty.

Professor Larry Marshall and Dick Dieter were eloquent, opposing death while suggesting improvements that would lessen the chance of wrongful execution. We missed Sister Helen Prejean, the nun whose book, *Dead Man Walking,* had breathed new life into the abolition movement. Dick said she'd missed her plane because of a hurricane. Only something like that, I knew, would keep her away.

Back home, I was awakened by a midnight call from the Liver Coordinator at Cedars, saying they had an organ for Shelley. We were to come to the hospital immediately. Stunned, I put her on hold and woke Shelley. Even after the earlier call, we still hadn't really come to grips with the idea. As off balance as I was, Shelley said she didn't think her condition was that critical and the organ should to go to someone who needed it. The woman was startled and had Dr. Vierling call us. I told him that we were pleased with how well Shelley was doing and didn't feel it was right for us at this point. He said we needed to talk.

A few days later, Dr. Vierling and the team's head surgeon gave us the facts. Despite all we had done and regardless of how well Shelley was feeling, her liver was a time bomb. The esophageal bleed that nearly killed her months earlier was a warning that her liver was so scarred and congested it was unable to process the toxins in her system. The strain on the other organs had caused the portal vein to protrude into her esophagus and burst. It was only a matter of time before something else would happen, and it might not be so easily detected. We were gambling with Shelley's life.

It was a terrifying conversation. Here in this small, clean, utilitarian room, these men we had come to trust were telling us there was really no choice. They were very sweet and completely understanding, for which I'll always be grateful, but they didn't pull any punches.

We had been avoiding the obvious at great risk. We looked at each other and knew the answer. And again, just like the day I told her that her hip had to be replaced, Shelley took it in, saw the reality and nodded, powerful in her calm acceptance. Tears ran down my face as she agreed to go forward, now with a very different understanding of what it meant. We left with one of the most insistent reminders of our new status: pagers we were to wear at all times so that we could be contacted immediately when an appropriate organ became available. And from that moment until the day we finally received the call, we could not be more than four hours away from the hospital.

Our lives changed completely and not at all. We continued to try to live normally and take care of each other. Shelley maintained her schedule of tests and checkups, while still helping the Alzheimer's Association, and I worked on the show. I told the producers that when the pager went off, I was headed for the hospital, and they said they'd do what they had to, to cover for me. From that day, the pager was an ever-present reminder of what lay around some unknown corner. When we shot a scene, I'd hand it to the assistant director, who'd hold it for me until the director said "cut."

Eventually our lives resumed a kind of normalcy. We didn't venture far from the city. Invitations to speak, requests to help, some urgent, still came our way, but we just had to say no more often, staying within the limits of our agreed tether.

I was thrilled in January of 2000 when Governor George Ryan of Illinois, a conservative Republican supporter of the death penalty, declared a moratorium on executions. An incredibly courageous step for a politician, Ryan had clearly been rocked by the mess in Illinois' death system, which had exonerated and freed thirteen condemned men, while twelve had been executed. He'd been deeply conflicted at having to preside over the execution of Andrew Kokoraleis, his first. Agonizing over the question but finally allowing the execution, he decided he couldn't in good conscience let it happen again without examining the system.

"I cannot," Ryan explained, "support a system which, in its administration, has proven so fraught with error and has come so close to the ultimate nightmare, the taking of innocent life." At last, a politician who understood the responsibility of leadership—and hadn't forgotten that he was a human being.

I didn't know the governor, but called his office to express my admiration. To my surprise, he took the call himself. He knew who I was, he knew of Larry Marshall's work at the Center on Wrongful Convictions, of the conference two years earlier and my part in it. One learns to be leery of the appearance of openness in a politician, but that was the beginning of a warm relationship with a man I have come to admire greatly.

Governor Ryan also understood that a moratorium on executions was meaningless without an examination of the system. He quickly named a bipartisan Commission on the Death Penalty to assess it and report back its recommendations. Evenly balanced with people on both sides of the issue, the Commission was chaired by retired Federal Judge Frank McGarr and my old friend, Senator Paul Simon. It was a major step.

2000 was an election year, and we were fed the usual nonsense. Unable to travel, I was lucky to be offered the chance to write a regular column for an online news site that allowed me to take aim at some of the more blatant hypocrisy I saw around me. In February I teed off on Al Gore, George W. Bush, and other presidential aspirants for their holier-than-thou, What-would-Jesus-do? posturing (see "Piety or Politics?" at www.mikefarrell.org/publications/piety.html), and in May I took a shot at a couple of governors while paying tribute to Ryan (see "Another Deaf Governor" at www.mikefarrell.org/publications/deaf.html).

On *Larry King Live* in June, I debated Reverend Albert Mohler, President of the Southern Baptist Theological Seminary, about the execution of Gary Graham, a.k.a., Shaka Sankofa. Dick Burr and others had been fighting to save his life for years, furious that no court would hear from eyewitnesses who directly contradicted the single woman on whom the prosecution relied. Courts and prosecutors use every technicality at their disposal to frustrate justice while condemning those who use the law for the defendant. It's mind-boggling.

It was awful to sit in the studio with Larry, listening to the smiling Reverend Mohler mouth pieties about God's will as another young black man was ushered into the killing room, strapped to a gurney and punctured to ease admission of the lethal chemicals. The "medicalizing" of this process is nauseating. Sanctifying it is blasphemous. I knew nothing we said would stop the horror, but I clung to the hope that some of those watching would see its utter inhumanity. We talked at each other; Graham died. Later, angered by Mohler's self-satisfaction, his smug manipulation of biblical lore, and his glorification of killing, I wrote an open letter twitting him (see "Open Letter" at www.mikefarrell.org/publications.openletter.html).

Through summer and into the fall, we fought the first federal execution in almost forty years. Every state makes its own decision about capital punishment; as of today, thirty-eight have it and twelve do not. The federal government has a death system, too, but it had not been used since 1963. A Justice Department study uncovered serious problems in the federal system, so before it could be used, a group of us began recruiting respected names to ask President Clinton to stop the execution of Juan Raul Garza and declare a moratorium on all federal executions. The Justice Department study showed that their system discriminated on the basis of race (eighty percent of the condemned were people of color) and geography (people charged with identical crimes in different regions get different penalties). We developed an enormous list of leading citizens, some supporters and some opponents of capital punishment, all of whom agreed that, at a minimum, it must be fair.

Clinton simply stayed the execution of Mr. Garza temporarily—effectively punting it to the incoming administration—and ignored the moratorium. A cowardly act, it turned a blind eye to the problems and left Garza's execution to the bloody hands of a man who had presided over the killing of more human beings—152 by my count—than any governor in our history.

Chapter 27
HERO

Around midnight on October 22, 2000, we got the call. All our consideration and planning flew right out the window. We went into autopilot, grabbed what we thought we might need, and headed for the hospital. Shelley was admitted; we were taken to a room and left alone to look at each other, think about what was coming, cherish everything that life together had meant, and struggle to put words to our thoughts. It was impossible. Every time I tried to tell her how much I loved her, my throat would close and I'd choke back the tears I knew would pour out with the words. Every time she tried to say, *If I don't . . .* the words wouldn't come, and I wouldn't have allowed myself to hear them if they had. We knew that it was, as the surgeon had said, the biggest, most serious, most difficult operation they do—more complicated even than a heart transplant. Her organs would be removed from her body and her entire blood system rerouted for hours. If anything went wrong . . .

Then they came for us, and I walked beside the gurney holding her hand, down to the operating room and into a cubicle to wait again. The donor organ had to be examined to be sure it was healthy and right for her. Up until the last moment, they could abort the process and send us home. God, I hoped they would. God, I hoped they wouldn't.

Staying calm, comforting and reassuring her, was all I could think of to do. And she helped with a bit of comic relief. For some time, Shelley had insisted that she didn't want to know anything about the donor. She'd somehow gotten it into her head that taking a donated organ into one's body brings with it some aspects of the person it came from. Being very suggestible, she was convinced that if anyone made the slightest mention of the fact that, for example, the donor was Italian, she'd wake up saying, *Hey, Goombah,* and gesticulating with every word. She told everyone who approached—doctor, nurse, it didn't matter—that she didn't want to know anything about the donor. Some people heard it five or ten times that night.

And then they took her away from me. I flashed back to the hollow, sick, helpless feeling I'd had many years earlier when they came to my brother's hospital room to take him down for lung surgery. I had wanted to stop them then, too. What if they didn't know what they were doing? What if he didn't come back? But he had come back, I reminded myself, and he was fine. And these were people I had come to know, as Shelley and I had been preparing for this moment for the past year and a half. And I had to be strong for her. But God . . .

So I went to the room they made available—and waited. Shel had given me a list of people to call, people who had asked to be told when the time came, but it was the wee hours, too early to make calls. When it was finally morning in the East, I started. And what the hell could I say? *She's in surgery. They told me it would be fine. But she wanted me to call.* I said I'd call back when I knew more. All were sweet; all were appreciative; all loved her deeply. So many love her.

Then, when it wasn't too early in the West, more calls. Some came immediately: Tom and Claire, Eugenie, my kids, Kathy, my brother Jim and Karen, Joe and Judy, Annie, Tracy. So many came. More wanted to come. And we waited and talked and probably prayed. And waited.

And after ten hours of surgery, the doctor came in and said everything was all right. She had come through fine. The procedure was a success. He was exhausted. She was fine.

Everything became a blur. She was moved into Intensive Care. Visiting with her was restricted to immediate family, so she suddenly sprouted brothers and sisters. But they could only pop in for moments. I think I slept on the floor of the ICU the first night. I think Eugenie did, too, one night, Claire another. I remember Shel in a stupor pulling the tubes out. Another time she tried to get out of bed. Neither was good. But I knew she was going to be fine when, early one morning, a cleaning woman arrived to mop the floor and Shelley announced: "I don't want to know anything about the donor!"

She came back to me—to all of us—slowly but steadily, with great determination and always with that astoundingly gentle spirit, that incredible decency and reassuring warmth that attracts people to her like bees to a flower.

There was pain, of course, and there were hard times—some very hard. After I brought her home, she had a violent reaction to a medication and had to be hospitalized again. But through it all she was powerful, indomitable, heroic. She gets embarrassed when I say she's my hero. But having seen her go through so much distress over these years, so many of the frightening and debilitating things that can embitter a person—and do so without ever losing her dignity, her incredible sweetness, and her illuminating core of decency—only underscores how lucky I am to have her in my life.

Watching for signs of rejection of the new organ became a constant. Nausea, vomiting, a temperature, a spike in the pain level—all were danger signals, and we saw them all and called the Liver Coordinator with questions, descriptions, and the need for reassurance. Shelley suffered through a confounding, nuts-making schedule of medications: anti-rejection, anti-infection, steroids, anticoagulant, antacid, vitamin, etc., some once a day, some twice, some more, all at a prescribed time, a specific number of hours apart, some with food, some after food, some before food. I made up a color-coded chart cross-referenced for time with each medication listed in a way that told us how many times it had to be taken and with or without what. She had a drain that needed to be cleaned and dressed. To say it was overwhelming understates the situation astronomically, but we muddled through. We went from terrified and overwhelmed to worried to fairly confident to feeling pretty damned good. And we laughed, and I admired and loved her more all the time.

* * *

The drama of the 2000 election was to some degree dimmed by the focus on Shelley's healing process, but it was excruciating to watch democracy sundered and the presidency stolen. The cowardice of the press, the arrogance of the Bush machine, and the outrageous gall of five political hacks on the Supreme Court forever changed this country—changed the world in ways that would only later become clear.

At this point I stepped into an awful union struggle that still has me shaking my head.

An insurgent group of angry actors, upset at not getting the attention they felt was their due, set out to take over the Hollywood Board of Directors of the Screen Actors Guild, the union I had proudly joined forty years earlier. Due to the inattention of the membership, they succeeded in chasing a bright and dedicated president, Richard Masur, out of office and installing their own Charlie McCarthy. Invited to sit in on a meeting, I was angered by the vulgar, bullying behavior of those now in control and joined a group of idealistic younger members hoping to set things right.

Elected to the union's first vice presidency as the running mate of reform candidate Melissa Gilbert, I served for the next four years— three as VP and one as national board member—with Shelley joining us there for the last three. We fought to bring reason and competence back to a legendary institution whose reputation—and ability to function—was being systematically sundered by a conniving, duplicitous group of narcissists.

Sparing you the four gory years, we lost. A storied organization with a wonderful, capable and dedicated staff was reduced to a brawling, self-annihilating shadow of its former self by the arrogance and incompetence of a gathering of petulant would-be's, used-to-be's, wanna-be's and worse . . . pitiful examples of the psychic injury that draws so many walking wounded to our business.

Feeling there were more important battles to fight, I left this struggle to others. I hope they can pull it together.

* * *

In January of 2001, four days after her ninety-fourth birthday, my mother died. Having lived with us through her declining years, she remained to the last a testament to simplicity, humility, and faith. Surviving my father by nearly fifty years, she never lost a certain girlishness, and in spite of some very tough times always accepted people as they presented themselves. Given the changes in the world she had witnessed, I found this remarkable. Her acceptance of others, I believe, grew out of an impoverished background that was nonetheless filled with family and love. From it she developed a sense of hopeful expectation, a belief that no matter how tough things got, there was always tomorrow. Watching her feed peanuts to the squirrels or sweep leaves in front of the little house we made for her, I was always touched by the sound of her humming the little ditty that never seemed far from her. *It's all right*, she seemed to say, *there's always hope, always something to sing about.*

Having her near for those years, especially as her need for independence gave way to our need to be sure she was safe, allowed for other gifts in our life. Our dear friend Patricia, a beautiful elf who came into my life as the baker in a vegetarian restaurant I owned for a while, became Agnes's companion, laughing with her, sharing stories about their lives, their kids, drinking in her wisdom and encouraging her to remember and recount, recording it all in her supple mind and loving heart. She made Mom feel visible and appreciated, always seeing that her needs were met without in any way violating her sovereignty. Her tenderness helped ease my mother's last year, an act of love I can never fully repay. And in the evenings Kathy or Jim and his wife Karen would come by. Other nights Shelley and I would be with her. Our kids, Jim's kids and grandkids, other family and friends dropped in. Agnes became again as she had been at the beginning: the axis around which our lives revolved and through whom we stayed in touch with one another.

When the inevitable came, I was lucky enough to be with her, to hear her last words: a whispered Act of Contrition. Faith to the last.

Though she had little about which to be contrite, it took me back to the priest in the confessional: "Now make a good Act of Contrition." There was never a better or less necessary act of contrition. As she passed the next day, I held her and offered my own prayer, singing, "When Irish Eyes Are Smiling," to send her on her way.

We paid our respects with family and many friends in a Celebration of Agnes, telling stories, reading loving notes, hearing anecdotes and words of praise and wonder for what she had been to so many. We laughed and cried and sealed the evening with that same song she so loved.

In the spring, Michael Kroll, a friend who works with death row inmates here in California, contacted me. Robert Massie had become a "volunteer" and would die soon. Michael said Massie had been using something I had written to justify his decision. He wanted to know if I'd be willing to go to San Quentin and talk to the inmate. "It's a long shot," he said, "but worth a try."

Shelley was fine, and I was able to get a day off work. I flew to Oakland and got a cab up to the East Gate of San Quentin. I'd been past the old wooden homes of San Quentin too many times, standing vigil against executions. This was different.

San Quentin, a dreary leaden lump, sits like a turd on the north shore of picturesque San Francisco Bay. Standing with your back to this house of misery allows in the unalloyed beauty of the bay, but turning around to face it brings back the depressing reality of our failed system like a cold slap. Walking toward the building, I found myself taking deep breaths, as if to store up oxygen from the free world.

Once through the now-familiar entry process, four of us arranged ourselves in a 6' x 12' cage on plastic chairs around a child-sized table and talked about law and life and death. An Episcopal priest was spiritual advisor to the condemned man. He hated the decision Massie had made but was there to offer support. Wishing Massie had not dropped his appeal, the lawyer, who had never handled a death case, said he respected his client's legal knowledge. Massie's argument was sound, he said, and, helpless before his client's choice, he had accepted the decision. The state would have its way.

Robert Massie was tense, sharp, edgy. The release of his cuffs revealed deep impressions on his wrists, which remained red and swollen through the nearly two-hour visit. My comment on them was met with a shrug and a smile. "They like to let us know who's boss," he said.

"I've seen them cause bleeding," added the minister, a regular here.

Even the little things, the little dehumanizing touches hardly noticeable to the untrained eye, erode the spirit. They were going to kill this man in a few days. Couldn't they afford him a shred of dignity?

Massie was contrary about the pack of "parasites" he claimed made up the death penalty defense bar, "taking money as they feed their clients into a voracious, rubber-stamp system." Ferociously proud of his grasp of the law, he was extremely articulate in defense of his claim: His issue was one of constitutional principle and his death would become a monkey wrench in the gears of the system. I'd heard it before. His contempt for everything he viewed as bowing to the courts' hypocrisy glowed with an intensity that leaped out from dark eyes, daring a lesser mind to counter a legal position keenly honed through years of study, analysis, and argumentation.

I was there, I said, to change his mind. I wanted him to rethink this decision that meant another killing. But his constitutional rights had been denied, he said. Convicted of murder, he had pled guilty against his attorney's advice, accepted the death sentence, and refused a state-mandated appeal. The court required that the appeal go forward despite his objection, appointed an attorney who had pursued the matter and overturned the verdict. In a second trial, he had again been convicted and sentenced to death. Thus his contention: He was a victim of double jeopardy. Because he hadn't agreed to the appeal and hadn't waived his constitutional rights, the second trial had violated his double-jeopardy protections.

"But," I argued, "isn't double jeopardy to protect someone who has been acquitted from having the state put him through the process in the hope of a 'better' result the second time around?"

No, said the attorney. "Double jeopardy is double jeopardy, whether the result of the initial proceeding is guilt or innocence."

This was nonsense, it seemed to me, and here, dangerous. The concept of double jeopardy is intended to protect someone from being tried twice for the same crime. But that wasn't what this was about. This is a self-destructive man who had killed another so the state would kill him in return.

Massie sloughed off my "state-assisted suicide" notion, saying his wasn't a death wish but a carefully drawn strategy. He was a soldier willing to die to take this hill, to bring down this hated and dehumanizing temple of hypocrisy.

Look at yourself, I wanted to scream. *What else does it say when you confess to murder against your attorney's advice and fight an appeal? What about your attempts at suicide?*

Massie's history was a festival of carnage, a testament to the enduring impact of degrading and abusive behavior on a young life. Born in Virginia to a fifteen-year-old mother and a man who chose marriage instead of jail for statutory rape, Massie was so abused by ignorant parents who took him to bars and fed him alcohol and drugs that he was placed in foster care at the age of five. For the next six years, he endured five different placements in hell. In one, his head was stuck into the toilet as a form of discipline. Another foster parent believed flogging a naked, spread-eagled child taught a lesson. It taught lessons, all right. In a juvenile institution where he was repeatedly gang-raped, he was put on a Virginia chain gang at the age of twelve, where he dug trenches and filled them in again. One day, a boy in his detail fell over dead. A guard loosed the shackles and tossed the dead body into the pit so the others could bury him. Upon release, the teenaged Massie was a ticking bomb ignored by society until car theft sent him to an adult prison. What followed—a series of psychological maladies that included manic-depression, schizophrenia, and suicide attempts—could have been plotted by Dickens.

Was there ever a clearer prescription for terminal rage, self-hatred, and a desire to end the pain?

Despite our debate, a few moments of earnest human contact occurred, and I found myself drawn to this tragic man, liking him despite his cocky posture and my frustration at his decision. I could not, as I looked into his eyes, help but see the echo of the tortured child, carefully hidden beneath the pasty white face with occasional red blotches, the perfectly combed hair. His voice still carried traces of his Virginia youth as he tirelessly expounded his legal litany of constitutional rights, state-paid parasites, and judicial hypocrites. But he wound down in response to an offhand comment, allowing the lonely Robert Massie to peek out.

"This old scarred body" was ready to rest, he said. He was going to die in jail anyway, and wanted to do it on his own terms. "Of course, I have doubts," he said. He hated the idea, sold by the media, that he and his fellow inmates were vicious, depraved, slobbering monsters. "I don't know none of them. I'm an old robber who's been inside most of my life. I'm not a big fella, but I've stood back to back with another when necessary and fought till blood ran the floor." His fellow inmates had value, he said. He knew men who had committed terrible crimes, but who were nonetheless thoughtful, spiritual, principled beings capable, if given the chance, of productive lives.

Then suddenly, jarringly, time was up. The guard appeared and prepared to take him away. The conversation that had become so quiet and personal ended. The man who had just allowed himself to become so vulnerable was to be taken away and disposed of. All of this crystallized as we were caught together in a moment in which time stopped. We both stood. Trying to grasp that he would soon be dead, I opened my arms and he stepped into them. I held him for a moment, an embrace he returned. And then he stepped away, was shackled, and quickly disappeared with no look back. The utter hopelessness of the place, the icy, uncompromising nature of it, came down like a shroud. We were escorted out into the daylight where we could breathe again, and I was able to walk away, free, sick, and disgusted that the country I love would rather kill the old man Robert Massie had become than save the boy with such promise.

Less than a month later, in recognition of the extraordinary step Illinois Governer George Ryan had taken—and in the hope that it would inspire the kind of leadership that would one day help us deal more humanely with the Robert Massies of the world—I presented the Death Penalty Focus Acts of Courage Award to him at our annual dinner. He was a tough nut. The fact that he came and accepted the honor even while hanging onto his theoretical support for the death penalty just made me like him more.

At home we were eight months out from the surgery and Shelley was doing well. She said it was time for me to get away for a bit, insisting that she wanted some quiet time alone. Greenpeace had asked me to do a tour of Cancer Alley, the polluted strip between Baton Rouge and New Orleans, Louisiana, to focus attention on the plight of the mostly poor, black residents who lived in the deadly offal spewed by the oil and chemical refineries that dot the region. My son Mike went with me.

Damu Smith, the spirited Greenpeace staffer (who was to suc-cumb to liver cancer in 2006), greeted us in New Orleans, full of enthusiasm. I was thrilled to hear that author Alice Walker was with us. Shelley and I had just seen her interviewed and were struck by her sweetness and clarity. She was a lovely woman. Yvonne Scruggs-Leftwich of the Black Leadership Forum was also on the tour, and I was delighted to hear that Congresswoman Maxine Waters would be joining us. A courageous and articulate woman, Maxine had been at the forefront of every important civil and human rights issue in recent memory. Haki Mahdbuti, a prominent African-American poet and writer, was also there.

The day was a trial. I was happy to have Mike with me so that, as in El Salvador, he'd have a personal experience of the things that so contradict what our nation claims to stand for. The Alley has dirt-poor patches and middle- and upper-middle-class communities, some mixed-race but mostly black, that are uniformly assaulted by gas, fumes, seepage, and other pollution from refineries and plants that crowd their homes and fields. Dangerous, disease-causing, chemically tainted water; dead and dying plant life; and rancid, foul-smelling air were a constant, as were snotty and unresponsive representatives of the offending businesses. Ragged children cried, "Please help us!" as their parents showed lists of dead and dying neighbors, complete with descriptions of the cancers and organ failures they'd suffered.

Though there isn't room here to include a full account (see "Cancer Alley" at www.mikefarrell.org/publications/cancer.html), a couple of memories stand out. A hot, vibrant, soul-stirring revival-style meeting at Myrtle Grove Community Church juxtaposed powerful song and a rafter-rattling sermon with calm, delicate words. Alice Walker called up the image of crumbling nuts inside poisoned shells in the pecan trees as an analogy to the disease-wracked Elle Plantation we had left an hour earlier.

Later in the day, we stood at Southern University, a black college in Baton Rouge, as a lovely young woman described years of suffering neural damage resulting from a benzene cloud that had covered the campus after a barge capsized on the river just below. Assured there was no cause for concern, the staff was instructed to keep the students in school, trapping this woman and hundreds of others in the noxious mist. No individual or company has ever taken responsibility for the damage, and no help has been provided its victims.

Next we met townspeople in a small bleak park in New Sarpy, just yards from a Shell Oil refinery. Acknowledging limited responsibility for the intolerable odor from their facility, Shell had offered to relocate the residents of two streets of the four-street town. Two! The mind boggled.

Our day stretched on with one heartbreaking stop after another until, toward evening, we toured Agriculture Street in New Orleans, a community built on a toxic dump. An astronomical cancer rate had finally triggered federal Superfund monies to dig out the dirt beneath the houses of the unsuspecting homeowners, who lived in filth for a year as contractors removed only the top two feet of poisonous waste that was known to be marinating more than a dozen feet below.

Death comes to us all and disease to too many. But it inverts the priorities of society to have one's life, home, and family invaded by the venomous debris of industries that hold themselves impervious to criticism, that can evade responsibility because they are wealthy and "essential." Businesses, no matter how necessary, cannot be more important than the lives and health of the people and the communities they claim to serve. Yet in the face of "progress," the people of Myrtle Grove, New Sarpy, Elle Plantation, Norco, and Agriculture Street were being deemed not only inconsequential, but invisible as they experienced a slow-motion Bhopal. They had become our human version of the caged canaries carried by miners to detect dangerous gases. When the birds died, the miners knew to get out. What are we waiting for?

Beyond outrage and shame, I was moved by the generosity of those who opened their homes and churches to us, fed us, and expressed warmth and appreciation for our concern. Again: attention and respect. Underlying their horror and disappointment, people there exhibited the stubborn belief that, because this was America and the victims were human beings, someone would see to it that things were made right. Would that it were so.

Months later, Mike, after some serious introspection, had the proverbial lightbulb go on. An interest in alternative healing came together with his study of martial arts and a fascination with Eastern philosophy to point him toward the study of Chinese medicine. He's now in school learning acupuncture and herbology, and I am a happy dad!

Chapter 28
SEPTEMBER 11, 2001

My concern about the hapless Bush Administration and the ineptitude of its band of Neanderthals was heightened after September 11, 2001. The horror of the attacks, the numbing human devastation, the sudden feeling of vulnerability, and the fear that such an assault could soon be repeated created a mix of emotions and opportunities. Fear could engulf the country, turn us inward, and provide a breeding ground for xenophobia. Rage could make us strike out blindly. Or there could be a coming together, an embrace of each other at home, and a grateful acceptance of the world's compassionate reaction. It was a critical time and everything depended on leadership.

I was briefly hopeful. Through the veil of pain that shrouded us, I thought for just a moment there was a willingness to take the high road, to demonstrate the necessary moral, inspirational leadership. By acknowledging our pain, accepting the world's embrace, and seizing the opportunity for international cooperation, the U.S. could exhibit greatness. But no. Instead, us-versus-them rhetoric poured from a cocky and immature leader. Forget international cooperation, we had a cowboy dead-set on recapturing lost face by launching a crusade.

The media leaped onto the bandwagon. With flags flying, television news became a megaphone for outrage, pumping up the impulse to strike back—and quickly. But against whom? War makes little sense on any human level, and war against a vaguely defined enemy no sense at all. But such horror raised the emotional temperature, challenged us, and sowed doubt. Who and what we were was in question, and pain and shock made us vulnerable.

During that awful period, I was on a talk show hosted by Pastor James M. Lawson, Jr., the nation's leading apostle of nonviolence. A pioneer from the early civil rights days, Jim had been Martin Luther King, Jr.'s friend, partner in the struggle, and his teacher of nonviolence, as recounted in David Halberstam's book, *The Children*. Jim was hosting a national dialogue on how to deal with this terrible assault, how to heal. The participants were frightened and angry, bitter and vengeful, moving and thoughtful. One, a chaplain, pointed out that we are all—not only those who had been directly wounded by the loss of a loved one in New York, Washington, or Pennsylvania—going through a grieving process. When in grief, he said, one shouldn't make big decisions or take definitive actions. We needed to take time to grieve, an important part of the healing process, before we could know what the next step should be. Our lives had to go on, but as a nation we were not in the state of mind necessary to make what would certainly be life-and-death decisions. His words helped me recognize my own grief, helped me understand why I was so very tired—and discouraged. The carnage, the God-awful loss of life, the violation of every principle of humanity, the heroism of so many—all of it had been deeply affecting, overwhelming.

But even in grief, one has to remain alert. Everything we had been working for could be swept away in a frenzy of fear and loathing. Certainly it had all been set back now. How much and for how long?

Another attack had to be considered. Logic alone said the ghastly "success" of 9/11 meant those involved—those who didn't die in the act—were devising ways to inflict yet more damage. And thought of another attack enhanced the talk of war. Striking back, the quicker the better, was promoted by those who believed a decisive act of violence would somehow make them whole again. Absent real leadership, I feared we'd soon see action taken that would be counterproductive. Because many of those on the receiving end of a military response would be ill-educated, impoverished, innocent people, an attack might drive them into the arms of the villains, who would only become better able to do their dirty work.

George Bush was clearly unequipped to live up to his "moment in history." His dualistic thinking ("either you're with us or you're with the terrorists"); his claim that the 9/11 assailants attacked because "they hate our freedoms"; his unwillingness to acknowledge any responsibility on our part for the smoldering resentment that precipitated the attacks; and his invoking God's name in our cause—presumably against Allah—revealed a frighteningly simplistic worldview. And then there was his thoughtless use of the word "crusade." One could only hope it was thoughtless.

Going after bin Laden made sense given the intelligence available, but publicly dictating inflexible terms to the Taliban was either an ignorant choice or a gambit that exposed Bush's intention of leaving the Taliban with no face-saving alternative but resistance. Reciting a litany of their strange—to us—religious requirements held them up to ridicule. Pretending their hold on power didn't result from our own meddling in the area was simply dishonest. None of it was necessary, none of it wise, and none of it likely to resolve the situation peacefully.

According to some reports, the Taliban refused to turn over bin Laden without being presented evidence of guilt—possibly a stall, though hardly unreasonable—but they were brushed off by Bush's "no negotiations, no discussion" posture. Attempting to show he meant business, Bush underscored our arrogance in the eyes of the rest of the world. Unless someone in Washington was wiser than we'd been given reason to believe, we were headed toward an action that would destroy innocents, alienate great numbers, guarantee more terrorism, and make a mockery of the rule of law.

Was there an alternative? Why not something bold, dramatic, far less costly in human life, and more likely to result in international support? Why not denounce the awful assault on September 11 for what it was: a grotesque and inexcusable crime? Rather than glorify it as warfare and elevate its architects to the realm of worthy adversary, why not label them as vicious, vulgar criminals unworthy of respect and deal with them in a manner consistent with our principles, our laws, and our international agreements? For their crimes against humanity, they were violators of world law, and there were appropriate responses that would buttress the concept of a world system and further solidify agreements placing terrorism, terrorists, and their sympathizers outside the bounds of the international community. Further, insisting that the perpetrators of this outrage and their allies, once hunted down and taken into custody, be tried in the International Criminal Court would deflect any claim of prejudice on the part of our courts or juries, while demonstrating our commitment to international law.

Bringing the perpetrators to justice would require the use of every viable legal detection and law-enforcement power in the world. Suicidal zealots armed with a belief in the glory of martyrdom for their cause would not be easily subdued. But the right of self-defense is understood, and using the force necessary to bring them to justice would not only be appropriate, but, importantly, would be seen as a valid response by people around the world.

Justice could have prevailed in this situation if only we'd had the character to demonstrate our willingness to act appropriately and fairly as the world's foremost power.

There is always a reason for human behavior. It was urgently important to grasp the history between the Western powers and the peoples of the Middle East. To understand is not to justify. Knowing the motivation of the actors involved could only help us avoid mistakes. Acting without knowledge, we fell into the very behaviors that caused us to be labeled "the Great Arrogance."

War talk, shorthand for retaliation, revenge, death, and destruction, only perpetuates the cycle of violence. We would have better served all we claim to believe by seeing to it that the awful episode of September 11 ended with a just resolution that affirmed the very values we were told were under attack on that day.

Instead, American flags were everywhere, on cars, on homes; people gathered on street corners with candles to express their . . . what? Some expressed solidarity with those who had suffered—were still suffering. Others looked for the comfort that comes from shared moments in a frightening time. But many, too many, became caught up in a jingoistic hysteria that was not so much an expression of solidarity with those in pain as a fist-shaking rage at "evildoers" that became hatred of "rag-heads" and "sand niggers." It was a time in dire need of thoughtful, inspirational leadership. Instead we got posturing, strutting, and cheap machismo.

It was a time of searching, a time of questioning, a time in which, I believe, the nation showed symptoms of Post-Traumatic Stress Disorder. And this may still be the case. Late that year, in an attempt at healing, Hugh Downs, the highly regarded newsman and commentator, asked for a contribution to *My Country*, his book dealing with our dilemma. I tried to raise some of these questions in the piece I wrote for him (see "Who Are You, America?" at www.mikefarrell.org/publications/america.html).

The wheels of the criminal justice system continued to crush people at home. In February 2002, Joe Ingle, the Tennessee minister who had sparked my work against the death penalty, sent a friend to the *Providence* set to film a clemency plea to Governor Sundquist of Tennessee for Abu Ali Abdur'Rahman. Here was another black man scheduled to die for a crime that, according to the evidence, did not happen as the prosecutor had claimed in court. The racial bias in the system is self-indicting. In order to entice the jury to order his death, the DA proclaimed that this indigent, mentally damaged man was "the kind of evil that the death penalty is here to eliminate." Our plea pointed out that evidence produced after the trial brought eight of those same jurors to join the appeal for clemency. The governor failed to act, politics cutting only one way, but the court did intervene, and Mr. Abdur'Rahman remains alive at this writing.

America's emotional tension found an outlet in the war in Afghanistan. And it played into the hands of media manipulators who transformed George W. Bush from an inept bungler to a war president. Just as they had done with LBJ after JFK's murder, the media bowed to the perceived need to calm the masses in a time of crisis. It was pathetic.

As the Taliban folded like a cheap tent and Al Qaeda slipped away into the night, innocent Afghans were reduced to collateral damage. Meanwhile, the Bush cohort used the opportunity to advance long-sought agendas. Legal charlatans secretly concocted a witches' brew of torture, assassination, round-ups, and imprisonment, without evidence, charges, lawyers, appeals, or courts. Vice President Cheney and his cadre of super-patriots shifted the focus from Afghanistan—lacking oil and trickier to deal with than expected—to Iraq, which had both oil and a loathsome leader, the perfect foil for the purveyors of Imperial America. "Everybody wants to go to Baghdad," boasted one unnamed official at the time. "Real men want to go to Tehran." As we waited for that shoe to drop, Attorney General John Ashcroft and his toadies neutered the Bill of Rights in the name of fighting the now all-consuming danger of terrorism by rushing the so-called Patriot Act through Congress like a stone skipped over water. Ari Fleischer, Bush's glib mouthpiece, laid down the threat to any citizen who had the temerity to speak up: "Americans should watch what they do, watch what they say."

Concerned that the antiterror frenzy was undermining our rights in every respect, I joined others in voicing opposition: at a national conference on the death penalty at DePaul University in Chicago; at a conference on border issues in Tucson; to former Senator Paul Simon's Public Policy Forum at Southern Illinois University; to Dispute Resolution Services in Albuquerque; and to the California Public Defender's Association in Los Angeles. In July, with Shelley feeling well enough to travel, I moderated a panel on the international implications of America's use of the death penalty in Geneva, Switzerland, hosted by Duke University's Law School.

In Illinois, Governor Ryan's Commission released its report listing eighty-five reforms necessary to correct flaws in their death system. But even if all eighty-five reforms were enacted, the Commission said, it would not eliminate the possibility of an innocent person's execution. A serious study by a bipartisan panel of respected professionals, this was further evidence that the death system fails to meet American standards of fairness and equal application of the law. The majority of the members of the Commission agreed that the only way to guarantee that an innocent person could not be executed would be to abolish capital punishment. Governor Ryan immediately sent the results to the state legislature, and the political jockeying began. Concerns about cost, police and prosecutors' fears of "having their hands tied," and legislators' truculence further unmasked the political nature of government killing in America.

Robert Greenwald, the producer of *A Deadly Silence,* a picture I had worked on years earlier, had become a friend. A highly regarded director and a keen critic of the social scene, he was generally contemptuous of political involvement, but shared my concern about Bush's bellicosity toward the "Axis of Evil" and his ever-narrowing focus on Saddam Hussein and Iraq. We wondered where the opposing voices were, the "loyal opposition" who could promote debate about the course Bush seemed intent on taking. With the media and the Democrats all marching in lockstep with the Administration, how could people know that there was another side to the White House's story?

Robert and I began probing for ways to break through the information-proof curtain the media was creating for the all-Bush-all-the-time viewpoint. In the hope of spurring some activity, we arranged a gathering at the home of Stanley and Betty Sheinbaum, the birthing platform for so many important movements in the past. On an August evening in 2002, a full house heard from Erik Gustafson, a Gulf War veteran from the Education Center for Peace in Iraq, David Cortright of the Fourth Freedom Foundation, and Scott Ritter, ex-Marine and former UN Weapons Inspector in Iraq. All were good, but Ritter, who had been roundly smeared for his no-holds-barred criticism of Bush's intentions, was withering in his attack and inspired great enthusiasm. In the end, however, there was energy and agreement, but no organization or leadership.

During the ensuing days, Robert and I came to the reluctant conclusion that, despite our hope for someone else to pick up the ball, it was left to us. We drafted a statement that we hoped would be signed by a few well-known individuals, thinking its release might break through the media curtain and at least get a dialogue started. Celebrities would get the media's attention, we knew, but they'd also be pilloried. To be taken seriously, we needed people with military, diplomatic, and political credentials as well.

Within a few weeks we had an extraordinary response. That fall, as part of a broad new coalition called Win without War, we launched Artists United to Win without War and released the following statement at a press conference in Hollywood.

> We, Americans proud of what our country stands for, are grateful for the honor brought us over the years by national leaders who have dedicated themselves to bringing peace, progress, and opportunity to the less fortunate in many parts of the world. In that spirit, we share President Bush's belief that the Middle East is an area of concern and that Saddam Hussein's Iraq is one of its main threats to stability. We agree with President Bush that the Iraqi regime cannot be allowed to acquire weapons of mass destruction and, given its history, must be effectively contained and disarmed.
>
> We part ways with President Bush, however, on the issue of whether America should threaten a preventative military attack against Iraq. We reject his Administration's newly declared doctrine— a reversal of long-held American history and tradition—that our country alone has the right to launch first-strike attacks. America is not that kind of country. We think that the arrogance displayed in President Bush's new "doctrine," his disregard for the views of many longtime U.S. allies and more broadly for "the opinions of mankind" represented by the United Nations, will make America less respected in the world. And *less*, not more, secure.

Rigorous, internationally backed "containment" and tough-minded UN-sanctioned arms inspections will meet the valid U.S. and UN objective of disarming Saddam Hussein. They are sufficient, they are appropriate, and they have the advantage of being legal. There is no need for a rush to war.

The President has not convinced us, and we believe he has not convinced most Americans, that Iraq poses an imminent threat to U.S. security or that of our allies. The United States should not initiate a war without the unanimous support and explicit authorization of the UN Security Council, nor should it act without the full cooperation and support of our major allies in Europe and the Middle East.

While it may be rare for a group of citizens outside government to come together and comment on foreign policy, we do so out of concern that those who normally bear that responsibility have shirked it—perhaps out of fear, perhaps for reasons of political expedience. But people will die, perhaps thousands of people— needlessly and tragically—unless Americans speak now. Some issues are simply too important to ignore for purposes of "business as usual." We believe that silence gives consent—and we do not consent. [See the full list of signatories at www.mikefarrell.org/publications.html.]

The strategy worked. The star-studded press conference got tremendous coverage and the statement was widely reported. Our hope of raising the level of debate was quickly realized as we were flooded with requests. We paired celebrities with experts as much as possible. Unfortunately, the electronic media was more interested in beating up on show-business types than discussing the pertinent issues, and we were often left to fend for ourselves. The result was both gratifying and horrifying. The debate began to be seriously engaged, but the discussion quickly turned ugly. While our appearances were at first dismissed with a smug "Who cares what celebrities think?" the realization that many cared a great deal—and not only cared but agreed—morphed arrogant dismissal into vicious attack. Unable to get the best of prepared, well-spoken, and thoughtful celebrities and others brave enough to speak out on television or in radio interviews, the opposition to us was reduced to name-calling and ridicule. "Saddam-lover," "America-hater," "Traitor," "If you don't like it, go back to France," and other moronic epithets began to pepper television and radio interviews, mail, newspaper columns, letters-to-the-editor, blogs, and e-mail. It was a hot time, in the midst of which I got a chance to help portray what was going wrong in America by playing the role of Ken Lay in *The Crooked E*, a TV movie of Robert's about Enron and the collapse of ethics in business.

And then Larry Marshall called. With Governor Ryan considering his options regarding those on Illinois' death row as he neared the end of his term, Larry was putting together another gathering of the exonerated. In the four short years since the original 1998 conference, the number had grown from seventy-eight to more than a hundred. In addition, Larry had arranged for a presentation of *The Exonerated*, a play dramatizing the stories of innocent people who had nearly died in America's chambers of death. He hoped to present the play to legislators and Governor Ryan and his staff, with as many of the exonerated in the audience as possible.

In mid-December 2002, I flew to Chicago and helped host the second Conference on Wrongful Convictions at Northwestern University, another painful pageant that heaped shame on our criminal justice system. The next night, Danny Glover, Richard Dreyfuss, and I joined the New York cast in presenting *The Exonerated* to Governor Ryan and an audience studded with those freed from death row, their families, and state legislators. It was a raw, deeply emotional, hugely powerful evening. Governor Ryan was clearly moved but remained characteristically tight-lipped.

Up to the end of the year, reports about what Governor Ryan might do before he left office seesawed back and forth. In January of 2003, as Shelley and I were driving home from our anniversary trip,

Ryan called, asking if I'd come to Chicago where he was going to make a statement. Thrilled at what the invitation implied, I got on a plane. I was privileged to be present in Northwestern's Lincoln Auditorium on January 11 when Governor Ryan condemned the "demon of error" and joined former Supreme Court Justice Harry Blackmun in no longer being willing to "tinker with the machinery of death." He pardoned four men completely and commuted the sentences of everyone else on death row, 167 in all, to life in prison. It was a momentous act by a courageous man and an historic day for the abolition movement.

Other days were less thrilling; other men less courageous. In the run-up to war, as the dishonesty of the Administration was further exposed, the reactions grew uglier. Massive demonstrations were casually dismissed. Thousands were stripped of their rights and imprisoned without charges or access to lawyers. People swept up in Afghanistan were shipped to Guantánamo Bay, Cuba, and tortured. Others were sent elsewhere for torture by proxy. Those who spoke out were libeled and suffered threats to their lives and livelihoods. Though we didn't stop the juggernaut, we made ourselves heard by those who, in their zealotry, were deafening themselves to democracy.

The war against a weakened Iraqi army was mercifully short, but Bush's "mission accomplished" stunt proved criminally premature. His rationale for the war decimated, new lies were tendered as the disastrous legacy of arrogance grew like cancer. With the body count multiplying, the Artists United statement proved sadly prophetic as American losses today near 3,000. Thousands more have been wounded and maimed, countless numbers left in mental distress, tens of thousands of innocent Iraqi civilians slain, billions of dollars wasted, the international community estranged, America's reputation shredded, Saddam's torturers replaced by our own, terrorism multiplied, and Muslims the world over reacting with fear, rage, and a volcanic hatred of Bush's crusade.

As the catastrophe laid waste to reason, the 2004 presidential contest devolved into an orgy of fear-mongering and slander in which the public's confusion was exploited without mercy. Fear of terrorism and shameless pandering were combined with a diversionary dive into homophobia to rule out reason. In Montreal that October, I chaired a panel on U.S. state killing at the Second World Congress against the Death Penalty and met Mrs. Mary Robinson, former President of Ireland and UN High Commissioner for Human Rights. She noted with satisfaction her sense that the people of the world had the ability to separate the views of the U.S. citizens from the actions of its government. However, she worried, if the result of the election proved an affirmation of Mr. Bush and his policies, that distinction might disappear.

Conclusion

THE SPIRIT OF AMERICA

Today, perhaps more than ever before, we face the task of determining what America truly is. So much of where we find ourselves now shows what we have failed to learn from mistakes of the past.

Zealots, whose dream of Imperial America has led us to the brink of moral and economic bankruptcy, continue to spin the plates and deny reality. Stuck in Iraq, American kids in uniform have become our version of Israel's "facts on the ground." With these brave fighting men and women in place, the architects of disaster refuse to admit any error. People must "support the troops," they insist, and forget that the reason for their going was a lie, forget that the loss of lives, the loss of limbs, the loss of minds, and the monumental destruction is completely unnecessary. Of course we should support the troops— by getting them the hell out of there (see "Bring 'em Home" at www.mikefarrell.org/publication/bringemhome.html).

The results we're told to celebrate could have been achieved at a fraction of the cost, human and economic, if our leaders had the courage to respect the law. Instead, truth has become lie, and lie truth. Echoing El Salvador's General Jose Guillermo Garcia's villainous claim that "all peasants are potential subversives," today's young soldiers are told that "all Arabs are potential insurgents." In Fallujah, Haditha, Baghdad, and elsewhere, our young again destroy the village in order to save it, while the Pentagon prepares the "Salvador Option," sending death squads to destroy selected targets. How low can we stoop and remain America?

* * *

Those in power have continued to gull the public by exploiting negative attacks, fear of terrorism, and apprehension about homosexuality, thus securing a victory for "moral values." Scorning tolerance, generosity and mercy, the new arbiters of morality disdain equality, sneer at poverty, and rape the planet to amass wealth for themselves and their friends. Playing bait-and-switch, they pare away rights, puncture the social safety net, and ignore Katrina's victims, wrapping the flag around an arrogant, authoritarian, might-makes-right approach to the world, all the while covering their tracks with attacks on traitors, appeasers, and "girly men" at home and Jihadists abroad.

All fundamentalism is dangerous: Christian, Jewish, Muslim, Hindu, or any other. The need to believe in something that gives meaning to life is understandable, and, per the learned Rabbi Leonard Beerman, fundamentalism provides "the comfort of being so much neater than the subtleties and nuances of everything that is human . . . [It] brings the illusion of certainty."

Struggling with the subtleties and nuances of life is the road to humility; the goal is becoming fully human. Religious certitude brings moral arrogance, and with it the fundamentalist Jews' expulsion of Arabs from their land; the fundamentalist Hindu's slaughter of Muslims; the Islamic Jihadists' suicide attacks; the fundamentalist Christians' bombing of clinics and assassination of family health providers. The belief that one speaks for God and can force his beliefs on another is a soul-destroying lie.

Today, a hyper-moralist triumphalism has gained ground in America, slipping in up the sleeve of imperialist zealots. Fundamentalist beliefs are insinuated into American life in Christian versions of the *madrassas* that inculcate young Muslims. If a religious belief or practice helps one deal with life's important questions, it is certainly of value, but it is a personal value. To impose a belief system on those who choose to find their answers in another way is to deny their basic human right—their "unalienable right"—to determine their own journey.

There are many different views of the proper way to express one's faith, and I applaud those who wrestle with the questions. I particularly appreciate the seekers. This seems to me closer to the concept of true faith than that of extremists who claim to have all the answers and, content in their settled wisdom, judge and condemn those who see things differently.

I've come to believe there is a divine spark in all of us, and it is this element of common humanity that we must honor and preserve, no matter the faith proclaimed. Decency and honor and compassion and hope can be the primary sacraments in our lives, respecting ourselves and the gifts we've been given in a way that empowers—rather than demeans—those around us. Honest pursuit of a meaningful, constructive, and productive life in ownership of such qualities is a purposeful way to honor and acknowledge whatever God may be out there—or in here.

In the meantime, we Americans have work to do. Making this nation live up to its principles requires the involvement of its citizens. It's a job that will either be taken seriously or taken away. If we want the nation we love to exemplify principles that make us proud to be Americans, we have to be true to those principles—and require that our leaders do the same. "All men are created equal" can't mean only men, can it? Or only white people? Only rich people? Only heterosexuals? Only Americans? If we're "endowed by [our] Creator with certain unalienable rights," among which are "Life, Liberty and the Pursuit of Happiness," can we be stripped of them by the powerful? By whoever happens to be the majority at a given moment? Should a government "instituted among Men" and deriving its "just Powers from the Consent of the Governed" lie to the very people who give it power? Should it manipulate its powers secretly to limit or take away people's sovereignty? Can "liberty and justice for all" and "equal justice under law" mean anything in a nation that imprisons people on suspicion, tortures them, holds them for years without charge, and denies them access to a court or a lawyer? Doesn't "Congress shall make no law respecting an establishment of religion, or prohibiting the free exercise thereof" say clearly enough that we're free to practice our chosen faith—or lack of faith—and that we will not allow the government to impose one on us? Just for fun, look up the word "fascism" in the dictionary.

The spirit of America is the vision of human possibility that inspires people across the world to reach higher. The American experiment is the attempt to achieve the goals set out for us hundreds of years ago. To pretend that we've already reached those goals—fully realized our potential—is to lie to ourselves and shirk our duty to our children.

The lessons taught me at The House so many years ago by whores, thieves, addicts, drunks, and other social outcasts have stood the test of time. They have since been underscored and validated for me by impoverished, illiterate peasants, caring angels of mercy, guerrillas, prisoners, care-givers, the abused, survivors, victims, criminals, the shamed, the hopeful, and the hopeless. Love, respect, and attention are necessary food for the human soul.

The opportunities and experiences noted above—and many not included—have provided an extraordinary education for this citizen, and I'm profoundly grateful for having been afforded them. My life is rich, made so by experience, by friendship, and mostly by love. And it will, I now understand, only get richer.

Through it all I've come to believe we are on a journey, you and I, a journey from the caves to the stars. There will always be those who choose to live in fear and try to frighten, force, or lure us back to the caves, but our future, our salvation, the realization of our potential, is in the stars. And love will light the way.

Activist? I prefer citizen. But just call me Mike.